British Economic and Strategic Planning
1905–1915

British Economic and Strategic Planning 1905–1915

DAVID FRENCH

Lecturer in Modern Political History, University College, London

London
GEORGE ALLEN & UNWIN

Boston   Sydney

George Allen & Unwin (Publishers) Ltd,
40 Museum Street, London WC1A 1LU, UK

George Allen & Unwin (Publishers) Ltd,
Park Lane, Hemel Hempstead, Herts HP2 4TE, UK

Allen & Unwin, Inc.,
9 Winchester Terrace, Winchester, Mass. 01890, USA

George Allen & Unwin Australia Pty Ltd,
8 Napier Street, North Sydney, NSW 2060, Australia

First published in 1982

British Library Cataloguing in Publication Data

French, David
    British economic and strategic planning 1905–1915.
    1. Great Britain – Economic policy – History
    I. Title
    338.9'41   HC256
    ISBN 0-04-942174-3

Set in 12 point Times by Performance Typesetting, Milton Keynes
and printed in Great Britain by
Biddles Ltd, Guildford, Surrey

Contents

Acknowledgements

In writing this book I have trespassed on the good nature and for-
bearance of many people and I should like to acknowledge the
most important of these debts here. First, I must thank Brian Bond
who supervised my original doctoral thesis, and I am grateful to
Professor James Joll, Dr Zara Steiner, Dr Norman Stone and Dr
Paul Kennedy for their advice and encouragement at various
stages during the preparation of this book. I should especially like
to thank Dr Martin Pugh who took time off from his own research
to read the entire typescript. They bear no responsibility for what
appears here, and I alone am responsible for any errors of fact or
judgement.

I am grateful to the Social Science Research Council and the
Carnegie Trust for the Universities of Scotland who both provided
me with research grants to enable me to write this book.

The following have kindly given me permission to quote from
material to which they own the copyright: Mr Mark Bonham
Carter (Asquith mss); Mrs Joan Simon (Emmott mss); Lord Esher
(Esher mss); the Trustees of the National Library of Scotland
(Haldane mss); Lord Gainford (Gainford mss); Mr David
McKenna (McKenna mss); the Master and Fellows of Trinity
College, Cambridge (Montagu mss; these papers are at present
uncatalogued and the references given in the footnotes are
temporary and will probably disappear when the manuscripts are
fully catalogued); Lord Mottistone (Mottistone mss); Mr Godfrey
Samuel (Samuel mss); Lord Harcourt (Harcourt mss); the
National Maritime Museum (microfilm of Slade mss); the Trustees
of the Liddel Hart Centre for Military Archives, King's College,
London (Edmonds and Spears mss); the *Spectator* (St Loe
Stratchey mss); the Trustees of the Imperial War Museum (French
mss, microfilm of the Wilson diaries and access to the microfilm of
the Fitzgerald mss); Mr A. J. P. Taylor and the Trustees of the
Beaverbrook Foundation and the Clerk of the Records of the
House of Lords Record Office (Beaverbrook, Bonar Law and
Lloyd George mss); the Trevelyan family for access to the C. P.
Trevelyan mss in Newcastle University Library, and to Newcastle
University Library for permission to quote from the Runciman
mss; Squadron Leader W. L. Griffiths, rtd (von Donop mss).

Professor B. McL. Ranft and Dr N. W. Summerton kindly gave me permission to refer to their unpublished doctoral theses and Professor Norman McCord gave me permission to quote an extract from his book *Free Trade: Theory and Practice from Adam Smith to Keynes* (Newton Abbot: David & Charles, 1970). The following publishers and agents gave me permission to quote from works they have published: Jonathan Cape Ltd (A. J. Marder, ed., *Fear God and Dread Nought. The Correspondence of Admiral of the Fleet Lord Fisher of Kilverstone);* Cassell Ltd (Earl of Oxford and Asquith, *Memories and Reflections);* David Higham Associates and Penguin Books Ltd (A. J. P. Taylor, *Essays in English History);* William Heineman Ltd (R. S. Churchill, ed., *Winston S. Churchill,* Vol. 2: *Companion);* Doubleday & Co., Inc., and Macmillan Ltd (excerpts from 'The Domestic causes of the First World War' by Arno J. Mayer which appeared in Leonard Krieger and Fritz Stern, eds, *The Responsibility of Power*); Macmillan Ltd (J. Morley, *Memorandum on Resignation*); Oxford University Press (D. W. R. Bahlmam, ed., *The Diary of Sir Edward Hamilton;* E. M. Lloyd, *Experiments in State Control at the War Office and the Ministry of Food;* A. Smith, *An Inquiry into the Nature and Causes of the Wealth of Nations,* edited by R. H. Campbell, A. S. Skinner and W. B. Todd).

Parts of Chapters 3 and 9 first appeared in a slightly different form in the *Journal of Strategic Studies* Vol. 2 (1979), pp 192–205. I am grateful to the editors and publishers for permission to reprint this material here.

Crown copyright material is reproduced by the kind permission of the Controller of Her Majesty's Stationery Office.

Despite my best efforts I was unable to trace the copyright-owners of the Grant Duff or Llewellyn Smith manuscripts. I offer my sincere apologies to them and to anyone else whose copyright I have unwittingly infringed.

Finally, I should like to thank Mrs Jean Roberts and Mrs Elizabeth Hughes for the way in which they typed the final manuscript under the most trying circumstances. My greatest debt of gratitude is recorded in the dedication.

DAVID FRENCH

For my parents

PREFACE

The political manoeuvres which brought about the collapse of Britain's last Liberal government in May 1915 have already been the subject of much scholarly debate. This book will attempt to go beyond the arena of strictly party and factional politics and will examine some of the administrative problems the Liberals faced on the home front. It will also relate them to the strategic policies they tried to pursue in the first nine months of the war. In a recent article in the *Royal United Services Institute Journal* Correlli Barnett has argued that the word 'strategy' changed its meaning during the First World War. In the late nineteenth century it had been a 'purely military' concept implying little more than the operational conduct of war by naval and military forces. But as the First World War became a struggle between whole peoples, strategy came to embrace the *active mobilisation* of the nation's entire economic resources as well.[1] This study will attempt to examine this change in British war plans and policies between the advent of the Liberal government in 1905 and its transformation into a Coalition government in May 1915.

The decade 1905–15 saw the government drift between three possible strategic policies. Before 1914 it rejected the option of sending a continental-scale army to northern France in favour of relying on naval and economic pressure and the assistance of its possible allies to encompass Germany's defeat. In this book this policy is labelled 'the strategy of business as usual'. Its supporters emphasised the role of the Royal Navy at the expense of the army. The navy was to bring about Germany's defeat by blockading its ports and causing its economy to collapse. Protected by its Dreadnoughts the British economy would be able to function almost as usual and so Britain would be able to supply its continental partners with all the munitions they required to conduct the land war. For a variety of reasons this strategy was unrealistic but this fact was not faced squarely until Kitchener became Secretary of State for War in August 1914.

Kitchener was responsible for persuading the Cabinet to take up a second strategic option. This entailed transforming Britain into a 'nation in arms'. He was intent on raising a continental-scale army and dispatching it to fight alongside the French. But by the spring of 1915 Lloyd George was convinced that even that would not be enough to defeat the Germans. Nothing short of an all-out economic *and* military effort would bring victory. By the time the Liberal government collapsed in May 1915 he was already insisting that Britain had no option other than to adopt a policy of total war. If any individual was responsible for changing the meaning of the word 'strategy' in the First World War it was Lloyd George.

Each of these three strategic policies called for steadily escalating degrees of state intervention in the economy. The government was severely dealt with by its critics for the way in which it tried to organise the home front for war. In particular it was accused of being too wedded to the ideology of *laissez-faire* to be able to marshal the nation's resources for the war effort. In 1924 E. M. Lloyd, formerly a civil servant at the War Office and Ministry of Food, wrote that the government had been

> committed to the doctrines of free trade and individualism. It is not surprising that the necessity of State intervention was only gradually admitted by Ministers who had spent the greater part of their political careers in exploding the fallacies of Protectionism on the one hand and Socialism on the other.[2]

This explanation of the manner in which the government acted, one which tries to tie all its policies on the home front to a particular ideology, has now become the accepted orthodox interpretation. In his Raleigh Lecture of 1959 A. J. P. Taylor characterised the problem facing the government thus:

> The great underlying conflict was between freedom and organisation. Could the war be conducted by 'Liberal' methods – that is by voluntary recruiting and *laissez-faire* economics? Or must there be compulsory military service, control of profits, and direction of labour and industry?[3]

Since those words were spoken research on the Liberals' economic and social policies between 1905 and 1914 has shown that they cannot be explained away by arguing that the party was addicted to *laissez-faire* economics. By this time the 'Old Liberalism' of Gladstone was rapidly being overtaken by the 'New Liberalism' of Lloyd George and Winston Churchill. H. V. Emy has shown that while the supporters of the 'New Liberalism' were not prepared to embrace a policy of full-blooded socialism they had also turned their backs on Gladstonian individualism. What they favoured was an attempt 'to use political tools in order to reverse the primacy of economic assumptions, to replace the role of political economy by a form of moral economy . . . '[4] G. R. Searle has shown that around the turn of the century there was a reaction against Gladstonianism which bore fruit in the movement for national efficiency and which captured the imagination of Liberals as well as some Conservatives.[5] Even earlier radical Liberals had come to believe that the solution of working-class problems through state action should be the primary objective of the party. These trends came to fruition after 1906 in two ways. The first was the budgetary proposals of Asquith and Lloyd George which overthrew Gladstonian principles. The second was the programme of social reforms which their budgets financed. By 1911 the days were long gone when Gladstone could condemn active state intervention to improve social conditions with the stricture that it would undermine the individual's independence[6] and expect to receive the unquestioning support of the majority of his party.

Similarly, it is impossible to explain away the government's economic defence plans in this period by reference to its supposed adherence to *laissez-faire* economics without doing violence to the facts. The starting point for its policies was not an economic ideology but the naval and military plans it hoped to implement. Its naval and military plans before 1914 did not call for any significant expansion of the army or navy, so there was no need to plan for the state to redirect economic resources from civilian production to support the armed services. During the period when Kitchener held sway, roughly from August 1914 to March 1915, it was somewhat slow to adopt state controls for a variety of reasons, none of which had much to do with a commitment to *laissez-faire* economics. Two reasons stand out as being of particular importance. The absence of a proper economic general staff meant that the government was very slow to recognise that uncontrolled recruiting was creating serious shortages in the economy which could only have been overcome if it had been prepared to dictate the allocation of manpower. And even if it had recognised that this was the only solution open to it, conscription was still politically impractical in the spring of 1915. Without conscription there was no way in which the government could be sure that both the army and industry got the men they needed. It is also worth noting that its policies concerning the state control of the railways and its secret purchases of large quantities of basic foodstuffs demonstrate conclusively that it had no doctrinaire commitment to *laissez-faire*.

It will also be argued that in the period March–May 1915, when Lloyd George was beginning to champion his own total war policy, the government was slow to use the wide powers conferred on it by the Defence of the Realm (No. 2 Amendment) Act to control industrial output. Once again its tardiness was not the result of any ideological scruples. The two main protagonists in the arguments surrounding the implementation of the Act, Kitchener and Lloyd George, were both happy to see the engineering industry come under closer government control. But what they could not agree on was which of them should control the industry and who the industry should supply, the New Armies or the allies. Sweeping generalisations which seek to explain the Liberal Cabinet's actions in terms of an outmoded economic theory simply do not fit the facts.

This book will also shed some refracted light on one of the controversies surrounding the work of Fritz Fischer. In 1961 and 1969 he published two books, translated into English as *Germany's Aims in the First World War* and *War of Illusions – German Policies from 1911 to 1914*. He provoked a furious debate amongst German historians by arguing that Germany bore a peculiar responsibility for the outbreak of war in 1914. Fischer claimed that from the 1890s Germany's policies were unique in that they were characterised by a 'persistent restlessness'.[7] He abandoned the diplomatic historian's traditional preoccupation with the work of the Foreign Ministry in favour of what he called 'the primacy of domestic policy'.[8] He argued that Germany was in a state of incipient domestic crisis which became particularly acute after 1912. To counter this its ruling class, the Prussian Junkers, the officer corps and leaders of big business, tried to consolidate their position by pursuing an imperialist policy abroad, and they 'hoped a war would resolve the growing social tensions. By involving the masses in the great struggle those parts of the nation which had hitherto stood apart (the Social Democrats) would be integrated into the monarchical state.'[9]

But his insistence on the uniqueness of Germany's policy must remain no more than a working hypothesis until it has been compared with the actions and motives of other governments in the July crisis. A start has been made in doing this by Arno J. Mayer. He shared Fischer's belief in the primacy of domestic policy and tried to apply it on a European-wide scale. He argued that as the right and left of the political spectrum became polarised, the vital 'compromise seeking centre of politics' was eroded. Its leaders, supported by groups who felt that their power and status were threatened by the left – the officer corps, the Foreign Office, the Ministry of the Interior and the church – came to regard a short, successful war abroad as the final antidote to their domestic problems. They hoped that it would rally all the dissident elements opposing them by presenting them with a common enemy against which they could unite.[10] As he wrote: 'During the decade, including the weeks immediately preceding July–August 1914, the

European nations experienced more than routine political and social disturbances.' And about Britain he continued: 'Even Britain, that paradigm of ordered change and constitutionalism, was approaching the threshold of civil war.'[11] Mayer was not alone in this belief. With Britain assailed from the right by the Ulster Unionists and from the left by the Triple Alliance of the railwaymen, the miners and the transport workers threatening a general strike, some historians have wondered whether, if war had not come in Europe, civil war might not have broken out at home.[12] The French and American historians Elié Halevy and George Dangerfield, and more recently the English historian Arthur Marwick, have broadly agreed with Mayer that 'Liberal England' was beginning to disintegrate under these attacks. Marwick argued that the result of this breakdown was that 'Everywhere there was bellicosity, signs of a will to war'.[13]

Mayer's assertions provoked a critical reply. This took two forms. M. R. Gordon established an alternative model based on a theory of economic development and political modernisation in opposition to Mayer's frankly Marxist frame of analysis. He argued that while Mayer's findings might be applicable to Germany they were not to Britain. The differing speeds at which the industrial revolution overtook the two countries ensured that Britain developed a political system able to resolve internal conflicts peacefully, while Germany did not.[14] Donald Lammers simply pointed out the internal inconsistences in Mayer's reasoning and denied that the socio-political tensions Mayer had discovered had any causal connection with the decision of the British Cabinet to go to war.[15]

The most recent survey of British policy on the eve of war demonstrated that neither the Foreign Secretary, Sir Edward Grey, nor his Cabinet colleagues felt tempted to use foreign policy to strengthen their domestic position.[16] It cannot be denied that there was indeed much talk of war before 1914. But this book will demonstrate that the expected social and economic consequences of a major war were regarded as being little short of catastrophic. Thus, far from the British Cabinet seeking war as a way of resolving its internal political problems, ministers were afraid that it would only add to them.

Notes: Preface

1 C. Barnett, 'Strategy and Society', *Royal United Services Institute Journal*, Vol. 121 (1976), pp 12–13.

2 E. M. Lloyd, *Experiments in State Control at the War Office and the Ministry of Food* (London, 1924), p. 21.
3 A. J. P. Taylor, 'Politics in the First World War', in *Essays in English History* (London, 1976), p. 229.
4 H. V. Emy, *Liberals, Radicals and Social Politics, 1892–1914* (Cambridge, 1973), p. xii.
5 G. R. Searle, *The Quest for National Efficiency* (Oxford, 1971), *passim.*
6 These words were spoken in 1889 and are quoted in A. Bullock and M. Shock (eds), *The Liberal Tradition* (Oxford, 1967), p. 208.
7 F. Fischer, *War of Illusions: German Policies from 1911 to 1914* (London, 1975), p. viii.
8 loc. cit.
9 ibid., p. ix.
10 A. J. Mayer, 'The domestic causes of the First World War', in L. Kreiger and F. Stern (eds), *The Responsibility of Power* (London, 1968), pp. 292–3.
11 ibid. p. 288.
12 ibid. p. 289.
13 A. Marwick, *Britain in the Century of Total War* (London, 1970), p. 47; see also E. Halevy, *The Rule of Democracy (Book Two)* (London, 1940), pp. 441–57; G. Dangerfield, *The Strange Death of Liberal England* (London, 1935), pp. 195–295. They also included the suffragettes as another group trying to undermine the status quo.
14 M. R. Gordon, 'Domestic conflict and the origins of the First World War: the British and German cases', *Journal of Modern History,* Vol. 46 (1974), pp. 191–226.
15 D. Lammers, 'Arno Mayer and the British decision for war in 1914', *Journal of British Studies,* Vol. 11 (1973), pp. 137–64.
16 Zara Steiner, *Britain and the Origins of the First World War* (London, 1977), *passim.*

1

Nineteenth-Century Political Economy and the Problem of War

When Britain's defence planners began to prepare for a war against Germany they had behind them a body of accepted ideas about war and economics which had originated in the late eighteenth century. These provided the intellectual framework within which they did their work. The classical economists believed that peace and prosperity were synonymous. But they were also realists and recognised that wars did happen and so their attitude towards them was ambivalent. On the one hand they deplored them because they destroyed capital and human happiness, but on the other hand they did occur and some ways of financing them were to be preferred to others because they minimised these unfortunate consequences.

By the 1840s much of the fundamental realism underlying this attitude was fading. There had not been a major war involving Britain for a generation. A new generation tried to explain this phenomenon by arguing that free trade had brought peace and prosperity in its wake and that universal free trade would bring about universal peace. Free trade would produce such a powerful material nexus between nations that wars would become obsolete.

But by the end of the century actual events were beginning to falsify these assumptions. The British Empire was being confronted by an increasing number of foreign threats. But Britain's position as the centre of a multilateral trade system made it impossible for it to abandon its policy of free trade. By the early twentieth century forecasts about the likely economic consequences of a major war fell into two contrasting camps. The optimists emphasised how great was the degree of economic interdependence between nations, and submitted that no aggressor could make economic gains from a war. They therefore concluded that because man was a rational being he would shun war. The pessimists agreed that nations were economically interdependent and that fact made a long war impossible because the belligerents' economies would quickly collapse under the strain. But they did not accept that men were ruled by economic self-interest or that the dire prospect of economic disaster would prevent nations going to war.

Adam Smith's book *An Inquiry into the Nature and Causes of the Wealth of Nations,* published in 1776, provided the starting point for the classical economists' analysis of the relationship between war and economics. It also provided the original theoretical foundations for Britain's economic strategy in the early months of the First World War. Smith made a sharp distinction between productive and unproductive labour. The former added value to raw materials, and hence the mechanic or the farm labourer was normally engaged in productive labour. Unproductive labour was that carried on by a 'menial servant',[1] and the largest employers of these were governments who enlisted them in their armed forces in great numbers. The armed forces added nothing to the material prosperity of society because 'in time of peace [they] produce nothing, and in time of war acquire nothing which can compensate the expense of maintaining them, even while the war lasts'.[2]

Hence it was always necessary to reduce the numbers in the armed forces to the lowest possible level commensurate with national safety. If they were allowed to multiply unchecked they would swallow up all the surplus goods produced by the rest of the population. Wars were economically wasteful because they diverted capital away from productive enterprises and because they multiplied the numbers of unproductive labourers in the armed forces.[3]

But while Smith shunned war on these grounds he had to concede that the state did need physical force to defend itself. Without this force it would forfeit its independence. Armed forces were a political necessity. 'The first duty of the sovereign, that of protecting the society from the violence and invasion of other independent societies, can be performed only by means of a military force.'[4]

And he was prepared to subordinate the dictates of prosperity to those of defence. This is shown most clearly in his attitude towards free trade and the Navigation Laws. Smith was an ardent believer in free trade between nations. Free trade benefited all countries because it enabled them to exchange their own surplus goods for those of other countries. But defence had to come before opulence and so he was prepared to defend the protectionist Navigation Laws because they helped to nurture the seamen upon whom Britain's security rested.[5] Although not all the classical economists were prepared to defend the Navigation Laws they did concede Smith's main point that the needs of national defence gave the state the right to overcome the dictates of economic freedom.[6] The theory of *laissez-faire* never prevented the state from interfering in the economy for the sake of national defence.

Smith was convinced that free trade and healthy export industries were the best ways to finance a war. He rejected the mercantilist argument that to pay for a war a government had to accumulate a hoard of gold and silver so that it could pay for the cost of its foreign military expeditions. Smith believed that whilst such a policy might be forced upon a predominantly agricultural country, Britain had no need to adopt it. It possessed a highly developed manufacturing and trading economy and could use the profits from these to pay for its war effort without ever having to export any specie at all.[7]

> Fleets and armies are maintained [he argued], not with gold and silver but with consumable goods. The nation which, from the annual produce of its domestick [*sic*] industry, from the annual revenue arising out of its lands, labour and consumable stock, has wherewithal to purchase those consumable goods in distant countries, can maintain foreign wars there.[8]

Bitter experience during the wars against France between 1793 and 1815 seemed to support Smith's contention that wars bred poverty. Writing in 1808, the economist James Mill said that war was a 'pestilential wind' which brought with it high poor rates, high taxes to support bloated armies and navies, and prevented profits from being reinvested in productive enterprises which might add to prosperity.[9] But the cessation of the war in 1815 did not bring about an immediate return to prosperity. The public blamed the continuing bad times on high taxation. They demanded retrenchment in government spending as the only way to return to prosperity.[10] In the face of such insistent demands Lord Liverpool's administration had little option but to comply. The army and navy were the largest spending departments and they suffered the most severe cuts. Defence expenditure fell from its wartime peak of just over £72 million to a plateau of £14–16 million in the 1820s, 1830s and 1840s. Proponents of this policy rested their advocacy of it on Smith's assumption that the ability to conduct a successful war depended not just on the army and navy but on the ability of the economy to support them, and that in turn rested on the lowest possible level of government spending in peacetime. Thus, for example, a parliamentary select committee of inquiry on finance tried to strike a balance between the competing demands of the armed forces and the economy. It conceded that the strength of the armed forces should be left to the government to determine in the light of any actual threats to Britain's security, but concluded that the army and navy alone could not ensure that security. Large quantities of money were also needed and they would only be forthcoming in wartime if, in peacetime, taxes were cut to the bone.[11]

Ten years later Sir Henry Parnell in his book *On Financial Reform* provided a fuller and more elaborate justification for the paradoxical policy of reducing the size of the armed forces in order to strengthen Britain's defences. Parnell argued that unless taxes were reduced the government would find it impossible to finance a major war without recourse to large-scale borrowing. This would mean a large addition to the national debt and a permanent addition to the tax burden needed to service that debt. If in the meantime the existing high level of taxation was continued in order to maintain an overlarge defence establishment it would destroy industry and produce national bankruptcy. The government did have a duty to prepare for war in peacetime but such preparations should be commensurate with the actual threats facing the country. In 1828 this was no longer the case because recent experience had shown all nations that wars did not lead to commercial gain. Hence the potent cause of past wars, commercial jealousy, no longer existed and no longer had to be guarded against. Every country now recognised that the path to prosperity lay not through war but through trade.[12]

This note of optimism became louder as memories of the wars against France faded and as Britain adopted free trade policies. In 1815 the Corn Laws had been imposed as a way of making Britain independent of foreign food supplies. But it very quickly became apparent that autarky was an impossible goal. Britain had no option other than to rely on foreign food imports.[13] The most convinced exponents of the argument that free trade would eventually make war obsolete and would replace it with an era of universal peace and prosperity were the spokesmen of the Anti-Corn Law League.[14] They argued that universal free trade would produce a material nexus between nations which would draw men together and enable them to overcome barriers 'of race, creed and language'.[15] Similar ideas were echoed by John Stuart Mill in his *Principles of Political Economy*. He looked forward to the happy day when commerce between nations would make war a thing of the past.[16] Richard Cobden explained this possibility by referring to divine providence. Providence had enabled some countries to produce particular goods in abundance so that they could exchange their surpluses for the produce of other countries, 'and that thus they may be united together in the bonds of peace and brotherhood'.[17]

Thus by the mid-nineteenth century several of the theoretical economic foundations of 'business as usual' had been erected. Manufactured exports, not a large war chest, were the best way to pay for a war. A small peacetime defence establishment was desirable because it would allow the government to reduce taxes and thus create the conditions necessary for economic prosperity and flourishing export industries. Free trade would open up the whole world to the goods produced by these industries and universal trade might even make war a thing of the past.

But after about 1850 the favourable economic and strategic circumstances enjoyed by the previous generation which had made such optimistic predictions plausible began to disappear. By the end of the century free trade still had plenty of devotees but many people were coming to see it as a potential strategic weakness rather than a source of strength.

This changing strategic situation first presented itself to Britain in the shape of a number of invasion scares. The first occurred in 1852 but the second, and much more serious one, began in 1858. The French began building the first ever ironclad warship and by 1859 the British public were deeply alarmed. Palmerston's government was divided on the question of how to meet the crisis. The Prime Minister was anxious to raise a large defence loan, but his Chancellor of the Exchequer, W. E. Gladstone, was loathe to add to the public debt by raising the money. As an apostle of Cobden's belief that free trade was Britain's best defence, Gladstone staunchly supported the free trade treaty then being negotiated in Paris by Cobden.[18] But although many of his colleagues were ready to pay lip service to Cobden's beliefs, few of them really shared Gladstone's faith in them. Instead they reverted to Smith's view that whilst free trade would bring prosperity, the best guarantor of security was a powerful fleet.

Even when he became Prime Minister himself, Gladstone was unable to persuade the majority of his followers that he was right. The latter might agonise over rising defence estimates but the estimates did rise. Three things conspired to bring this about. The increasing pace of technological change made weapons obsolete more rapidly and tended to ensure that their replacements were always more expensive. Secondly, the number of invasion scares multiplied as did the number of colonial wars the army undertook. And finally, the enlarged electorate began to demand that the government pay more attention to the state of Britain's defences. Gladstone's persistent desire to reduce defence expenditure may have been appropriate to the 1830s and 1840s but by the last quarter of the century it made him look old-fashioned and increasingly out of touch with both his colleagues and the electorate. By 1882 he could only lament that

> The cry of economy is a thing of the past. The want of it is the worst characteristic in the modern Liberal or Radical, and makes him in this respect compare badly with the old Whigs, with whom economy and retrenchment were part of their creed.[19]

Fittingly, the occasion for Gladstone's final break with his own government came in March 1894 over the navy estimates. Alone in the Cabinet he refused to agree to increasing them to meet the threat from the combined Franco-Russian fleets.

In the final analysis Gladstone's approach to strategic problems was firmly rooted in the past. The situation facing Britain in the 1890s was very different from what it had been in the 1840s and now gave much cause for pessimism. Since the 1840s the British economy had moved rapidly away from self-sufficiency. After 1870 Britain had built up a system of multilateral trade links which spanned the world. By the beginning of the twentieth century its continued prosperity depended on the smooth and continuous flow of goods into and out of the country. Stocks of vital raw materials and staple foodstuffs retained in Britain were small. For example, at the turn of the century 45 per cent of all meat consumed in Britain was imported, and cold stores only held one month's supply. Pork and bacon stocks would only last for two weeks. Half of all of the cheese eaten in Britain was imported, as was two-thirds of all butter. Stocks of these and other dairy produce would only last for between four to ten weeks.[20] Britain was even more dependent on imported grains, a crucial factor because the population consumed more bread than any other foodstuff. In 1904 only 20 per cent of the country's flour requirements could be met by home-grown wheat. Between 1870 and 1904 imports had risen threefold in order to keep pace with declining home production and rising demand. Stocks sometimes fell to as low as two and a half weeks supply and they would be quickly exhausted if the smooth flow of international trade was interrupted.[21] And as for industrial raw materials, in 1903 it was estimated that all of the United Kingdom's raw cotton was imported and if imports were stopped stocks would run out in six or seven months. Three-quarters of all wool used in weaving was imported and stocks of that would only last for three months. The iron industry relied on imports for 40 per cent of its raw materials and had stockpiled reserves for only four weeks. Without imported manganese all steel manufacturing would very soon cease.[22]

Thus Britain was totally dependent on the continued flow of international trade for its economic survival, a fact of which its political leaders were well aware. In October 1903 the future Prime Minister, H. H. Asquith, told an audience that

> There was no other means by which they could maintain the comfort of the people and the prosperity and progress of their commerce both at home and in the foreign markets than by securing the freest and fullest possible influx into these islands of the food and raw materials which were the very basis of our industry.[23]

Asquith could have added that it was equally vital for Britain to retain its position as the financier, shipper and insurer of the world's trade. Without the profits from these undertakings its balance of payments would have been regularly in deficit. Britain's success in these particular undertakings owed much to the fact that it stood at the centre of the international gold standard. The name gold standard was, in reality, somewhat misleading. The late nineteenth-century gold standard was actually a sterling standard, although sterling bills were convertible into gold on demand.[24] In the 1860s and 1870s British merchants and financial institutions began to expand abroad and foreigners began to take up the opportunity this offered them to settle their international debts through London using sterling bills of exchange. This increasing use of sterling was given extra impetus by the establishment of major commodity markets in London as Britain became the world's largest importer of food and raw materials.[25] Essentially the sterling system worked because traders all over the world recognised that London was, in practice, the world's only free market in gold. This made them confident that if they wished to they could exchange their sterling bills for gold on demand, and because they were confident of that fact, they did not exchange them.

Britain's enormous dependence on international trade was not thought to be a major strategic weakness in the second quarter of the nineteenth century because there was then no other power which seriously threatened its international position. But by the early twentieth century that was no longer the case, and by 1900 the question of whether or not free trade still added to Britain's security was open to debate.

Between 1815 and 1846 Britain had gained little in terms of international security from protection. Given the increasing size of its population and the ever-present possibility of crop failures at home, Britain's only real security lay in encouraging the development of foreign sources of supply. The only alternative would have been to have reduced the size of its population to keep it in line with domestic food production. Far from increasing its security this policy would have reduced the men available for the army and navy; it would have retarded the development of its manufacturing economy upon which its prosperity finally depended; and it would have produced such serious social tensions in Britain that they would have threatened national unity at a time of crisis. By contrast, free trade promoted Britain's security by enabling it to develop diverse sources of supply for food and raw materials and to establish markets for its manufactured goods, and so ultimately helped it to expand its industrial base. And finally, free trade and overseas commerce encouraged the development of the Royal Navy, the force upon which its final security rested.[26]

However, by the 1880s Britain was no longer the world's only major industrial power. Its competitiors now began to close their markets to British exports by erecting tariff barriers. And by the end of the century other navies were threatening the supremacy of the Royal Navy. The economic and strategic certainties of the mid-Victorian era were all called into question. During the Boer War of 1899–1902 the defence estimates spiralled upwards, and after the war they obstinately refused to fall back to their prewar levels.[27] The problem of meeting this heavy burden was compounded after 1908 by the cost of new social services. Rising government expenditure brought about a new and fundamental cleavage in British politics. To raise the necessary money many Liberals were prepared to resort to progressive taxation. More orthodox financiers in both the Unionist Party and the Treasury were horrified at this. The Treasury was committed to the interdependent goals of preserving free trade and keeping public expenditure at the lowest possible level.[28] Free trade precluded the government's placing a large share of the tax burden on commerce, and so the government had to raise money through taxes on income. These gave a strictly limited yield, and the Treasury feared that if they were raised too sharply they might harm industry and enterprise. Equally important in this context were the fears expressed by many Unionist MPs that the strain these new burdens placed on the income tax would undermine Britain's ability to pay for a major war. Since the days of Pitt the Younger the British tradition of war finance had dictated that the national debt should be kept down to the lowest possible level by paying for wars out of current taxation, and in particular through an income tax.[29] But on the eve of the First World War many Unionists feared that the government's social policies would leave no reserves in the income tax which could be drawn upon in an emergency. In 1913 Lord

Cromer, one of Britain's most distinguished experts in public finance, wrote of Lloyd George's budget that

> it was our superiority in resources that really pulled us through our old wars. The most damaging criticism of the whole of Lloyd George's policy unquestionably is that if he has not entirely destroyed he has enormously weakened our fiscal reserves.[30]

Others went on even further and voiced the gloomy prediction that the existing high levels of direct taxation meant that Britain had already shot its financial bolt and that there were no reserves left to pay for a major war.[31]

The lack of unlimited finance therefore became an important constraint on defence preparations before 1914. Almost everyone was persuaded that defence spending in peacetime was, at the very best, a necessary evil. It was believed that it should be kept as low as possible commensurate with a reasonable margin of safety. The Foreign Secretary, Sir Edward Grey, explained this point when he wrote: 'I call expenditure on armaments unproductive because it brings in no direct return. I do not say that it is unnecessary. It is, of course, a form of insurance.'[32]

Many Unionists saw a return to protection under the guise of tariff reform as the only escape from this dilemma. But such a solution was still anathema to the Liberal Party, the Treasury and the Foreign Office. By the early twentieth century the Foreign Office had elevated free trade to being one of the cornerstones of British foreign policy. On 1 January 1907 Sir Eyre Crowe, the Senior Clerk at the Foreign Office, wrote a long memorandum exploring the basis of British foreign policy in relation to Anglo-German relations. Crowe argued that throughout the nineteenth century Britain's foreign policy had revolved around three facts. It was an island off the coast of Europe; it possessed a vast colonial empire; and the security of both Britain and its empire rested on its possession of a preponderant navy. Crowe believed that Britain's possession of the world's most powerful navy was bound to arouse the hostility of other powers and that if they ever combined against it, it was certain to be overthrown, because 'no single nation could in the long run stand, least of all a small island kingdom not possessed of the military strength of a people trained to arms, and dependent for its food supply on oversea commerce.'[33] The only way the British could avoid such a hostile combination coming together was if it did all in its power to ensure that British policy harmonised with that of a majority of the other powers. The first interest of all independent states was to preserve their independence. Hence Britain had to be the enemy of any state threatening the independence of its neighbours. But second only to national independence was 'free intercourse and trade in the world's markets'.[34] So free trade was a strategic necessity for Britain. If it threw a tariff barrier around its empire it would eventually call into being a hostile coalition bent on its downfall. But Crowe's reasoning still left two problems. It did not really provide an answer to the Unionist jibe that the Liberals had wrecked Britain's finances. The latter could only retort that Britain's credit was still good and so the cost of a long war could be met by borrowing. Nor did it reassure people who believed that Britain's central position in the international economy would be a source of grave weakness on the outbreak of war. At the very heart of that economy lay the Bank of England, the centre of Britain's and ultimately the world's banking system. The Bank was Britain's central bank, and acted as a lender of last resort to all other bankers in Britain. The Bank held the ultimate reserves for the whole banking system, and the stability of the entire edifice depended on the Bank's being able to meet all its customers' demands for gold in exchange for the notes and bills they presented to it. But it could not do this simply by relying on the gold it held in its vaults. In 1891 the Bank's gold reserves were only £24 million. The liabilities facing, for example, only eleven of the larger joint-stock banks totalled about £170 million and their own cash reserve only covered about a tenth of their liabilities. In a crisis, if their depositors demanded gold, they had to call in their short-term loans to merchants and manufacturers, and ask the Bank to advance them money.[35]

The latter was only able to function, and to protect itself against a prolonged drain, by selling securities on the open market or by raising the bank rate. Both operations attracted gold to its vaults.[36] But international trade could present a second threat to the Bank's reserves. Joint-stock bankers made short-term loans to merchant bankers and bill-brokers on the security of their bills of lading. On completion of the transaction the bills were discounted by the joint-stock banks. The danger to the Bank's reserves lay in the fact that if a merchant anywhere in the world wanted gold in exchange for a sterling bill, the Bank was obliged to pay in gold, which then left the country.[37]

The problem of the size of the gold reserves was first brought to the attention of bankers during the Baring crisis of 1890. The crisis had shown that the Bank's reserves were too small to meet a real emergency, and the Bank had been forced to adopt the expedient of going to the French and Russian central banks for gold. In the aftermath of the crisis G. J. Goschen, the Chancellor of the Exchequer, wanted to double the reserve to £40 million by issuing one pound notes, in the hope that these would drive gold sovereigns out of circulation and into the Bank's vaults.[38] Nothing came of this suggestion because, by the middle of the 1890s, the panic was over. The joint-stock banks had increased their reserves with the Bank of England, and furthermore, as world gold production increased, some of it found its way to London. The result was that between 1891 and 1895 the Bank's reserves did double without the need to print pound notes.

But this did not put an end to all disquiet. During the Boer War the joint-stock bankers again made substantial increases to their reserves. The Russo-Japanese War seemed to pose another threat. Shortly after the Dogger Bank incident in October 1904 Sir George Clarke, the first secretary of the Committee of Imperial Defence, sent a memorandum to the Treasury arguing that national security would be in serious danger if the gold reserves collapsed. He was worried that the immediate result of Britain being dragged into the Russo-Japanese War would be large withdrawals of gold from the Bank of England by the French and German banks. This would produce a sharp rise in the bank rate and a corresponding fall in the price of securities. American securities would be sold in New York and the money raised would be remitted to London, but as soon as this process had begun there would be financial panic in New York and the British government would have no hope of raising loans there. With the French and German markets already shut, New York would be the only place Britain could turn to for money, but if his forecast proved to be correct, then Clarke's gloomy prediction was that 'I doubt whether we are in a position to be able to finance such a war if it were sprung on us without notice, which is part of the hypothesis'. Secondly, he feared a pre-emptive strike against the Bank's reserves. The governors of the Bank of France and the Reichsbank were known to exercise very close control over their countries' private banks. He thought that they were quite capable, just prior to the declaration of war, of ordering their banks to withdraw all of their deposits in London. In that way they could cripple Britain's finances. And finally, he feared that the outbreak of war would be marked by an internal drain of gold from the reserves as private depositors panicked and hoarded gold against unforeseen emergencies. All of this, he believed, made the problem

> an integral part of any scheme of Imperial defence, and, with all due deference, I would submit that just as you have a two or three Power Standard for your Navy, so you must have one for your finance.[39]

And by the outbreak of war Clarke was only one voice amongst many advocating a return to mercantilism and the amassing of a war chest.[40]

The last faint notes of Cobden's optimistic belief that free trade would produce universal peace were sounded by Ralf Lane in 1909. Under the pseudonym Norman Angell he published a book called *Europe's Optical Illusion.* It was republished several times before 1914 under the title *The Great Illusion,* and it sold over 2 million copies between 1910 and 1913.[41] Angell's book was widely reviewed and most reviewers shared his conviction that war would bring about economic disaster through the collapse of international credit. But they did not agree with his underlying assumption, namely, that this fact made it pointless to go to war for economic gain and that recognising this to be true, nations would shun war. Reviewing Angell in 1910 a writer in the *Quarterly Review* argued that if Britain went to war with a major naval power like Germany, 'the London money-market would be immediately subjected to a financial panic which could hardly fail to involve the whole community in incalculable losses . . .'.[42] Credit would collapse, stock-market securities would rapidly depreciate, foreign trade would come to a standstill, and finally unemployment and starvation would stalk the country. The upshot would be a short war for, 'in the light of modern experience, it does not appear that such a war could be much prolonged, and nine months would probably be a reasonable period to anticipate'.[43]

.This pessimistic analysis had penetrated deeply into politicians' consciousness by 1914. Speaking to the Manchester Chamber of Commerce in February 1914, Grey remarked that war was the worst possible thing that could happen to trade. He noted that there existed in Britain the Norman Angell Society, 'which produced most attractive arguments, appealing most strongly to the intellect on this question of armaments and of war generally', but he shrewdly concluded that on questions of war and peace men were often ruled not by their intellects but by their emotions.[44] And Grey was not the only politician who feared the economic and social consequences of a major war. Many of the types of people A. J. Mayer believed looked forward to a war as a way of shoring up their domestic political position were actually afraid that a war would have exactly the opposite effect. For example, in April 1897 two Unionist MPs, H. Seton-Kerr, a longstanding advocate of imperial preference, and R. A. Yerburgh, a former president of the National Agricultural Union and a man who became president of the Navy League in 1901, tabled a motion in the House of Commons calling attention to the United Kingdom's wholly inadequate food supplies. Yerburgh painted an apocalyptic picture of what might happen if Britain's food supplies were interrupted in wartime.

Starving mobs would riot and force the government to surrender unconditionally. He asked:

> would the Army be able to operate with any efficiency if it had behind it a sullen, discontented population, ready to take to riot and pillage under the stress of hunger and the fear of starvation? The Army could not hope to operate effectively, and there would be no recourse but unconditional surrender and loss of empire.[45]

The early setbacks of the Boer War only added to these fears. Britain was denuded of regular troops and there was an invasion scare. The Navy League was foremost in asking whether the navy was as ill-prepared as the army to face a major war.[46] Prominent members of the League combined with other interested parties to demand that the government take steps to ensure the safety of food supplies. On 2 February 1903 a group calling themselves the Association to Promote an Official Enquiry into the Security of our Food Supply in Time of War was formed. Its purpose was to do just what its title suggested. The association rested its case on three points. Half of Britain's population lived on incomes of between fifteen and fifty shillings per week. This meant that 'any considerable rise in the price of food would make it impossible for any of these people to support themselves'. Many would be thrown out of work if the navy could not keep open the sea lanes, and they would starve. This would have catastrophic political results.[47] The membership of the association indicates just how widespread these fears were. The association comprised not only Unionist MPs who favoured protection, but Liberal free-traders as well. Corn merchants, shipowners and insurance brokers rubbed shoulders with members of trades councils and at least one member of the parliamentary committee of the TUC.[48] All of them looked towards a war with deep foreboding and their fears underlay most of the government's economic plans for war. But before the latter can be fully understood it is necessary to explain how the government expected the purely naval and military aspects of the war to develop.

Notes: Chapter 1

1   A. Smith, *An Inquiry into the Nature and Causes of the Wealth of Nations*, ed. R. H. Campbell, A. S. Skinner and W. B. Todd (London, 1976), Vol. 1, p. 330.
2   ibid., p. 342.
3   ibid., pp. 344–5.

4   ibid., Vol. 2, p. 689; see also D. Winch, *Adam Smith's Politics* (Cambridge, 1978), ch. 5, *passim.*
5   Smith, op. cit., Vol. 1, pp. 464–5
6   Lord Robbins, *Political Economy, Past and Present* (London, 1976), pp. 153–5.
7   Smith, op. cit., Vol. 1, pp. 444–5.
8   ibid., pp. 440–1.
9   D. Winch (ed.), *James Mill. Selected Economic Writings* (Edinburgh, 1966), p.157.
10 N. Gash, 'After Waterloo. British society and the legacy of the Napoleonic Wars', *Transactions of the Royal Historical Society,* 5th ser., vol. 28 (1978), *passim.*
11 C. J. Bartlett, *Great Britain and Sea Power, 1815–53* (Oxford, 1963), pp. 13–14; see also B. Hilton, *Corn, Cash, Commerce* (London, 1977), ch. 8, *passim.*
12 Sir H. Parnell, *On Financial Reform* (London, 1831), pp 211–13.
13 Hilton, op. cit., pp. 20–2, 109–17.
14 N. McCord, *The Anti-Corn Law League* (London, 1958, repr. 1975), p. 24; idem, 'Cobden and Bright in politics, 1846–57', in R. Robson (ed.), *Ideas and Institutions of Victorian Britain* (London, 1969), p. 90.
15 K. Bourne, *The Foreign Policy of Victorian England* (London, 1970), p. 269.
16 J. S. Mill, *Principles of Political Economy, with Some of their Applications to Social Philosophy* (London, 1848), pp. 581–2.
17 J. A. Hobson, *Richard Cobden. The International Man* (London, 1919, repr. 1968), p. 47.
18 J. Morley, *The Life of William Ewart Gladstone* (London, 1908), Vol. 1, pp. 487–504.
19 D. W. R. Bahlman (ed.), *The Diary of Sir Edward Hamilton* (London, 1972), Vol. 1, p. 71.
20 *Report of the Royal Commission on Supply of Food and Raw Materials in Time of War,* Cd 2643 (1905), pp. 4–6; *Minutes of Evidence of the Royal Commission on Supply of Food and Raw Materials in Time of War,* Cd 2644 (1905), QQ. 2972, 9527, 3957, 3988, 1937, 1952, 2249, 2269, 2982, 2988, 3742, 3006, 3036–8, 4236.
21 Cd 2643, op. cit., pp. 6–16; Cd 2644, op. cit., QQ. 270, 508, 2672.
22 Cd 2643, op. cit., pp. 2–4; Cd 2644, op. cit., QQ. 4375, 4383, 4385–6, 4585, 4629, 5024, 4280, 4292; C. E. Fayle, *A History of the Great War. Seaborne Trade* (London, 1920), Vol. I, pp. 1–5.
23 N. McCord, *Free Trade, Theory and Practice from Adam Smith to Keynes* (Newton Abbot, 1970), p. 138.
24 M. de Cecco, *Money and Empire. The International Gold Standard, 1890–1914* (Oxford, 1974), pp. 1–7, 20–1.
25 D. Williams, 'The evolution of the sterling system', in C. R. Whittlesey and J. S. G. Wilson (eds), *Essays in Money and Banking in Honour of R. S. Sayers* (Oxford, 1968), pp. 266–77.
26 A. H. Imlah, *Economic Elements in the Pax Britannica* (New York, 1958, repr. 1969), p. 186.
27 B. R. Mitchell and Phyllis Deane, *An Abstract of British Historical Statistics* (Cambridge, 1962, repr. 1976), p. 398; A. T. Peacock and J. Wiseman, *The Growth of Public Expenditure in the United Kingdom* (London, 1967), p. 168.
28 H. Roseveare, *The Treasury. The Evolution of a British Institution* (London, 1969), p. 187; H. V. Emy, 'The impact of financial policy on English politics before 1914', *Historical Journal,* vol. 15, (1972), pp. 103–27.
29 W. K. Hancock and M. M. Gowing, *British War Economy* (London, 1949), pp. 4–5.
30 PRO FO 633/22, Lord Cromer to B. Mallet, 28 Nov. 1913. (I am grateful to Dr P. M. Kennedy of the University of East Anglia for drawing my attention to references in the Cromer mss to this subject.)
31 See, for example, 52 HC Deb., 5s., col 2137.
32 PRO FO 800/109, Sir E. Grey to Sir B. Mallet (n.d.).

33 G. P. Gooch and H. Temperley (eds), *British Documents on the Origins of the War, 1898–1914* (London, 1926–38), Vol. 3, p. 402.
34 ibid., p. 403.
35 PRO T 168/97, 'The insufficiency of our cash reserves and of our national stock of gold', speech by G. J. Goschen given at Leeds, 9 Jan. 1891; see also de Cecco, op. cit., ch. 5 *passim*.
36 R. S. Sayers, 'The development of central banking after Bagehot', *Economic History Review*, 2nd ser., vol. 4 (1951), *passim*.
37 De Cecco, op. cit., pp. 85–6, 103–6; R. H. Brand, *War and National Finance* (London, 1921), pp. 14–16; PRO T 168/97, 'Our gold reserves', speech by Sir Felix Schuster, vice-president of the Institute of Bankers, 19 Dec. 1906.
38 PRO T 168/97, 'Address to the London Chamber of Commerce by the Rt Hon. G. J. Goschen on the Metallic Reserve', 2 Dec. 1891; J. H. Clapham, *The Bank of England, a History, 1797–1944* (London, 1944), Vol. 2, pp. 343–4.
39 PRO Cab. 17/81, Financial effects of the outbreak of war, G. S. Clarke (n.d. but *c*. Jan. 1905)
40 See, for example, Sir R. Giffen, 'The necessity of a war chest in this country, or a greatly increased gold reserve', *Royal United Services Institute Journal*, vol. 52, (1908), pp. 1,329–40.
41 N. Angell, *The Great Illusion. A Study of the relation of Military Power to National Advantage* (London, 1909), *passim;* see also H. S. Weinroth, 'Norman Angell and the "Great Illusion"; an episode in pre-1914 pacifism', *Historical Journal*, vol. 17 (1974), *passim*.
42 E. Crammond, 'International finance in time of war', *Quarterly Review* (Oct. 1910), p. 303.
43 ibid., p 316.
44 *The Times*, 4 Feb. 1914.
45 48 HC Deb., 4s., col. 655.
46 A. J. Marder, *The Anatomy of British Sea Power* (London, 1964), pp. 376–92.
47 *Royal Commission on Supply of Food and Raw Materials in Time of War. Appendices*, Cd 2645 (1905), App. 49, Papers supplied by the Association to Promote an Official Enquiry into the Security of our Food Supply in Time of War.
48 ibid.

2

The Strategy of
'Business as Usual'

In 1901 the British Empire was isolated in a hostile world. Its defence planners were only too conscious that their resources were too limited to allow them to meet all the commitments facing them. But between 1902 and 1907 British diplomacy skilfully reduced the threats facing the empire to a more manageable size. The Anglo-Japanese Treaty of 1902, the Entente Cordiale of 1904 with France and the Entente of 1907 with Russia placated all but one major hostile power: Germany.[1] But just because the dangers facing Britain had been narrowed that did not mean that its strategic plans were fully prepared to meet them. Before the First World War Britain's naval and military plans were both ambiguous and based on some doubtful premisses. In the first place the Cabinet avoided deciding before August 1914 whether, in the event of a war with Germany, Britain would stand by France, and if it did so, whether it would fight a purely maritime war or commit its very small Expeditionary Force to the continent. The planners at the War Office and the Admiralty were thus compelled to work within a political vacuum. And secondly, the plans they produced were unrealistic given the resources available to them. The War Office firmly embraced the continental commitment but it was without a continental-scale army to carry it out and it did not even have any plans to raise one. The Admiralty insisted that a blockade would bring Germany to its knees, but in saying so it omitted to assess just how vulnerable the German economy was to a blockade.

And yet out of this assortment of dogma and half-thought-out plans a national strategy for a war against Germany did emerge. A small group of ministers would have been prepared to accept the General Staff's case for a major land commitment to the continent but the prejudices of the majority of the Cabinet, the Liberal Party and probably most of the population, against continental entanglements and in favour of carrying on wars by naval and economic means, meant that their strategy was politically impossible before

1914. Thus by August 1914 Britain intended to fight the war by blockading Germany and causing its economy to collapse. Simultaneously the Royal Navy would keep open Britain's sea lanes and so the British economy would be able to supply its allies with all the munitions they needed to carry on the land war. These were the naval and military premisses which underlay the strategy of 'business as usual'.

The General Staff first examined the possibility of acting in concert with the French army against the Germans in April 1905. From a strategic war game they played they discovered the principles which underlay all their prewar plans. They believed that an eventual German advance through Belgium was probable because the strength of France's eastern frontier defences precluded a successful advance there. Belgium could not stop such an advance without British military help, but if that aid was to be of any use it would have to arrive quickly.[2]

However, while the General Staff wanted to send direct military assistance to Belgium, the Admiralty, in the person of Admiral Sir A. K. Wilson, the commander in chief of the Channel Fleet, wanted to exploit the supposed flexibility inherent in the use of sea power to assist France. In June 1905 he told the Admiralty that no action by the fleet alone could help the French army in the decisive theatre of operations, on the French frontier. However, the Royal Navy could blockade German ports, which would weaken Germany by disrupting its trade. More significantly he recommended that combined operations against objectives on Germany's coast should be launched in an effort to force it to divert large numbers of troops from France.[3]

The War Office completely rejected the use of its troops in this way. Wilson's plan was unrealistic because it ignored the dangers a fleet operating near the German coast would face from mines and submarines. Nor had he taken any account of the ease with which the Germans could have used their excellent railway communications to rush troops to any threatened point on the coast. But conversely, as Colonel Callwell, an assistant director of military operations, explained to the Admiralty in October 1905, if the General Staff's plan was adopted

> an efficient army of 120,000 British troops might just have the effect of preventing any important German successes on the Franco-German frontier, and of leading up to the situation that Germany, crushed at sea, also felt herself impotent on land. That would almost certainly bring about a speedy, and from the British and French point of view satisfactory, peace.[4]

The General Staff thus saw the British Expeditionary Force as the final element in the allied strategy which would tip the scales in their favour. The Germans, faced by a stalemate on land and sea, would have no option other than to make peace. But in reasoning along these lines the General Staff were being highly optimistic. The Expeditionary Force was tiny by the standards set by the size of the armies of the other great powers. And the General Staff had also overlooked the possibility that the Germans might simply dig in and let the allies exhaust themselves by attacking them rather than make peace.

If these possibilities had been recognised before the war it might have been borne home more clearly to some members of the Cabinet that the size of the army was not based on a realistic assessment of the task it would have to perform in a European war, but on the money and the numbers of men available to pay for it and to man it.

When the new Liberal Secretary of State for War, R. B. Haldane, began to reorganise the army in 1906 the need to economise was uppermost in his mind. He was determined that the army estimates should not exceed £28 million p.a. and he was relatively successful in achieving this aim. They fell from £29,813,000 in 1905/6 to £27,435,000 in 1909/10.[5] But even if more money had been available to pay for a larger army it is doubtful whether more men would have been willing to volunteer to enlist. In the period 1910–13 the army recruited an average of 28,557 men each year.[6] In reporting to the Committee of Imperial Defence in April 1913 the Secretary of State for War admitted that the army needed 34,000 men each year to maintain its strength. In their annual reports successive directors general of recruiting lamented thet good trade years meant lean recruiting. More pay did not seem to be the answer.[7] In 1912, in an effort to attract more recruits to the Royal Engineers, a private's pay was raised by one shilling a day to two shillings and threepence halfpenny, but even this failed to attract more recruits.[8] Prospects for the future looked bleak. Unemployment insurance and the establishment of labour exchanges, emigration and increased recruiting by the Royal Navy made the army even more a last resort for the unemployed than it had always been.

If voluntary recruiting failed to fill the ranks of the army then conscription was the only alternative. But before 1914 this was never politically practical. Lord Roberts, the chairman of the National Service League, publicly advocated conscription for home defence, and privately for a war in Europe. The reply Winston Churchill, then First Lord of the Admiralty, sent to him refusing his request to support conscription shows the dilemma in which supporters of the continental strategy found themselves.

> I was when I first went into Parlt, opposed to the principle of compulsory service. I am disposed somewhat differently now towards it. As to the right of the State and the duty of the citizen there can be no doubt. But I am far less certain that it is necessary or that it wd be convenient. Further even if I were satisfied on these points, I do not see at this moment what steps shd be taken or what combination of force wd be available to support them.[9]

His letter illustrated both the illusions and the sound grasp of practical politics that the supporters of the continental commitment had. He was wrong in believing that Britain did not need a larger army but he was correct to assume that peacetime conscription was impossible. In 1910 Lloyd George argued that compulsory training even for home defence was beyond the bounds of possibility, 'because of the violent prejudices which would be excited even if it were suspected that a Government contemplated the possibility of establishing anything of the kind'.[10] The truth of this remark was shown by the parliamentary and Cabinet debates on a Bill to introduce compulsory training for the Territorial Army in March 1913. Of its twelve sponsors only one was a Liberal; the remainder were all Unionists. The Bill foundered during its second reading, but not before both its supporters and its opponents had expressed their views on it. Supporters of the Bill argued that in the face of Germany's growing naval strength voluntary recruiting for the Territorials had failed, and that every citizen had a duty to defend his country. Opponents of the Bill came from both the Liberal and the Labour parties. J. H. Whitehouse, the Liberal MP for Mid Lanark, and George Roberts, the Labour MP for Norwich, opposed the Bill in almost identical terms, that as the Royal Navy was Britain's defence against invasion compulsory service for home defence was unnecessary; supporters of the Bill were being less than honest because they would not admit that they really wanted it so that Britain could take part in aggressive adventures on the continent. As Whitehouse explained,

> Those of us who disbelieve in compulsory military service regard compulsory service as wholly unnecessary. We see in it means by which not the defence of this country is secured but many adventurous designs are undertaken apart from this country, possibly contrary to the will of the great majority in this country.[11]

Keir Hardie, the Independent Labour Party MP, added a purely socialist argument to the debate. He believed that the ruling classes, feeling that their control of the masses was weakening, wanted to introduce 'compulsory militarism' to maintain their hold over the people.[12]

No division ever took place on the Bill, so it is difficult to estimate the exact degree of opposition and support for it within the Liberal Party. When the Cabinet discussed it on 10 April they found themselves divided. Churchill, Lloyd George and Haldane supported the measure, Runciman, McKenna, Harcourt and Hobhouse were amongst those who opposed it. Conscription was thus clearly a contentious issue which could not be pursued without causing disruption within the Liberal Party and the Cabinet and probably the country too. It was an issue which Asquith, who almost always placed party harmony above all else, was not prepared to pursue except under the pressure of the most dire pressing necessity. The situation before 1914 was not one of dire and pressing necessity and so the problem was quietly dropped.

Thus before 1914 Britain had to be content with the army it had. Conscription was ruled out as being politically impractical and voluntary recruiting had failed to fill the ranks of the peacetime army. No one had cause even to dream of the success Lord Kitchener would have in 1914–15 in raising a huge new army by voluntary means. And not only did the General Staff not believe that men would volunteer in large numbers, even if they did, they did not believe that they could be trained in time to be of any use at the front. It was expected that even the partially trained Territorials would require between four and six months' training before they could match enemy regulars. Raw recruits would need even longer, and there probably would not be sufficient instructors available for them.[13]

But even if the problems of finding the recruits in the first place could be overcome and then instructors found for them, the General Staff were convinced that all this would be to no avail. The war would have been decided before the new troops could take the field. In April 1906 the director of military training, Major General F. W. Stopford, estimated that in a European war an Expeditionary Force of 140,000 men would suffer casualties of 65–75 per cent within one year. Hence drafts of 91,000–105,000 men would be required to keep it up to strength. Between 40 and 50 per cent of these casualties were expected to occur in the first six months of the campaign when it was expected that the decisive battles of the war would be fought, and so these drafts would have to be trained and ready to proceed abroad at the same time as the Expeditionary Force was mobilised. There would be no time to

raise and train them once the war had started. His recommendations were subsequently written into the *Field Service Regulations*
and became official doctrine.[14] Because the General Staff did not
expect to be able to raise and train large numbers of fresh troops
once the war had started, they made no plans to do so.

In 1906 Haldane had toyed with the notion that the Territorials
might be used to expand the Expeditionary Force, and on 1
February he informed the Army Council that 'Should further
expansion of the striking force be eventually required in the later
stages of the war, it is on the Territorial Army that we must rely
...'.[15] But this plan fell into limbo when he refrained from asking
Parliament to pass legislation to compel the Territorials to serve
outside the United Kingdom. Lloyd George admitted in his *War
Memoirs* that 'No one before the war contemplated our raising
hundreds of thousands of men for any war in which we were ever
likely to be involved'.[16] Lloyd George's 'No one' did not include
Lord Roberts, but it does accurately reflect the absence of any
government plans. Giving evidence to the Dardanelles Commission
in 1916, Sir Reginald Brade, who had served before the war at the
War Office first as an assistant under-secretary and then as the permanent under-secretary, admitted that no plans had been prepared
before 1914 for any great increase in the size of the regular army
on the outbreak of war.[17] Such plans as there were to increase
recruiting were all set within the modest limits of the existing
Regular and Territorial armies. In 1912 the War Office's War
Book laid down that recruiting in war would be modest. It
mentioned the possibility that some special contingents might be
raised, but it could not have been expected that these would be very
numerous, as the director general of recruiting was to be given only
three new clerks to cope with them.[18]

The General Staff had embraced the continental commitment without having the means at their disposal to carry it out. The
Admiralty, on the other hand, were determined to pursue a
maritime strategy, even though it was far from certain that this
would force Germany to come to the peace table.

Between 1906 and 1908, just when the General Staff were preparing plans to send the British Expeditionary Force to the continent to support the French left flank in the event of war, a small
committee working under the supervision of the First Sea Lord, Sir
John Fisher, was drawing up the Admiralty's war plans. In the
winter of 1906–7 they worked under the chairmanship of Captain
G. A. Ballard and prepared four plans, each with two versions,
depending upon whether France was neutral or an active ally.
Although the plans made some passing references to giving direct

military help to Belgium or Holland if the Germans tried to absorb them, Ballard's committee clearly believed that Britain's main role in such a war should be a maritime one. It recommended that the Royal Navy should be used to put economic pressure on Germany by driving its merchant marine from the world's oceans and so disrupting its overseas trade. This was to be done by the establishment of a close blockade of Germany's ports, and, if necessary, by bombarding its Baltic coastal towns and by seizing offshore islands as advanced naval bases.[19] These plans were based on the premiss, which was asserted without any detailed supporting evidence, that Germany was as vulnerable as Britain to an attack on its seaborne trade. The committee believed that

> The density of population per square mile in Germany is rapidly attaining such proportions that she is becoming more and more dependent on the sea for feeding her people. She is ceasing to be an agricultural nation, and is becoming a vast industrial nation. This means that she must have the raw materials with which to keep her industries going, and if the import [*sic*] is stopped financial difficulties will be entailed which will seriously affect her capability of carrying on a great war. Therefore besides direct action on her flanks, our efforts must be concentrated on the destruction of that trade. The flow of raw materials and foodstuffs inwards, as well as manufactured articles outwards, is almost becoming as much a necessity for her as it is for us.[20]

The committee was greatly impressed by Germany's supposed vulnerability to economic pressure, although as its secretary admitted some years later, 'we could not judge whether it would be possible to squeeze her into submission, or how long it would take, particularly in view of the assistance she could obtain from her continental neighbours'.[21]

This vital question, which was fundamental to any judgement about the effectiveness of the blockade, was never properly answered before 1914. The Admiralty did make a half-hearted attempt to answer it in May 1908 when the director of naval intelligence suggested that an investigation should be made 'to gauge her [i.e. Germany's] actual dependence on these overseas supplies'.[22] But he took it as 'an accepted fact' that Germany was vulnerable to a blockade and he merely wanted to know whether or not it would be possible for it to supply itself through neutral ports by rail.[23] In fact two separate inquiries were conducted which arrived at diametrically opposite conclusions. As part of a Committee of Imperial Defence inquiry into the naval and military needs of the empire the Admiralty carried out its own investigation.

It concluded that even if the blockade was not complete it would produce a serious economic depression in Germany. This was largely wishful thinking. Before the war Germany's total imports amounted to only about 20 per cent of its net national product and its exports to 18 per cent. The Admiralty underestimated the relative ease with which Germany was able to obtain by rail supplies from neutrals and territory which it had conquered between 1914 and 1918.[24] The blockade did deprive the Central Powers of some strategic raw materials like cotton, saltpetre and various non-ferrous metals. But the implicit analogy on which the Admiralty's plans were based, that the Central Powers were a beleaguered fortress, was false. Their economy was too broadly based within Europe for a naval blockade alone to cripple it. The decline of the German economy between 1914 and 1918 was due at least as much to the inordinately heavy burdens made upon it by the demands of the war for labour, food and munitions as it was to the blockade.[25]

The Admiralty was in fact provided with a more realistic assessment of the likely economic effects of a blockade on Germany by the Foreign Office. Three British consuls, at Hamburg, Frankfurt and Antwerp, were asked to give their opinions on the problem. After an extensive survey of the available German trade statistics they all reported that although a blockade would produce temporary shortages, these could be overcome. After an initial period of readjustment Antwerp and Rotterdam would be able to act as neutral channels for German trade. Sir Francis Oppenheimer at Frankfurt drew the obvious conclusion from this: a blockade would only be effective if all contiguous neutrals were included in it.[26]

A Committee of Imperial Defence subcommittee set up in January 1911 to determine how trade between Britain and Germany could be stopped in wartime reached the same conclusion. The possibility that Britain might have to blockade neutrals as well as its enemies raised important questions concerning Britain's relations with other powers. In the event of the Triple Entente facing Germany and Austria-Hungary, the neutrals most likely to be involved were Holland, Denmark, Norway, Sweden and, above all, the USA. The subcommittee, presided over by Lord Desart, recommended blockading Holland and Belgium (should the latter be neutral) but refused to be dogmatic on the subject. Desart and his colleagues contended themselves with the enigmatic comment that these were matters 'which must be governed and modified by geographical considerations and commercial relations with particular states'.[27]

What Desart meant was that any gains accruing to Britain from the blockade might be offset by the hostility to Britain it aroused amongst the neutrals. For example, it would do the British cause no good at all if they damaged the German war effort by preventing the import of American cotton through Holland if the Americans retaliated by placing an embargo on their trade with Britain. This was the very point which was seized upon when the report was considered by the full committee in December 1912. Asquith contemplated with horror the possibility of blockading neutral Holland or Belgium in order to stop their transit trade with Germany. To do so would be tantamount to treating them as belligerents. But Churchill and Lloyd George were quite prepared to blockade them. The Foreign Office sympathised with the Prime Minister. Sir Arthur Nicholson and Sir Eyre Crowe thought that such acts would place Britain in the wrong in the eyes of neutral world opinion just when it needed all the support it could get.[28] Eventually the committee reached a tentative compromise. If Belgium and Holland remained neutral Britain would ration their imports and so ensure that they had no surplus goods they could tranship to Germany.[29] That might work with relatively weak powers like these, but the committee did not consider what the likely American reaction would be to this policy.

Thus the plans of both the army and the navy were riddled with elements of wishful thinking. The army wished to play a major role on the continent but did not have the troops to do so or even plans to raise them, while the navy had greatly overestimated Germany's vulnerability to a blockade. And, of course, the plans of the two services were incompatible. The British Expeditionary Force was simply too small to be in northern France and in transports waiting to pounce on the north German coast at the same time. This basic incompatibility between their plans was made explicit by a sub-committee of the Committee of Imperial Defence set up to investigate the military needs of the empire in 1908–9. The General Staff deployed all their arguments for rejecting the Admiralty's plans. Landings in the Baltic were impracticable because of the German railway system and because of the superiority of the Landsturm. A blockade would not be effective in time; France would be defeated long before the German economy had ground to a halt. They told the Committee that

> The General Staff believe that it is a mistake to suppose that command of the sea must necessarily influence the immediate issue of a great land struggle. The Battle of Trafalgar did not prevent Napoleon from winning the Battles of Austerlitz and Jena and crushing Prussia and Austria, whilst in more recent times we have

seen that but for the adequacy and efficiency of her armies, Japan would have been left with command of the sea and Russia in possession of Port Arthur and Manchuria.[30]

Sir John Fisher refused to disclose the substance of the Admiralty's plans to anyone, including the Prime Minister. He told Lord Esher that their success would 'depend on suddenness and unexpectedness and the moment I tell anyone there's an end of both!!!'[31]

The General Staff insisted that the Expeditionary Force should be dispatched to the French left. If it arrived by the twentieth day of mobilisation it would offer at least some prospect of bringing success to the allies, as it would give the French the confidence they had lacked in 1870. All the Admiralty did was to submit a paper in which it recommended that Germany should be blockaded, and Fisher argued that landings should be made on the Pomeranian coast.[32]

The committee failed to persuade the two services to harmonise their plans. It concluded that the War Office's plans were valuable and told the General Staff to work out the necessary details so that they could be put into effect if the situation ever demanded it. But whether the situation would ever demand it was not something that a committee of naval and military experts and a handful of ministers, even if their chairman was the Prime Minister, could decide alone. Hence their report said that

In the event of an attack on France by Germany, the expediency of sending a military force abroad, or of relying on naval means, is a matter of policy which can only be determined, when the occasion arises, by the Government of the day.[33]

Exactly why the final decision on whether to adopt a maritime or a continental strategy had to be a matter of expediency which could only be decided by the Cabinet was made clear in the aftermath of a meeting of the Committee of Imperial Defence on 23 August 1911. At the meeting Sir Henry Wilson (the director of military operations) spent several hours outlining the War Office's plans to give direct military assistance to the French by sending them all six infantry divisions and the one cavalry division of the Expeditionary Force. The Admiralty's representatives at the meeting, Reginald McKenna, the First Lord of the Admiralty, and Admiral Sir Arthur Wilson, now First Sea Lord, then revealed that their ideas were completely at variance with the army's. McKenna said that the navy could not guarantee the safe passage of the army to France on the outbreak of war, and Wilson argued that the dispatch of the Expeditionary Force to France would result in an invasion scare in Britain which would force the navy to maintain a defensive posture and deprive it of the troops it needed to seize advanced bases off the German coast. However, the Admiralty's plans were supported by none of the reasoned arguments which Henry Wilson had employed in his exposition. They gave the impression of having been concocted on the spur of the moment, and Asquith dismissed them as being 'puerile'.[34]

As a result of the meeting Asquith replaced McKenna with Churchill at the Admiralty. Plans to land on the German coast were shelved for the time being but it was not until March 1914 that an interdepartmental committee to arrange plans to ship the Expeditionary Force to France was established. It did not present its report until 30 July 1914, barely one week before the troops were dispatched. A blockade still remained part of the Admiralty's strategy.[35] But what the meeting had not decided was that, in the event of war with Germany, troops would inevitably be sent to France. Even Asquith was dismayed by the General Staff's insistence that the whole Expeditionary Force should go to France; he wanted to retain two divisions in Britain.

The reason why the Committee of Imperial Defence never decided before the outbreak of war that British troops would inevitably be sent to France was because too many Cabinet ministers were opposed to such a policy. Asquith was well aware of this. Early in October 1911 he discussed the General Staff's plans with Lord Esher and he admitted that because the majority of the Cabinet knew nothing of their ideas it would be impossible to persuade them to sanction the dispatch of troops in time to help the French.[36] Those who had attended the meeting on 23 August had been very carefully chosen: with the exception of McKenna and Sir Arthur Wilson, all those present already believed that Britain had to send direct military aid to France. Two groups of ministers were excluded from the meeting. They were regular members of the committee like Crewe, Harcourt and Morley, who it was expected would be harshly critical of the army's plans, and non-members of the committee like Runciman and J. A. Pease. When rumours of the meeting leaked out they began to show just why they disliked a military commitment in France. On the day after the meeting Runciman wrote to Harcourt outlining his position. He was alarmed at the warlike tendencies he perceived in the French Cabinet, and even more so amongst some of his own colleagues. He thought that the only way to avoid war with Germany was for Britain to make it quite clear to the French that it would not support them in this crisis. But he then added an important qualification to his argument. He was not opposed to war against Germany at all times.

What he did oppose was, firstly, war with Germany at the present moment over the Moroccan crisis, and secondly, the continental strategy which Asquith, Grey, Haldane and Churchill seemed so eager to implement.

> The one thing to keep these rampageous strategists in check would be a definite decision of the Cabinet that under no circumstances conceivable in the present Morocco controversy would we be prepared to land a single British soldier on the continent. I draw a sharp distinction between acting by sea, and the certain destruction of British troops in Belgium or France; and I believe that if we emphatically forbid the latter we shall check the mad desire for war which has overtaken some unreliable politicians.[37]

Harcourt agreed with him and described the possibility of sending troops to France as 'criminal folly'. A week later Runciman amplified his earlier reference to drawing a distinction between naval and military support for France. He told Harcourt that

> What I have been most anxious about has been that this week which is critical should not pass without the French knowing that whatever support we may have to give her, it cannot be by six divisions, or four, or one on the Continent. The sea is our natural element and the sooner they realise that we are not going to land troops the better will be the chances of preserving Europe's peace.[38]

In stressing that Britain was predominantly a naval power, that its contribution to a future war should be confined to the navy, and that it should avoid beforehand committing itself to the dispatch of an Expeditionary Force, Runciman was only repeating ideas which were common in radical circles both within and outside the Cabinet.[39] In a memorandum written some time after the Agadir crisis, Charles Trevelyan, who resigned his office as parliamentary under-secretary at the Board of Education in August 1914 in protest at Britain's entry into the war, set out similar ideas. He was convinced that if Britain did have to support the French it should not send the Expeditionary Force to France because it would be swallowed up in the battles on the French frontier. In place of this he advocated a judicious blend of maritime and amphibious warfare.[40] Opponents of the continental commitment wanted to build their strategy around the navy. They wanted the navy to protect Britain's overseas trade from German interference, to sweep Germany's trade from the seas, and to bring victory by strangling its economy, ideas which were very similar to those of the Ballard Committee's. The former secretary of that committee, Captain M. P. A. Hankey, provided the fullest exposition of this strategy in a memorandum he wrote in March 1913. It was prepared to help the Secretary of State for War, Colonel J. E. B. Seely, reply to the Territorial Forces Compulsory Training Bill in the House of Commons. After rehearsing the usual navalist arguments he added a powerful new one. He told Seely:

> we are not compelled, as other countries are, to make these tremendous drains on our labour supply in war. Our aim should be to continue our trade, and so to keep the economic conditions of life in this country tolerable, whilst they are becoming progressively more intolerable to the inhabitants of the enemy's country. By this means not only shall we enable ourselves to outlast the enemy, but we shall be in a position to render to our allies (if we have them) assistance of a material nature, which as in the Napoleonic Wars, may be no less welcome than the assistance we can render by sea and land, enabling them to sustain the burden of war while the enemy is rapidly consuming his resources.[41]

Thus Hankey saw Britain's proper role in an alliance as being the economic powerhouse of the powers ranged against Germany. But the *sine qua non* of this was that the economy must not be deprived of manpower by futile and dangerous attempts to raise a large army. If that were attempted the economy would be ruined and Britain would be pitched into a costly land war. At home, 'the transport service would be demoralised, [and] the mills, mines and agriculture would all be short of labour at a time when it was specially required'.[42] The burden of his argument was that there was simply no point in Britain's paying the blood tax of a full-scale land war if the navy and the French and Russian armies, equipped with British-made supplies, could win the war without it. And indeed it could be a disaster for Britain and its allies if large numbers of men were taken from the factories and put in the army, because 'This might result in a general and universal destitution and starvation and the Government would be subjected to heavy pressure to bring the war to an end at all costs.'[43]

But although the internal logic of these arguments was quite sound the premises on which they rested were not. The navalists and Radicals did not consider what would happen if the French and Russian armies were not powerful enough to compel the Central Powers to make peace. Nor did they ask themselves how long Britain's allies would be prepared to fight the land war alone whilst the British enriched themselves by supplying them with munitions. A cash nexus was not a stable basis for a wartime alliance. They were fond of looking back to the Royal Navy's successes during the Napoleonic War, but they had forgotten or misunderstood one of the most important lessons of that war. Britain's naval and economic strength alone had not been enough to ensure victory. It had also needed powerful military allies to defeat the French. Between 1793 and 1815 Britain spent nearly £66 million subsidising various continental allies but money alone could not give them the will to resist the French. Only in 1813, when they had found that will from within themselves, did they make effective use of British aid, and it was only when Napoleon had been defeated on land that he surrendered.[44] But even so, as late as 28 August 1914, J. A. Pease still believed that 'we could win through by holding the sea, maintaining our credit, keeping our people employed and our industries going – by economic pressure, destroying Germany's trade, cutting off her supplies we would gradually secure victory'.[45]

These were the fundamental strategic premises on which 'business as usual' rested. Britain could play its full part in defeating Germany by relying on the Royal Navy to protect its own economy and on its allies to fight the land war whilst the British provided them with all the munitions and supplies they required. Victory would be assured because the Royal Navy would slowly but surely strangle the enemy's economy. It would be wrong to assume that the Cabinet made a determined and conscious decision to opt for this strategy before 1914. It did not. It drifted towards it as the only alternative which was put forward to the ideas of the General Staff which were unacceptable to a majority of ministers. The antipathy exhibited by many Liberals to sending troops to the continent was, to some extent at least, the traditional response of radicals and navalists to military entanglement on the continent. Given their political influence within the government Asquith could not dismiss their ideas. The immediate effect of their opposition was that at two Cabinet meetings on 1 and 15 November 1911 the supporters of the General Staff, Asquith, Grey, Haldane, Lloyd George and Churchill, found themselves heavily outnumbered by a group of their colleagues led by Morley, McKenna and Harcourt. They believed that the Anglo-French staff talks had committed Britain to a future course of action without their knowledge or consent. A major Cabinet split was only avoided when Asquith agreed that there would be no further communications between the General Staff and the staff of any other army without the previous approval of the entire Cabinet.[46]

However, in some respects this victory for the radicals and navalists was more apparent than real. As Henry Wilson noted in his diary, 'This will stop me going to Paris, I think, but not much else'.[47] The Cabinet's decision had not precluded the possibility that troops would be sent. The option to do so was still open and could still be taken, as indeed it was in August 1914.

But for the time being the Cabinet had committed itself to 'business as usual', and this had several important implications for the kinds of economic and social plans for war the Cabinet felt it was necessary to prepare. It meant that its plans fell into two categories. Firstly, they were either those, such as the censorship of the press, the arrest of supposed spies, the preparation of the War Book and the drawing up of an Emergency Powers Bill, which would be necessary on the outbreak of any war, no matter how Britain decided to deploy its naval, military and economic resources. Or, secondly, they were adjuncts to 'business as usual'; studies of how the disruption of the international economy, which was the expected concomitant of a European war, would affect Britain, and how this could be overcome so that the economy would continue to function. This meant that before 1914, in several important respects, the government failed to plan for the war which actually happened. No one dreamt that in 1914–15 Lord Kitchener would be able to raise a huge volunteer army or that the civilian economy would have to be converted to war production to equip his men, or that a stalemate would ensue on the western front which would necessitate the expenditure of enormous quantities of munitions. Hence the reason why Britain went to war in 1914 without any national plan for economic mobilisation under government direction was not because the Cabinet was addicted to *laissez-faire* economics. The strategic plan which it had drifted towards did not call for a massive mobilisation of civil society to support the armed services so the need to make plans to do this was simply not recognised.

Notes: Chapter 2

1 M. Howard, *The Continental Commitment* (London, 1974), p. 30; G. W. Monger, *The End of Isolation* (London, 1963), *passim*.
2 Howard, op. cit., p. 42; J. Gooch, *The Plans of War* (London, 1974), p. 280; PRO WO 33/364, Records of a strategic war game, War Office, 1905; see also N. W. Summerton, 'The development of British military planning for a war against Germany, 1904–14' (PhD thesis, University of London, 1970), pp. 23–52.
3 A. J. Marder, *The Anatomy of British Sea Power* (London, 1964), pp. 504–6.
4 PRO WO 106/46/E2/1, British military action in case of war with Germany, Col C. E. Callwell to Captain Ballard, 3 Oct. 1905; Gooch, op. cit., p. 280.
5 Haldane mss 6109 (II), Memorandum of events 1906–15, R. B. Haldane, Apr. 1916;

ibid., 5907, Haldane to Asquith, 28 Dec. 1905; ibid., 6108A, A preliminary memorandum on the present situation. Being a rough note for the consideration of the members of the Army Council, R. B. Haldane, 1 Jan. 1906; ibid., 5908, Haldane to Cabinet (and enc.), 4 Dec. 1909.

6   *General Annual Reports on the British Army (including the Territorial Force from the Date of Embodiment) for the Period from 1 October 1913 to September 1919,* Cmd 1193 (1921).

7   Mottistone mss box 13, Attack on the British Isles from Oversea. Memorandum by the Secretary of State for War, April 1913; *The General Annual Report on the British Army for the Year ending 30 September 1913,* Cd 7252 (1914).

8   Mottistone mss box 13, op. cit.

9   R. S. Churchill (ed.), *Winston S. Churchill,* Vol. 2: *Companion, Part II* (London, 1969), pp. 1,499–1,500. Churchill to Roberts, 23 Jan. 1912.

10 Lloyd George mss C/3/14/9, copy of Lloyd George's memorandum to Balfour on basis for possible coalition government, 17 Aug. 1910.

11 51 HC Deb., 5s., col. 1533, 11 Apr. 1913.

12 ibid., cols 1591–3.

13 PRO Cab. 16/3A, Report of a sub-committee of the CID appointed by the Prime Minister to reconsider the question of oversea attack, 22 Oct. 1908.

14 PRO WO 32/8813, Wastage in war, F. W. Stopford, 26 Apr. 1906.

15 Haldane mss 6108A(I), Second memorandum, R. B. Haldane, 1 Feb. 1906; see also Note on army reorganisation, R. B. Haldane, 1 Dec. 1906, and H. Cunningham, *The Volunteer Force* (London, 1975), pp. 140–1.

16 D. Lloyd George, *War Memoirs* (London, 1934), Vol. 1, p. 128.

17 PRO Cab. 19/33, Dardanelles Commission, Minutes of evidence, Q. 4045 (Sir R. Brade).

18 PRO WO 32/5966, War Book, 1912 (Provisional).

19 P. Haggie, 'The Royal Navy and war planning in the Fisher era', *Journal of Contemporary History,* vol. 8 (1973), pp. 118–21; P. Kemp (ed.), *The Papers of Admiral Sir John Fisher* (London, 1964), Vol. 2, pp. 315 *ff.*

20 Kemp, op. cit., Vol. 2, p. 360.

21 Lord Hankey, *The Supreme Command* (London, 1961), Vol. 1, p. 40.

22 A. C. Bell, *A History of the Blockade of Germany, Austria-Hungary, Bulgaria and Turkey 1914–18* (London, 1937), p. 25.

23 ibid.

24 G. Hardach, *The First World War, 1914–18* (London, 1977), p. 32; P. M. Kennedy, *The Rise and Fall of British Naval Mastery* (London, 1976), pp. 253–5, Hankey, op. cit., Vol. 1, p. 70.

25 Hardach, op. cit., pp. 30–4.

26 Bell, op. cit., pp. 25, 27; Marion C. Siney, *The Allied Blockade of Germany, 1914–16* (Ann Arbor, Mich., 1957), p. 14.

27 PRO Cab. 4/4/33/160B, Report of a sub-committee of the Committee of Imperial Defence on trading with the enemy, 30 July 1912.

28 G. P. Gooch and H. Temperley, (eds), *British Documents on the Origins of the War, 1898–1914* (London 1926–38), Vol. 8, docs nos 320 and 321.

29 PRO Cab. 2/3, Minutes of 120th meeting of the CID, 6 Dec. 1912.

30 PRO WO 106/46/E2/20, Reply by the General Staff to CID Paper E.5 by Lord Esher, Feb. 1909.

31 A. J. Marder (ed.), *Fear God and Dread Nought. The Correspondence of Admiral of the Fleet Lord Fisher of Kilverstone,* Vol. 2: *Years of Power* (London, 1956), p. 175.

32 PRO WO 106/47/E2/17, British military policy in a war between France and Germany. Memorandum by the General Staff, 26 Nov. 1908; N. d'Ombrain, *War Machinery and High Policy* (London, 1973), p. 94; S. R. Williamson, *The Politics of Grand Strategy* (Cambridge, Mass., 1969), pp. 108–9.

33 PRO Cab. 4/3/1/109B, Report of a sub-committee . . . on the military needs of the Empire, 24 July 1909.
34 Haldane mss 5909, Asquith to Haldane, 31 Aug. 1911; Williamson, op. cit., pp. 169–91; Gooch, op. cit., pp. 290–2.
35 A. J. Marder, *From the Dreadnought to Scapa Flow* (London, 1961), Vol. 1, pp. 367–72; PRO Adm. 116/1331, Expeditionary Force arrangements, Inter-departmental Committee, Minutes of 1st meeting, 6 Mar. 1914; PRO Adm. 116/1324, Expeditionary Force, Report of Inter-departmental Conference relating to despatch, 30 July, 1914.
36 M. V. Brett (ed.), *Journals and Letters of Reginald, Viscount Esher* (London, 1934–38), Vol. 3, pp. 61–2.
37 Runciman mss box 63, Runciman to Harcourt, 24 Aug. 1911.
38 Runciman mss box 63, Runciman to Harcourt, 4 Sept. 1911.
39 A. J. A. Morris, *Radicalism against War, 1906–14,* (London, 1972), pp. 10, 33; H. S. Weinroth, 'The British radicals and the balance of power, 1902–14', *Historical Journal,* vol. 13 (1970), pp. 653–79.
40 C. P. Trevelyan mss box 30, Trevelyan to Runciman (n.d. but *c.* 1911–12).
41 Mottistone mss, Hankey to Seely, 15 Mar. 1913, and (enc.), Some new aspects of the National Service question.
42 ibid.
43 ibid.
44 Kennedy, op. cit., pp. 146–7; J. M. Sherwig, *Guineas and Gunpower. British Foreign Aid in the Wars with France, 1793–1815* (Cambridge, Mass., 1969), pp. 345, 352.
45 Gainford mss diary entry, 28 Aug. 1914.
46 Gainford mss, diary entries for 24 Oct. and 1 Nov. 1911; E. David (ed.), *Inside Asquith's Cabinet – from the Diaries of Charles Hobhouse* (London, 1977), pp. 107–8; Haldane mss 6011, Haldane to Elisabeth Haldane, 13 and 16 Nov. 1911.
47 Wilson mss diary, (reel IV), entry for 17 Nov. 1911. Wilson was correct. Haldane did allow the talks to continue. See Haldane mss 6109 (I), W. G. N[icholson] to Haldane, 21 Nov. 1911.

3

Munitions and the Edwardian Army

It has long been recognised that one of the government's most important failures in the first nine months of the First World War was to supply the army with the shells and guns for which it asked. By the winter and spring of 1914–15 the army in France believed that it had insufficient numbers of guns and shells, and those that it did have were of the wrong type, to break through the German lines. At home there was a shortage of all kinds of munitions with which to equip the growing New Armies.

The blame for these deficiencies has normally been squarely laid at the feet of Lord Kitchener and his master-general of the ordnance, Sir Stanley von Donop. Their most prominent critic was Lloyd George. He accused them of delaying supplies through administrative incompetence and through jealously trying to retain the whole organisation of supplies in their own hands. He found their supposed reluctance to give orders to firms outside the circle of their prewar manufacturers inexplicable. In his *War Memoirs* he portrayed himself as the only member of the Cabinet who had a realistic vision of what ought to be done.[1] But his polemic against Kitchener and the staff of the War Office was a serious distortion of reality. Undoubtedly they did make some mistakes. But Lloyd George's criticisms were ill-founded on at least two points. He failed to understand that munitions could not be manufactured at the drop of a hat. Their production required a considerable lead-in time and the real root of the problem lay in the government's pre-war plans. These were based on two assumptions, that ammunition expenditure would be strictly limited and that no new forces would have to be equipped. But in 1914–15 the reality of the war in France and the formation of the New Armies falsified both of these premisses.

The Boer War came as a rude shock to the Royal Artillery. It discovered that its horse and field artillery guns were far inferior in range and rate of fire to the Boers' Krupp and Creusot guns. The army tried to rectify this situation and in January 1901 Lord Roberts set up a committee under Major General Sir George Marshall to re-equip the horse and field artillery with modern weapons.[2] By July the committee had agreed on the specifications it wanted, and by March 1904 the manufacturers' final designs had been accepted. Shortly afterwards the gunners began to receive the two main weapons they were to take to France with them in 1914, the 13-pounder horse artillery gun and the 18-pounder field gun.

Both weapons were designed to meet the needs of mobile warfare. Artillery tactics, as laid down in successive prewar manuals, were largely confined to providing supporting fire for the infantry as it engaged in its own fire and movement tactics. The gunners were told to use short bursts of fire directed against known points of resistance which were holding up the infantry's advance. The infantry commanders devised the plan of assault, and the artillery had to assist them as best it could. The manuals contained no mention of the elaborate barrage plans which became commonplace on the western front during 1916–18.[3] One reason for this omission was that such operations required enormous quantities of ammunition and the transport to carry it would have meant a great sacrifice of mobility. In 1905, when the Army Council came to fix the ammunition allocations for the new quick-firing guns, it was confronted by a number of imponderables. The army had no practical experience of using such weapons. Information about their use in Manchuria was discounted as being unreliable. It knew that a battery of the new guns could fire between 3,600 and 5,400 shells in one hour; no horse-drawn supply system could sustain that rate of fire for more than a couple of hours and still remain mobile. The quartermaster-general explained that

> Every wagon, with the road space it occupies, and the increased difficulties of supply which the men and animals for it entail, affects to some degree the mobility of a force. We anticipate great results from the fire effect of a field gun, but we must recognise that its adoption must to some extent involve loss of mobility.[4]

Consequently the Army Council placed a self-denying ordinance on the artillery. The introduction of quick-firing guns, able to fire three times as fast as weapons of Boer War vintage, was not recognised as an opportunity to bring heavier fire to bear upon the enemy. Instead, the new guns were seen as a temptation to waste ammunition, and one which battery commanders had to resist. Artillery officers were constantly told to be sparing with the ammunition they used. If they were not they would quickly exhaust their entire supply. As *Field Artillery Training 1906* said:

> When it is borne in mind that guns can be fired at such a rate as to exhaust the whole of the ammunition taken into the field with an army in less than an hour, it is hardly necessary to point out the grave responsibility resting on those who allow ammunition to be wasted.[5]

This was a lesson most battery commanders seem to have learnt. One of them, writing just before the war, believed that 'the *raison d'être* of a quick-firing battery is not to fire quickly but to get to effective fire quickly'.[6] In 1905 the Army Council decreed that each gun should be provided with 500 rounds of ammunition in the field. By 1914 this figure had been doubled. In addition a further 500 rounds per gun was kept in a stockpile in Britain. This was two and a half times larger than the reserve of ammunition which had been kept in 1899. By Boer War standards it represented a prodigal supply of ammunition. In January 1910 the Secretary of State for War, R. B. Haldane, was convinced that 'the supply of ammunition is amply sufficient and very different from what it was at the outbreak of the Boer War. Now everything has been calculated and the whole of the supplies for war including ammunition are there.'[7]

Such confidence was only possible because artillery was regarded merely as a supporting weapon. In their evidence to the Elgin Commission a few infantry commanders with recent experience in the Boer War said that they believed that their men had been at a disadvantage when engaging Boers who were dug in. The British artillery had no effective high explosive shells and the shrapnel shells it did have were largely ineffective against earthworks. Sir Arthur Paget, who had commanded an infantry brigade, told the commission that whilst shrapnel could force an enemy to cower in the bottom of his trench while he was actually being shelled, only high explosive shells could kill him when he had gone to ground.[8] But in general there was little agreement amongst the infantrymen on whether their supporting field guns should be able to fire high explosive shells. Many were frankly disappointed with the performance of the existing lyddite-filled shells and others discounted the need for them completely. Many thought that Paget's expectations of what the artillery should do were exaggerated. They were content if friendly artillery could cover the advance of their own men by firing shrapnel and forcing the enemy to cower in his trenches.[9] In selecting ammunition for the new guns the Marshall Committee showed that it agreed with this assessment of the gunners' true role. It believed that the job of the artillery was not to win a battle by the weight of its fire, or by killing men in trenches, but to assist the advance of friendly infantry to the point where it could deliver a decisive assault with the bayonet. It could best do this by firing shrapnel and so neither of the new guns was supplied with high explosive shells. Marshall, commenting on the demand voiced by a handful of commanders for high explosive shells, wrote:

> The demand appears to be founded upon a theory that field guns alone should, by their fire, be able to drive an enemy out of his entrenchments. If the enemy's infantry is good, I do not think that there is anything in the experience of the war, or of the practice ground, to show that this can be done.[10]

Thus when the army went to war in 1914 most of its artillery was equipped with light, shrapnel-firing guns. They were effective against men advancing in the open, but they were unable to level earthworks or to kill men in them.[11] Those who supported the use of shrapnel shells to subdue the enemy's fire overlooked the fact that there was bound to come a time when the supporting guns would have to lift their fire for fear of hitting their own men. At that moment the defenders would no longer be forced to shelter in the bottom of their trenches and would be able to emerge and turn their own weapons on their advancing assailants. The predominance of shrapnel-firing field guns in the army was only partly offset in 1914 by the presence of a small number of medium guns and howitzers able to fire high explosive shells. One of the great discoveries of the Boer War was that medium guns weighing as much as 4 tons could keep pace with marching infantry. But even after the war opinions were still divided as to whether such guns were necessary. Sir Ian Hamilton voiced one extreme minority view. He wanted to abolish field artillery and to replace it with heavy guns able to travel at a walking pace. At the other extreme was Major General Barton, the former commander of 6 Division. He discounted the need for heavy guns completely because he thought that they were too immobile. He argued that the army had only needed them in South Africa because the Boers had used them. The fact that the army might require them in the future for a similar reason seems to have escaped him.[12]

Most other observers of the South African War, the gunners included, stood about halfway between these two positions. Marshall agreed that the fact of being outranged by the Boer's heavy guns did demoralise the British. He also agreed that some howitzers, firing both shrapnel and high explosive shells, were necessary. Only weapons such as these could actually drop shells directly into a trench or gun pit. Finding suitable weapons took some time, but eventually infantry divisions were given a number of 4.5-inch howitzers and 60-pounder breech-loading guns.[13] Both weapons were chosen with a view to bringing the heaviest possible shell into the field consistent with the gun being light and mobile enough to march with the infantry.[14] But the 18-pounder remained the most numerous gun. In 1914 each infantry division went to France with fifty-four 18-pounder guns and only eighteen 4.5-inch howitzers and a single battery of four 60-pounder guns.

Seige artillery (that is, guns and howitzers of over 6-inch calibre) was a neglected weapon in the Edwardian army. After the Boer War the seige train consisted of five batteries of obsolescent 6- and 9.45-inch howitzers. In 1908 the commandant of the Siege Artillery School at Lydd, Colonel von Donop, recommended that, for the first time, one of these batteries should be permitted to take part in the annual manoeuvres. Four years passed before his advice was taken. The British army had little practical or theoretical knowledge of how to use heavy siege guns. Von Donop also suggested that the 6-inch howitzers should be scrapped and replaced by more modern weapons. The General Staff quashed his suggestion on the grounds that it was very doubtful whether siege artillery would play a major part in any future European war. They believed that the Japanese experience in Manchuria, where they had been forced to use siege guns at Port Arthur, was exceptional. They did not consider that in a future European war the British army would be faced by frontier fortresses or strong lines of field entrenchments which would necessitate the use of siege guns. Hence when the army went to war in 1914 the siege artillery consisted only of these obsolescent weapons and one sole prototype of a modern 9.2-inch howitzer.[15] It was not even planned to send these guns to France with the Expeditionary Force; the first siege batteries were not sent across the Channel until the end of September 1914.[16] The British were at an immediate disadvantage. Because the Germans had anticipated that they would have to assault frontier fortresses and earthworks each German division and corps had a regular supply of medium and heavy howitzers.

In addition to the stockpiles of ammunition held ready for the artillery on mobilisation, the War Office also intended to issue emergency contracts on the outbreak of war for more ammunition. It was expected that within six months these would provide the gunners with another 500 rounds per gun and 400 per howitzer.[17] This six-month waiting period was based on Boer War experience. Before the Boer War the War Office had been starved of money for reserve stores and had been unable to keep any substantial reserves of munitions. It believed that its two sources of supply, the government ordnance factories and the private munitions manufacturers, would be able to supply what was required when the time came.

Sir Henry Brackenbury, the director-general of ordnance, later confessed: 'I thought that you could get anything you wanted out of the trade of this country at short notice. I found it was impossible . . . '[18] The Cabinet reacted by hastily setting up a committee under Sir Frances Mowatt (the permanent secretary to the Treasury) to investigate Brackenbury's recommendations about the need to keep increased reserve stocks. They agreed that just over £11.5 million should be given to the War Office to ensure that there should be a reserve of guns, carriages, stores and ammunition on hand sufficient to keep a force of three corps in the field for six months.[19] The figure of six months was chosen *not* because it was thought to be the maximum possible duration of a war but because it was considered that munitions manufacturers would need a lead-in time of six months to increase their production to meet wartime demands. It was adhered to right up until the outbreak of war for the same reason.[20] The Treasury cut £1 million from the committee's recommendation, but the remaining money was spent between 1901 and 1904.

Mowatt's committee also examined the relationship between the government purchasing departments, the ordnance factories and the private arms manufacturers, and their ability to increase their output quickly in an emergency. Throughout this period there were only a handful of private manufacturers who supplied arms to the government. Between 1908 and 1913, for example, the government placed orders with only twenty-one private munitions manufacturers. Only four produced guns, nine produced shells, three produced small arms, five produced small arms ammunition and seven produced explosives.[21] The purchasing departments refused to go outside this small circle of manufacturers because they believed that no outside supplier had the skill or expertise to work to the extremely exacting specifications they demanded. Government demand was at best unpredictable, and the Mowatt Committee found that one of the major obstacles to increasing production quickly was the extreme reluctance of the private manufacturers to lay down the necesssary plant and equipment in anticipation of a crisis.[22] They were afraid that the government would simply cut off orders to them when the emergency had passed, and their men and machines would stand idle.[23] Representatives from Vickers and Armstrongs, the two largest private manufacturers, pointed out to the Elgin Commission that if they had been in receipt of substantial War Office orders before

1899 it would have enabled them to keep sufficient trained men and machines to have made it relatively easy for them to expand production quickly to meet the emergency of the Boer War. As it was, because they had been given insufficient peacetime orders and were given little or no prior warning of the need to increase production before the war began, it took them a considerable time to do so. They found, to their cost, that men could not be trained overnight, nor could tools and gauges be prepared immediately.[24]

The private manufacturers were very jealous of the government ordnance factories. They saw them as competitors who received many of the orders which they needed. In 1903 Trevor Dawson of Vickers suggested that in peacetime the government should place all munitions orders with the private firms and just keep the ordnance factories as a reserve in case of war.[25] Beneficial as this would have been to the private companies, the government had already decided upon a different course. The Mowatt Committee was not prepared to make the government a hostage to the private firms, but at the same time it was inclined to help them. Mowatt recommended that orders should be spread rather more evenly than hitherto between the two sectors of the industry. He was not prepared to abandon the public sector because it benefited the government in several ways. It allowed it to set standards of workmanship which the private manufacturers had to match, and it enabled it to ascertain what was a fair price for each class of munitions. But above all the ordnance factories represented a reserve capacity which could be called upon immediately on the outbreak of war to tide the army over until the private manufacturers had geared themselves up to full production.[26]

However, a policy of trying to spread orders between the ordnance factories and the trade so as to preserve the ability both to increase their levels of production rapidly in an emergency would only have worked if there had been sufficient orders to spread. But after 1905 this was no longer the case. By 1907 the post-Boer War rearmament of the army had come to an end and the government was reluctant to spend more than it absolutely had to on land armaments. Consequently War Office expenditure on munitions dropped by over one third between 1905/6 and 1912/13. This meant that much of the productive capacity that both the trade and the ordnance factories had built up during the Boer War was now surplus to government requirements. The public and private sectors of the industry dealt with the problem in different ways. Machinery and manpower at the ordnance factories were reduced. In 1905 a whole rifle factory, at Sparkbrook in Birmingham, was sold to a private concern, the Birmingham Small Arms Company.[27] In 1907 a committee under Sir George Murray,

Mowatt's successor at the Treasury, began ruthlessly to prune what it regarded as surplus ordnance factory capacity. It paid lip service to the belief that expenditure on the ordnance factories 'is part of the necessary insurance of the nation against the possible failure of supplies in time of war', but it still recommended economies on a large scale.[28] The total workforce of the ordnance factories was cut from just over 14,000 men to 10,600. This latter figure was a little under 40 per cent of the total workforce needed to ensure maximum production in wartime and it was also 4,500 men fewer than the chief superintendent of the ordnance factories wanted as his peacetime nucleus of men.[29] However, the committee ignored his criticisms.

Within two years there was an even more sweeping abandonment of the principle that the spare capacity of the ordnance factories was preserved as an emergency reserve. A committee under the master-general of the ordnance, Major General Sir C. Hadden, recommended that as much of the machinery and many of the buildings at the ordnance factories were kept only for emergencies, it was better to scrap them rather than have to pay for their upkeep out of the cost of current production. Retaining them only added to the cost of production in peacetime. The report argued that 'the deliberate building up of a reserve of machinery in the Ordnance Factories is much to be deprecated'.[30] This was tantamount to standing earlier strictures about the need for just such a reserve on their heads.

Despite these reductions in capacity, the government still experienced difficulties in keeping the factories that remained employed. The ordnance factories never received less than half of all War Office orders in the lean years between 1907 and 1913, but even this was barely enough to keep the minimum establishments occupied. In November 1909, for example, Haldane had to plead with the Admiralty to place supplementary orders for munitions at Woolwich rather than with the trade, because 'The Ordnance Factories count on receiving some of these supplementary orders in order to keep their minimum establishments going as those allocated at the beginning of the year are never sufficient.' The Admiralty refused this request, just as it did a similar one in October 1913, on the ground that products brought from the trade were cheaper.[31]

If the government did have any qualms about what it had done its members must have comforted themselves with the unbounded faith they had in the ability of private enterprise to rise to the occasion in any national emergency. This was an opinion shared by the witnesses from Vickers and Armstrongs who appeared before the Hadden Committee; and the committee took them at their word.[32]

Hadden carried out his task with the conviction that things had changed greatly since the bad days of the Boer War. The Mowatt reserve supposedly ensured that the army had enough ammunition to last for six months, and the private manufacturers were thought to be able to produce emergency orders quickly. But in a period of steeply declining orders for land armaments this last point was just not true. In August 1907, in the wake of the Murray Committee's report, and in order to keep the ordnance factories occupied, the Army Council decided that they were to be given the pick of all new orders. The trade was to be left to survive as best it could,[33] and it was, in effect, returned to its pre-1899 position when War Office orders were too small to make it worthwhile to keep significant reserves of men or machinery available to meet emergencies. Thus in the lean years after 1907, although both sectors of the industry suffered from declining orders, the trade suffered most severely.[34] The master-general of the ordnance had to fight for every penny he spent. In terms of the quantities of munitions actually produced these orders were tiny. In the financial year 1913–14 only four complete guns and two outfits of ammunition were produced by the trade for the War Office.[35]

In the face of the British government's indifference to their problems, the private manufacturers had no option but to look elsewhere for work. The Birmingham Small Arms Company, for example, turned much of its machinery over to the production of bicycles, motor-cycles, sporting guns and machine tools. Hadfields turned nearly all of its machinery over to producing private orders. Many firms, like Vickers and Armstrongs, looked abroad for outlets for their capital and products, and Armstrongs also branched out into motor-car production.[36] Thus, although in 1914 the War Office relied heavily on the trade to provide it with most of its equipment in a war, the government's reluctance to spend money on land armaments meant that the trade had been discouraged from keeping ready the men and machines necessary to meet the War Office's needs.

By 1914 the British army was relying on a policy of 'armament in width' to supply its needs for munitions. It had stockpiled shells to meet the expected expenditure, and it looked to a small circle of public and private manufacturers to supply its modest wants. Such a policy was thought to be realistic because ammunition expenditure was expected to be small. The master-general of the ordnance had been told that it was only necessary to prepare for the needs of the existing forces. His task once war began was expected to consist of bringing existing artillery units up to full strength, providing ammunition for Territorial Army batteries to use in practice firing, and replacing guns and ammunition expended or lost in the field by the regular army. As for placing fresh orders for new guns, 'it is not likely', wrote the director of artillery in 1912, 'that guns would have to be ordered at the outbreak of war for land services, but in any case the trade could supply any ordinary requirements'.[37] He made no mention of what was to be done if the army's requirements proved to be extraordinary. There were no plans to adopt a policy of 'armament in depth. The government had no plans to expand the size of the army, and so logically enough, no plans to meet the ordnance requirements of such a force either. Beyond expecting the existing armaments industry to produce small emergency contracts, the government had given the industry no warning of any other demands the war might place on it. No plans existed for enlisting the help of engineering firms outside the small circle of the government's regular suppliers, nor for providing them with the necessary machine tools, skilled labour, gauges, or raw materials.[38]

Notes: Chapter 3

1 D. Lloyd George, *War Memoirs* (London, 1939), Vol. 1, chs. 5 and 6 *passim;* an exception to this generalisation is G. H. Cassar, *Kitchener: Architect of Victory* London, 1977), ch. 16 *passim.*

2 *Minutes of Evidence of the Royal Commission on the War in South Africa,* Cd 1790 (1903). See the evidence of Lord Roberts and Sir G. Marshall, QQ. 10564, 18508 and 18556; Gen. Sir J. Headlam, *The History of the Royal Artillery, (1899–1914)* (London, 1937), Vol. 2, pp.13–15.

3 General Staff, War Office, *Combined Training, 1905,* p. 112; idem, *Field Artillery Training, 1906,* pp. 226–7; idem, *Field Artillery Training, 1912 Provisional,* pp. 224, 235–9; idem, *Field Service Regulations, Part I, Operations (1909 revised 1914),* pp. 135–45; Lt. Col. C. N. F. Broad, 'The development of artillery tactics, 1914–18'. *Journal of the Royal Artillery,* vol. 49 (1922), p. 62; Lt. Col. A. F. Brooke, 'The evolution of artillery in the Great War'. *Journal of the Royal Artillery,* vol. 51 (1924–5), p. 36.

4 PRO WO 32/7003, Quartermaster-General to Chief of the General Staff, 2 Jan. 1905.

5 *Field Artillery Training, 1906,* p.218.

6 Maj. H. Rowan-Robinson, 'More accurate methods with field artillery', *Royal United Services Institute Journal,* vol. 58 (1914), p. 111.

7 Haldane mss 6011, Haldane to Elizabeth Haldane, 12 Jan. 1910; see also *History of the Ministry of Munitions, I: Industrial Mobilisation 1915–18; Part I, Munitions Supply* (London, 1918), p. 21; von Donop mss, The supply of munitions to the army, notes by Maj.-Gen. Sir S. von Donop, Aug. 1915, para. 14.

8 Cd 1790, op. cit., Q. 16520 (Maj.-Gen. Sir A. Paget).

9 ibid., Q. 16835 (Maj.-Gen. W. F. Gatacre); Q. 16109 (Maj.-Gen. H. J. T. Hildyard); Q. 15850 (Lt.-Gen. Sir C. Warren).

10 *Appendices to the Minutes of Evidence Taken before the Royal Commission on the War in South Africa,* Cd 1792 (1903), App. 31.

11 S. Bidwell, *Gunners at War* (London, 1970), p. 23.
12 Cd 1790, op. cit., Q. 13941 (Lt.-Gen. Sir I. Hamilton); QQ. 16308, 16310, 16312–3 (Maj.-Gen. Barton).
13 Headlam, op. cit., Vol. 2, pp.81–3.
14 Col. F. G. Stone, 'The heavy artillery of a field army: a comparison', *Royal United Services Institute Journal*, vol. 52 (1908), p. 925.
15 Stone, op. cit., p. 927; von Donop mss, op. cit., para. 33; PRO Cab. 19/32, Supplementary statement on the provision of guns and gun ammunition by Maj.-Gen. Sir S. von Donop, 15 Feb. 1917.
16 Maj. A. F. Becke, 'British heavy and siege batteries in France, August to November 1914', *Journal of the Royal Artillery*, vol. 50 (1923–4), pp. 168–70.
17 *History of the Ministry of Munitions*, op. cit., p. 21; von Donop mss, op. cit., para. 14.
18 Cd 1790, op. cit., Q. 1732 (Maj.-Gen. Sir H. Brackenbury) and Q. 8945 (Lord Wolseley); C. Trebilcock, 'War and the failure of industrial mobilisation: 1899 and 1914'. in J. M. Winter (ed.), *War and Economic Development* (London, 1975), pp. 145–8; C. Trebilcock, *The Vickers Brothers* (London, 1977), pp. 66–8.
19 Cd 1790, op. cit., Q. 1616 (Maj.-Gen. Sir H. Brackenbury); PRO WO 33/163, Interdepartmental Committee on reserves of guns, stores, etc. for the Army (Mowatt Committee), 31 Mar. 1900.
20 PRO Cab. 17/37, Minutes of 1st meeting of the Inter-departmental Committee for Reserve Stores for Ordnance Factories, 17 Mar. 1913.
21 PRO T 181/50, annex II, Pre-war orders, Sir M. Hankey, May 1935.
22 C. Trebilcock, 'A special relationship: government, rearmament and the Cordite firms', *Economic History Review*, 2nd ser., vol. 19 (1966), pp. 366–7.
23 Trebilcock, 'A special relationship', pp. 373–8; Cd 1790, op. cit., Q. 20915 (Lt. A. T. Dawson, Vickers Ltd); QQ. 20862, 20899 (Sir A. Noble, Armstrongs Ltd).
24 ibid. See also PRO WO 32/4734, Minutes of Evidence taken before the Departmental Committee on Government Factories and Workshops, QQ. 2188–9 (Murray Committee).
25 Cd 1790, op. cit., Q. 20918 (Dawson); see also Trebilcock, *Vickers Brothers*, p. 76.
26 PRO WO 33/163, Mowatt Committee, op. cit., Report; see also O. F. Hogg, *The Royal Arsenal* (London, 1963), Vol. 2, pp. 895–6.
27 PRO WO 32/4734, op. cit., para. 13; David French, 'Some aspects of social and economic planning for war in Great Britain, *c.* 1905–15' (PhD thesis, University of London, 1978), p. 60.
28 PRO WO 32/4734, op. cit., para. 30.
29 ibid., Q. 433 (H. Davidson, Chief Superintendent Ordnance Factories), and para. 38.
30 PRO WO 33/476, Interim report of Committee on Cost of Ordnance Factories' Production (1909).
31 McKenna mss 3/3, Haldane to McKenna, 11 Nov. 1909; Mottistone mss box 21, J. E. B. Seely to G. C. N. Nicholson, 31 Oct. 1913.
32 PRO WO 32/4734, op. cit., QQ. 2182–4, 2201 (Sir A. Noble); Q. 2325 (A. T. Dawson).
33 ibid., R. H. Brade to the Secretary of the Admiralty, 14 Aug. 1907.
34 PRO T 181/50, app. 5, Notes on private arms manufacture in the Great War, Sir M. Hankey, May 1935.
35 PRO MUN 5/6/170/15, Statement showing orders placed with the trade during the financial year 1913–14 and during the war period, August 1914 to July 1915, 30 Aug. 1916.
36 PRO T 181/61, G. D. Burton (Birmingham Small Arms Coy.) to the Royal Commission ... 25 July 1935; C. Trebilcock, 'Spin-off in British economic history. Armaments and industry, 1760–1914', *Economic History Review*, 2nd ser., vol. 22 (1969), pp. 481, 486–90; J. D. Scott, *Vickers, History* (London, 1962), p. 93; C. Trebilcock, 'British armaments and European industrialisation, 1890–1914', *Economic History*

Review, 2nd ser., vol. 26 (1973), pp. 256*ff.;* R. J. Irving, 'New Industries for old? Some investment decisions of Sir W. G. Armstrong, Whitworth & Co. Ltd., 1900–1914', *Business History,* vol. 17, (1975), pp. 150–75.

37 PRO Cab. 13/1, app. 3, Memorandum by the Director of Artillery, 4 Jan. 1912; von Donop mss, op. cit., para. 26; PRO WO 32/5966, War Book, 1912, Master-General of the Ordnance Department.

38 PRO T 181/50, app. 5, Indirect causes of failure, May 1935.

4

Economic Planning for 'Business as Usual'

British thinking about a war against Germany was thus dominated by two ideas. The first was that Britain would fight in conjunction with France and Russia and it was they who would bear the main burden of the land war. Britain might contribute a token, although strategically important, force to the continent, but its main war effort would be confined to blockading Germany and providing its allies with munitions and money. The second idea was that these intentions could be reduced to nothing if the economy collapsed on the outbreak of war and if masses of starving and unemployed workers forced the government to make peace. Hence much of the government's prewar planning was directed towards mitigating the potentially disastrous effects the outbreak of war might have on the economy. Unless there was peace at home Britain might not be able to wage war abroad.

Even before the Liberal government assumed office in December 1905, the possibility of economic and social collapse on the outbreak of war had been the subject of one official inquiry. In 1903 the Association to Promote an Official Enquiry into the Security of our Food Supply in Time of War had persuaded Balfour to establish a Royal Commission to investigate this problem. Through extensive inquiries it documented in great detail Britain's dependence on visible overseas trade. It then examined ways in which that trade could be interrupted in wartime. The Royal Commission expected that in a future naval war both sides would adhere to the ideas of Admiral Mahan. They would refrain from attacking their opponent's merchant ships until they had destroyed his battle fleet. Only then would the victor turn his attention to unarmed merchant ships. To the commission it was unthinkable that the Royal Navy could lose such an encounter, for if it did Britain would have lost the war and then there would have been no point in worrying about the economy. However, it was possible that isolated enemy cruisers would succeed in capturing a few British merchant ships in the period between the outbreak of war and the time when the Royal Navy had gained control of the seas.[1] Even small losses in this period of uncertainty might lead to vastly inflated food prices. Panic buying caused by the fear of shortages to come would raise prices and the increased cost of marine insurance to cover war risks would also have to be passed on to the consumer.[2] The dislocation of international trade that was expected to occur on the outbreak of war was also bound to lead to higher unemployment and a decline in working-class purchasing power. If this happened the commissioners and the Admiralty feared that public pressure on the government to give direct protection to merchant ships might be irresistible. The navy might be forced to divert warships away from their proper task of hunting and destroying the enemy's battlefleet.[3]

Hence the Royal Commission saw its main task as being to find a way to avert this panic. It considered two possible solutions. One was that national granaries should be established by the government in which supplies of wheat could be stored in peacetime for distribution in an emergency. This was a popular idea with supporters of tariff reform in the Unionist Party and with the National Agricultural Union. The Unionist MPs who were in the forefront of the Association and who sat on the commission saw it as a backdoor way towards their goal of tariff reform.[4] However, the Royal Commission's main report rejected granaries, ostensibly on the grounds that they were impractical. In fact Balfour had been very careful to balance the tariff reform supporters on the commission with free-traders. Thus only a minority report signed by four members came down in favour of granaries whilst the majority report turned its attention to the question of a national guarantee for the war risks of shipping.

This solution had been under discussion for some time. In the early 1890s Vice-Admiral Sir George Tryon had published an article in the *United Services Magazine* in which he argued that there was a pressing need for a government-financed scheme under which the state offered to reimburse ship-owners for the increased cost of war risk insurance in wartime. Tryon said that unless this was done the sense of insecurity caused by just a few captures would cause panic to overtake the insurance market. Premiums would be out of all proportion to the real risks involved and owners would be forced to transfer their vessels to neutral flags to escape capture, or even perhaps to lay them up for the duration of the war. Owners bold enough to keep their ships at sea would have to pass on the cost of the insurance to the consumer, and the latter would have to pay rising food prices just when the rising cost of scarce imported raw materials made British exports uncompetitive on the world market and when British factories were closing for lack of orders.[5]

Tryon's article was a little premature because until 1898 war risk insurance could be bought at Lloyd's for little extra cost as part of an ordinary marine insurance policy. But in 1898 the Fashoda crisis caused the market to panic and henceforth it could only be had by special agreement.[6] This had very serious implications for Britain's foreign trade. International trade was carried on by credit, and bankers demanded insurance policies as part of the collateral for their loans. Without war risk insurance policies in wartime, finance for international trade might dry up.[7] Ship-owners now began to share Tryon's fears and in retaliation against the Lloyd's decision a group of them established the North of England Protection and Indemnity Society in 1899 to provide their own war risk insurance. But this was only a partial solution to the problem because their policies covered ships at sea on the outbreak of war only until they reached the nearest safe port. They did nothing to enourage owners to keep their vessels at sea during a war.[8]

The Royal Commission investigated two types of national guarantee. One was a national insurance scheme under which the government either reimbursed ship-owners and merchants for the cost of war risk insurance, or set itself up as the purveyor of such insurance on a non-profit-making basis. The other was a scheme for a national indemnity, by which the government promised to make good to ship-owners and merchants the cost of any property they lost at sea due to enemy action. Owners favoured the second scheme because it gave them everything for nothing,[9] but the commissioners were not so certain in their views. In their report of August 1905 they concluded that the only real safeguard for Britain's overseas trade was a powerful Royal Navy but they agreed that some form of national guarantee was needed to avoid panic. However, they recognised that any scheme could be beset by pitfalls. It might encourage ship-owners to run unnecessary risks, knowing that the government would meet any losses. The state might be defrauded by unscrupulous ship-owners who over-valued old ships and then sent them to sea in the hope that they might be captured. The state would also find it very difficult to separate war risks from ordinary marine risks. Any government insurance office would be bound to be dogged by red tape and routine, whilst a successful scheme would have to operate quickly. And finally, those underwriters who were still willing to underwrite war risks because they hoped to make large profits from them were bound to feel themselves unfairly treated because the government threatened to rob them of part of their business.[10]

These last points proved to be important considerations in the deliberations of a Treasury Committee which sat between 1906 and 1908 to try to carry out the Royal Commission's recommendation to formulate a practical scheme. As early as December 1904 Sir George Clarke at the Committee of Imperial Defence had drafted a national insurance scheme. He wanted the state to offer war risk insurance at a low fixed premium in the hope that competition between the state and the open market would keep the latter's rates down below what the government was offering. Thus those underwriters who did want to sell war risk insurance would be free to do so, but they would be forced to keep their rates down. Within a few months the Admiralty and the Board of Trade had accepted Clarke's scheme.[11] Permanent officials at the Committee of Imperial Defence, the Admiralty and the Board of Trade all agreed that their function was to protect the whole community in wartime by freeing the Royal Navy from having to give close protection to merchant ships and so allowing them to hunt the enemy's battle fleet. They were not prepared to let the particular interests of insurance underwriters stand in their way. Therefore, they accepted that the state should step over the dividing line between public and private business if the national interest seemed to demand it.

But the Treasury had a different concept of where the national interest lay. It was not convinced that rising prices on the outbreak of war would necessarily have dire results and it believed that an indemnity 'was not equitable' because it unfairly favoured shipowners at the expense of the rest of the community. And in principle it considered it axiomatic that it was 'undesirable too, to increase the scope of the State's activities and responsibilities if such a course can be avoided', especially if it meant the state taking on new and uncertain financial liabilities just when its finances would already be strained trying to pay for the war.[12] Austen Chamberlain endorsed the Treasury's view both when he was Chancellor of the Exchequer and also when he became chairman of the Treasury Committee in March 1906. Not surprisingly the committee was biased against state action from the outset. It tried to pretend that a case for a national guarantee of some kind still had to be made out, even though the Royal Commission had already done so. All shades of expert opinion were consulted and the result was only to confuse the issue further. As Chamberlain noted in his diary, 'we had a very good witness, but Lord! as Mr Pepys says, to see how these people do contradict one another'.[13] In the face of all these contradictions the authors of the majority report confessed that they were baffled, and contented themselves with stating that no case had been made out in favour of the government's doing anything. They dismissed most of the evidence as conjecture and then virtually repeated the Treasury's case against insurance or indemnity.[14]

The committee concluded its report in March 1908 and it was accepted without demur by the Cabinet. The reason for this is easy to see. Balfour had established the Royal Commission because he hoped that it would scotch once and for all what he called 'some unfounded fears'.[15] Asquith's appointment for a leading opposition front-bencher as chairman of the Treasury Committee was proof enough that he did not believe that the problem deserved urgent government attention.

But that does not mean that by 1908 everyone in official circles was indifferent to the possible economic consequences of a great war. As the naval and military planners began to prepare for a future war their attention was inevitably drawn to these problems. In September 1908 the director of naval intelligence became concerned about what would happen if the Germans succeeded in blockading the east coast. Ships would have to be diverted to the west coast, something he did not think was immediately practical.[16] Three months later the director of military training, who was responsible for preparing home defence plans, became concerned about how to preserve public order in the event of an invasion. London, the very heart of the empire, was thought to be particularly vulnerable. He was afraid that if Britain was invaded the civilian population might panic, food would run short, and the unemployed would riot. Foreign agitators and saboteurs might also add to the disturbances. He even listed a number of areas in the metropolis which would have to be guarded in wartime against civil disturbances. They included the Houses of Parliament, all main-line railways stations, docks, food stores and shipping on the River Thames. If these vulnerable points were not safeguarded

> with the vast number of ignorant, underfed and discontented unemployed, together with the alien and criminal population, the Government might have a weighty question on its hands at a time when all the energies of our naval, military and civil authorities should be devoted to repelling the enemy.[17]

These possibilities served to keep concern alive in official circles but both these officers looked at the problem from their own narrow departmental points of view. They did not see them as only small parts of the much wider question of how to safeguard the economy in the event of war. Such a breadth of vision was first provided by a man who stood outside the government.

Sir Frederick Bolton was a ship-owner and a former chairman of

Lloyd's. He had given evidence before the Royal Commission and the Treasury Committee and in January 1909 he asked the Prime Minister to undertake what amounted to a complete survey of the possible ways the economy might be dislocated by the outbreak of war. He highlighted three areas which deserved particular attention. He wanted to know how Britain's tiny gold reserves would serve to cover its huge home and foreign liabilities in the event of a panic run on them. Without adequate war risk insurance shipowners, merchants and bankers would not be able to carry on their business. If that happened the flow of imports into Britain would cease, hundreds of thousands would be unemployed and hungry, and 'the country will be faced with the problems of civil commotions'. London was particularly vulnerable. If the port was closed by enemy action, stocks of food would soon run low, starvation would be imminent and the population might force the government to end the war. To avoid these dangers he wanted immediate inquiries started into the adequacy of Britain's gold reserves, a practical war risk insurance scheme prepared, and he wanted to develop alternative lines of supply to any east coast ports liable to be blockaded. To do this the capacity of the west coast ports to land extra cargoes normally handled on the east coast, and the adequacy of the railway system to move them, would have to be ascertained.[18]

By February 1910 his suggestions had been brought to the attention of the War Office. It was particularly concerned with his final point because if extra pressure were put on the railway system at the start of a war it would disrupt its mobilisation plans.[19] A new Committee of Imperial Defence subcommittee under the chairmanship of the Under Secretary of State for the Colonies, Colonel J. E. B. Seely, was set up to look at this possibility, but its work proceeded at a leisurely pace. It took another eighteen months for the government to be imbued with any real sense of urgency. Then, between June and August 1911, there were widespread strikes throughout the country. They coincided with a period of acute diplomatic tension during the Agadir crisis. On 16 June a seamen's strike began, and the government was surprised at the support the seamen received from dockers, carters and railwaymen. At the end of the month the government's chief industrial adviser, Sir George Askwith, told the Cabinet that the situation could only become worse and might culminate in a general strike. Churchill, the Home Secretary, believed that his observations were 'a most interesting and disquieting report'.[20] Even more disquieting was the effect such strikes had on the food supplies of many of the country's major cities. On 21 July Ben Tillet of the Transport Workers' Federation threatened that his members would paralyse the conveyance of food.[21] On 26 July strikers in south Wales placed an embargo on flour and perishable foodstuffs. Within eight days strikers in Liverpool had done the same, and the Isle of Man, crammed with 50,000 summer visitors, was seriously short of food. By 17 August the Mayor of Liverpool demanded extra troops to escort badly needed food convoys through strikers' pickets. On the same day a national railway strike began, and very soon similar reports reached the Home Office from other cities. For example, the chief constable of the North Riding of Yorkshire warned the Home Secretary that if the strike lasted for only another few days the iron industry of Cleveland and Middlesborough would have to close down, 100,000 hungry men would be unemployed, and he would need troops to preserve order.[22]

On 11 August the Cabinet decided that it would have to use troops to protect the transport of food supplies from the strikers. Haldane soon had 30,000 men standing by, 'to save London from starving'.[23] The Cabinet had felt compelled to intervene in the strike 'in order to prevent the paralysis of trade and to ensure the distribution of food'.[24] When the strikes were over and the government was able to review the situation it realised that the strikers' embargo on foodstuffs had shown just how small were the stocks of food held in cities like London, Liverpool and Manchester. This led some ministers to become convinced that the Royal Commission of 1905 and Sir Frederick Bolton were right in contending that public order in wartime would depend on adequate food supplies reaching the major cities. Churchill had been closely involved in preserving public order during the strikes and in October he wrote to the Prime Minister:

> During the last few months circumstances with which you are well acquainted, have forced me to consider the question of the country's food supply in the event of a general strike or of war. In either event the Home Secretary would be responsible for the maintenance of order throughout the country; in the event of war he might have to maintain order without the military assistance which is available in ordinary circumstances; and nothing would more inevitably lead to riots and disturbances than a shortage of food supplies, or even a considerable rise in the necessaries [sic] due to mere panic.[25]

Thus the strikers had convinced the government that there was an urgent need to act to prepare the civilian population to withstand the economic dislocation of a war.

As a result of its experiences in the summer of 1911 the

government began to look with renewed interest at the work of Seely's subcommittee. Seely had plunged straight into the middle of the problem. Rather than first discovering how many tons of extra cargo might have to be diverted from the east to the west coast and moved across country by rail, he secretly asked half a dozen general managers of the major railway companies if they could cope in such a situation. In August 1911 they replied that, in theory, if London was blockaded, they could supply it by rail from Liverpool, Manchester, Southampton and Bristol. But in practice this would mean trains belonging to one line running over tracks belonging to another. This would present problems of traffic co-ordination which could only be solved if some form of central direction were established and if the companies were told in good time of the extra traffic they would have to carry. To avoid any confusion they recommended that a permanent committee of railway managers and representatives of the War Office, Admiralty, Home Office, Board of Trade and the Treasury should be established. When war came they recommended that the government should take control of the railways through the Committee of Imperial Defence but leave their daily running in the hands of the existing management.[26]

Churchill considered that their report was very valuable. Asquith confessed in private that he could not 'make head or tail of the report', but he wanted the work to continue. He was anxious to know exactly how naval, military and civil demands on the railway might clash.[27] A second subcommittee, also under Seely, therefore began by collecting information on the likely military and naval demands on the railways. In January 1912 the Admiralty estimated that its minimum needs would be about four dozen trains each day. These would be needed to carry part of the fleet's coal reserves from south Wales to the Humber, Tyne and Forth. It might also require 30,000 wagons to be placed at its disposal permanently to hold further coal reserves.[28] The War Office told Seely that its heaviest demands on the railways would be confined to the first two weeks of the war. It needed 1,000 trains to bring reservists to their units on mobilisation, 700 to take the Expeditionary Force to its ports of embarkation, and another twenty to thirty trains every day to carry the Expeditionary Force's stores from London to Newhaven. Finally, between the thirteenth and sixteenth day of mobilisation, it required another 300 trains to concentrate the Central Force of the Home Defence Force in East Anglia. After that movement it predicted that 'Subsequent military demands for railway transport [could] not possibly be upon such a scale as to impose any great strain upon the railways save in case of invasion or emergency'.[29]

Predicting the likely civilian demands on the railways proved to be more difficult. These depended upon an unknown factor which Seely's Committee did not investigate, namely, the capacity of the west coast ports to unload the extra cargoes in the first place. Because Seely did not do this his committee failed to develop alternative lines of supply for the east coast. But what the Seely Committee did do was extremely valuable; it devised a practical plan by which the government could take control of the railways in wartime in the national interest. This was the first workable scheme which witnessed the government crossing the line between public and private business. During the Boer War the army had learnt that co-operation with the management of the South African railways paid handsome dividends. It was also a necessity. The army simply did not have enough trained men to run the South African railways itself. So instead of even attempting to do so the director of railways acted as a channel of communications between the army and the railway managers who actually ran the lines. This system of remote control worked well and the lesson was remembered.[30] In Britain, until 1909, liaison between the War Office and the railway companies was carried out by the War Railways Council, a committee of War Office and Admiralty officials and railway managers.[31]

The plan of control Seely's Committee decided upon followed closely the South African model. In April 1912 Frank Ree, the general manager of the London and North Western Railway, suggested that a committee of eight general managers of the largest companies should meet under the chairmanship of the President of the Board of Trade to form the link between the railways and the government. This committee, which became known as the Railway Executive Committee (REC), was to act as a court of last resort to co-ordinate the demands of the War Office, the Admiralty and the civilian population on the railways. Under two almost forgotten Acts of Parliament passed as long ago as 1870 and 1888, it was given the power in wartime to order individual companies to re-route their trains on to the lines of other companies if they were likely to clash with more important traffic.[32]

In adopting this scheme Seely's subcommittee was motivated by pragmatic rather than ideological considerations. It had discovered a problem concerning the armed services, the whole civilian population and a private business interest, the railway companies. It tried to solve it by countenancing the minimum of state action consistent with both the expected scope of the problem and the ends the government desired to achieve. Such limitations were dictated by the government's limited ability to act. It was not equipped to carry on the administration of the railways by direct control through the civil service. Only the railways themselves could provide the skilled men and managers necessary to run them. The government's only choice was to co-operate with these people and work through them or do nothing. Thus willy-nilly the government was pushed towards the concept of planning to control an industry in wartime through a mixture of compulsion and industrial self-government. This was a pattern of state control which was to be followed many times during the war, not only in Britain but amongst the other belligerents as well.[33]

Opposition to state action, just as in the case of a war risk insurance scheme, came from the Treasury. Sir Robert Chalmers, the new permanent secretary, was nervous that the government might be making itself liable to pay large sums in compensation to shareholders of the companies they took over if their wartime earnings dipped below their peacetime earnings. However, Ree beguiled away his fears by promising that if the government did take them over the companies would pool their accounts, and the government could then compensate them as a whole for any lost earnings. These would be calculated on the basis of their average annual peacetime earnings.[34] Each company could then claim its fraction of the pool, also based on the same peacetime average. The two parties continued to haggle over the exact basis of compensation, but this formula appears to have calmed Chalmer's fears. The fact that they were to retain day-to-day control of their lines and that they were to be compensated in this way probably accounts for the companies' willingness to accept government control. They believed that their dividends would suffer during a war and so the government's offer to guarantee their peacetime earnings must have seemed too good to refuse. Asquith and the Committee of Imperial Defence accepted this plan in August 1912.[35]

Although Seely's subcommittees had sat for two years they had only dealt with one small aspect of the whole problem. The heart of the matter, how Britain's trade would be affected by the outbreak of war, still remained to be investigated. Asquith was not slow to see this and on the same day that he accepted Seely's final report he told the Committee of Imperial Defence to establish another subcommittee under Walter Runciman to do all the work Seely had failed to do. Runciman's main task was to predict the likely consequences if Britain's North Sea trade was disrupted and to recommend ways of mitigating any hardships this caused. He was also asked to advise on how ships could be controlled and diverted away from the east coast to the west coast and to ascertain the capacity of the major west coast ports to handle this diverted traffic.

When the Runciman Committee began its work it had in front of it the report of another subcommittee which had sat under Lord Desart in 1911–12. This had been established to investigate whether or not British subjects should be permitted to trade with the enemy in time of war. The subcommittee's work was important because it restated the central importance of a blockade to British strategy and at the same time frankly admitted that such a strategy could hurt Britain almost as much as Germany. Desart had tried to reconcile two irreconcilable positions. On the one hand his subcommittee had wanted to do all that it could to help the Royal Navy blockade Germany. But he also recognised that Britain and Germany were active trading partners, and he wanted the blockade to have as few harmful effects on Britain as possible. To try to achieve both of these ends the subcommittee recommended that on the outbreak of war all trade with Germany must stop. This would accord with public opinion and Britain's naval policy. If the Royal Navy kept open Britain's sea lanes it would suffer much less than Germany would from the blockade. The subcommittee's report noted:

> It follows that it would be inconsistent with the principles of the offensive in war, and consequently with the highest interests of the nation at a crucial moment, to permit the commercial community to trade with the enemy (either directly or through neutral countries) at a time when the Army and Navy were trying to exhaust and crush him. By prohibiting trade with the enemy we should no doubt be augmenting the inconvenience and loss sustained by our own people, but in as much as the British Empire is assumed to be able to preserve its communications with the rest of the world uninterrupted, we should feel the loss and inconvenience less acutely than Germany, whose communications with the outside world would be largely diverted to indirect routes.[36]

However, Desart recognised that a total blockade would provoke protests both from neutrals and from British merchants who had done business with the Germans. Hence he recommended that in the later stages of the war a more flexible policy of permitting a certain amount of trade with the enemy should be pursued if it were found to be in Britain's political or economic interests.

Runciman and his colleagues accepted his policy, just as they accepted that food, employment and public order were intimately connected. At his subcommittee's first meeting Runciman told his colleagues that 'the first anxiety of those who were responsible for internal order was at all times to ensure a plentiful supply of foodstuffs and raw materials'.[37]

The subcommittee discovered that in 1911 Britain had imported

16 million tons of goods from Germany and countries bordering the Baltic, and had exported to them just over 29 million tons of goods. This trade represented just over a quarter of all Britain's imports by value and just over a fifth of its exports. When these crude figures were broken down they showed that, for example, over half of all butter and margarine eaten in Britain came from here, as did no less than 70 per cent of all sugar. If trade across the North Sea were suspended, the timber industry would lose half its raw materials and the flax spinning industry would lose all of them. Germany supplied Britain with over 30 per cent of all of its steel, 60 per cent of its zinc, half of its electric motors and no less than four-fifths of its coal tar dyes. The Board of Trade predicted that although some British manufacturers might welcome any respite from German competition a war would bring them, there was no way in which home suppliers could make good the resulting deficiencies in sugar beet and coal tar products. The only optimistic side of the picture was that a war would have a much less damaging effect to Britain's exports. Foodstuffs and coal which had previously been sent across the North Sea would be needed at home.[38]

Between December 1912 and March 1913 three members of the subcommittee visited almost every major port on a line around the south and west coasts from Southampton to Greenock, asking local port officials whether they could deal with more cargoes in an emergency. In London other members of the subcommittee collected figures to enable them to estimate the likely amount of tonnage which might have to be diverted. They calculated that anything between 19 and 28.7 million tons of cargo annually might have to be handled on the west coast over and above its normal traffic. But 9.7 million tons was a wide margin of error, and the subcommittee was compelled to admit that 'the unknown factors in the problem are so numerous that it is impossible to arrive at any satisfactory estimate of the amount of the deduction to be made from the East Coast trade'.[39]

Of the twenty-six ports it surveyed it found that only four, Manchester, Bristol, Liverpool and Glasgow, had the capacity to handle significant amounts of extra traffic. A handful of others could manage to deal with more coal but not with general cargoes. But it would certainly be impossible for them to deal with all the traffic which might have to be diverted.

Thus the Runciman Committee was able to show how and to what extent trade would be disrupted but it could only make a few positive recommendations about how to overcome the resulting problems. The subcommittee recognised that if shipping were diverted to the west coast one of the most intractable bottlenecks would be at the ports. Prompted by one of its members, C. W.

Gordon, the chairman of the United Kingdom Shipping Federation, its report recommended the establishment of 'some overriding authority who could control the whole machinery of the port and its vicinity, so as to ensure its use to the best possible advantage'.[40] But the war broke out before the subcommittee could emulate the Railway Executive Committee and put each port under the control of a unified management.

In such a labour-intensive industry as the docks an ample supply of labour and the co-operation of the trade unions was vital. But the subcommittee paid scant attention to this issue. It was handicapped by its acceptance of the widely held belief that there would be large-scale unemployment on the outbreak of war. Hence they could recommend almost in passing that as east coast ports shut down their labour could be 'transferred' to the west coast. As Gordon told the subcommittee's secretary, Hankey, it was not worthwhile interviewing trade union leaders, 'for it may be taken for granted that in any time of stress such as we are contemplating wages would be high, and labour probably quite plentiful'.[41]

This conclusion turned out to be facile, but it only became so because of the way in which the New Armies soaked up the unemployed in the winter and spring of 1914–15. Far from labour being plentiful it was soon in short supply. But had there been no New Armies, Gordon's conclusions would have been correct. There would have been a pool of surplus labour to draw upon, although whether it could have been redeployed quite as easily as Runciman anticipated is open to doubt.

The subcommittee conceded that war would lead to high prices, unemployment and the closure of some markets, but it made no detailed recommendations about how to mitigate the social hardships which were bound to result from this. There seemed to be so many imponderables in the situation that it could only lamely conclude that 'these are not matters [for] which it appears possible to make arrangements beforehand'.[42] It firmly rejected government price-fixing as a way of keeping down the price of scarce imports. It argued that if the government fixed prices it would interfere with the workings of the free market economy, which, if left to itself, would right the deficiency in time. Higher demand, expressed through the medium of higher prices, would stimulate enterprising suppliers to run the extra risks of sending replacements to Britain. Without the stimulus of higher prices the shortages would be prolonged, because 'if prices were kept low by artificial means, the principal stimulus to enterprise in bringing supplies to this country would be withdrawn, and an actual shortage might result'.[43]

These ideas represented the received economic wisdom of generations, and it is perhaps too much to expect that they could have been abandoned before the exigencies of war showed that they were obsolete. But the subcommittee can be faulted for failing to investigate specifically where Britain was supposed to find alternative sources of supply for the imports it had hitherto bought from Germany. If the work of the Runciman Committee can be faulted it is because it failed to make discreet inquiries in, for example, the USA about the ability of the American economy to make good Britain's deficiences. Such inquiries would have paid handsome dividends in 1914–15. Nor did the committee take a sufficiently broad view of the economic aspects of the coming war. It did not consider that our potential allies would also cease to trade with Germany and that they too would be trying to secure replacement goods in the world market to make good their own shortages, and that unless allied purchasing policy were co-ordinated the result would be that they would only succeed in pushing prices up against each other.

In the final analysis the Runciman Committee trusted to the Royal Navy and the enterprise of British businessmen to ensure that everything came right on the day. As long as the Royal Navy ruled the waves it would be able to help businessmen find new markets for Britain's exports and new sources of raw materials. The navy would cut Germany off from its own former markets and colonies and so, out of necessity, they would be forced to trade with Britain. If this happened the disruption to the economy caused by the war might be serious, but it would not be catastrophic. 'Business as usual' in the literal sense of those words might not be possible, but business of some sort on a worldwide scale would continue. This final conclusion gave the subcommittee's report an optimistic glow, but in reality it was only a gloss. The members of the subcommittee still feared the worst. Hankey summed up their feelings when he wrote in January 1914 to one of the committee's members: 'I rather agree with you that the draft report is pessimistic, but I have endeavoured throughout to interpret the general feeling of the subcommittee, which, I fear, is rather on the pessimistic side'.[44]

Perhaps one of the reasons for this pessimism was that no generally acceptable solutions had yet been devised to meet the two most critical problems raised by Bolton's original memorandum: a national guarantee for the war risks of shipping and the paucity of Britain's gold reserves. Possible solutions to both problems were discussed before August 1914, but even on the eve of war there was no agreement about what should be done.

There was one dissenting note at the end of the Runciman Committee's report. C. W. Gordon refused to sign the main report and in January 1914 he appended his own minority report calling on the government to adopt a war risk insurance scheme.[45] Since 1908 the war risk insurance market had shrunk almost to insignificance. After the Agadir crisis most underwriters were no longer interested in war risk insurance business because they thought that the risks shipping would run in wartime were too dangerous to make it profitable. In December 1911 the chairman of Lloyd's had told the Committee of Imperial Defence that on the outbreak of war there would be at most a tiny and expensive market for war risks, and so the free movement of ships and cargoes might be crippled. Ship-owners agreed with his assessment. In 1912 two new mutual indemnity associations were formed, and within one year 70 per cent of all British tonnage had enrolled in them. However, like the original association, their policies covered vessels only until they had reached the nearest safe port, and so they still offered owners no encouragement to keep their ships at sea.[46]

When Gordon signed his minority report the campaign for a government scheme appeared to have come to a standstill. In 1911 Bolton had convinced Churchill of the need for a government-sponsored scheme, and he had taken up the idea with enthusiasm.[47] He persuaded Asquith to sanction a third inquiry. Churchill and his professional advisers at the Admiralty were convinced that the naval situation had deteriorated considerably since the Treasury Committee's report. They were aware that the Germans possessed a number of large and fast liners fitted with gun mountings. On receipt of a wireless message on the outbreak of war they could mount their guns and attack British vessels without warning. Hence it was possible to imagine many more vessels than the Treasury Committee had envisaged falling victim to German commerce raiders, and ship-owners by their own testimony would run their ships into port. The result, according to Churchill, 'would be a general cessation of trade, and a sharp rise in prices, which might lead to such internal difficulties as to force us to conclude an early peace on disastrous terms'.[48]

When his subcommittee began its work in December 1911 Churchill believed that 'the question is really quite simple'. In fact it was anything but simple. Treasury opposition continued. Chalmers and Runciman worked together to oppose the First Lord and they fought a successful rearguard action which lasted until the outbreak of war. They refused to sign the subcommittee's report and entered a minority report of their own. They did not accept that the naval situation had changed for the worse, nor did they believe that a rise in war risk insurance rates would drive up food prices. They thought that exactly the opposite would occur, and that the laws of supply and demand, expressed through higher freight rates and food prices, would combine to encourage ship-owners to send their vessels to sea regardless of the danger. A national guarantee was an invitation to ship-owners to defraud the government and 'the Treasury would be exposed to plunder'.[49]

The task of producing a workable scheme was given to Sir Herbert Llewellyn Smith, the permanent under-secretary of the Board of Trade. Drawing heavily on the proposals Clarke had made to the Treasury Committee, he tried to avoid all the numerous criticisms which had been made against a national guarantee in the preceding ten years. It had to avoid appearing to be a gratuitous handout by the state to ship-owners, it had to interfere as little as possible with underwriters' businesses, and it had to minimise the amount of work the government would have to undertake. Inevitably he recommended the same mixture of compulsion and industrial self-government which had already been applied to the railways. He suggested that the government should offer to insure British ships and cargoes at the relatively high premium of 10 per cent per voyage. The result of such an offer, he wrote:

> would be that the vast bulk of marine and war insurance would still remain in private hands, since the usual risks, even in wartime, are much below ten per cent. But the offer of the State would effectively prevent rates rising above ten per cent.[50]

The latter figure was also sufficiently high to deter ship-owners from defrauding the government by overvaluing their ships. So few risks would come to the state that the whole scheme could be run by a small committee of experts acting as agents for the government.

But even this did not satisfy Runciman and Chalmers. They carried their opposition to a full meeting of the Committee of Imperial Defence in February 1913. 'The battle began before luncheon and was continued after an adjournment till 5 p.m.', wrote one of the committee's assistant secretaries.[51] In favour of the Llewellyn Smith scheme were Churchill and his professional advisers, Seely, and Sydney Buxton, the President of the Board of Trade. Opposing it were Runciman, Chalmers and McKenna. (The latter denied that German merchant cruisers presented the real threat that Churchill thought they did.) Their opposition was so strenuous that Asquith, who remained studiously impartial throughout the meeting, eventually seized upon an idea Runciman had put forward. An expert committee was to take Llewellyn Smith's proposal and base a practical scheme on it, but the decision on whether or not to implement it was to be left to the whole Cabinet to decide. Runciman was certain that his Cabinet colleagues would crush Churchill's pet idea.[53]

Because of the sharp divisions between the Admiralty and the Treasury there were no departmental representatives on the new committee. Its chairman was Frederick Huth-Jackson, the Governor of the Bank of England. His committee had three inestimable advantages over all its predecessors. Its members were united in wanting a national insurance scheme. The fact that most British vessels were already members of one of the three mutual indemnity clubs relieved the government of the burden of administering the scheme because it could use the clubs as its agents. And finally, because Lloyd's underwriters were now shy of accepting war risk business, they no longer opposed a government scheme because it interfered with their legitimate business. Thus the Huth-Jackson Committee was able to arrange with the clubs that their policies should be extended to cover all voyages after the outbreak of war, and that they could reinsure 80 per cent of all risks with the government. The clubs themselves were prepared to cover the remaining 20 per cent. Once war was declared the government would offer a varying premium of up to 5 per cent per voyage on all voyages the Admiralty considered safe. This would have the effect of keeping most of the business in the market. Ship-owners who flouted the Admiralty's orders and sailed into danger were to be penalised. On the outbreak of war a state insurance office would be opened in London to insure cargoes as well. A board of experts was to be appointed to administer the scheme on behalf of the government. The committee believed that if the government's intention to fix a 5 per cent ceiling on war risks was known before the outbreak of war it would keep the market open, because 'the natural instinct of competition would tempt the insurance market to quote a slightly lower rate than what the state was working at in order to get the business'.[53]

But at that point the matter was allowed to rest. On 14 July the matter came before the Committee of Imperial Defence again. Asquith, ever ready to minimise discord, abode by his original decision. The Cabinet would first have to agree to the scheme before details of it could be made public. Thus when the crisis broke two weeks later no one knew whether the government would act or not.

In a similar manner the question of the gold reserves on the outbreak of war had also been discussed but nothing definite had been decided. The problem of the gold reserves had intruded into the work of the Desart Committee. The British consul-general at Frankfurt, Sir Francis Oppenheimer, had told the committee that in the event of a war the Reichsbank would declare a moratorium on all debts including those due to be paid by German banks abroad.[54] The subcommittee interviewed several leading British bankers on this possibility and found that they were all alarmed at the prospect. Germany owed about £1 million of bills each day in London. If it refused to meet its obligations the result could be disastrous. Acceptance houses would be unable to meet their short-term debts to their joint-stock bankers, and the latter would need to call in that money if their own depositors panicked and demanded gold. Many important firms would have to suspend payments completely, and the whole fabric of international trade might be endangered. However, witnesses were divided on how serious any drain of gold from London might be. Huth-Jackson thought that it was unlikely that the Reichsbank would be able to drain enough gold from the Bank of England to cripple its reserves, because the German banks only held £1–2 million of securities which they could sell in a hurry. But Sir Felix Schuster, the president of the Institute of Bankers, believed that the drain would be considerable and dangerous. All the bankers who gave evidence were convinced that the outbreak of war would be accompanied by panic and they had been discussing for some years ways of strengthening the reserves. But their proposals had one great weakness which prevented anything being done: it was impossible to persuade the Bank and the Treasury to agree to them.

The only thing that all interested parties did agree on was that a simple embargo on gold exports on the outbreak of war would do more harm than good. It would mean that London would lose its position as the world's only free market in gold, and along with it the profits from the financing of a great deal of international trade. But the joint-stock bankers were reluctant to increase their own cash reserves at the Bank of England because this would diminish their profits by limiting the amount of money they could lend, and at the same time increase the Bank's profits by increasing the money it had available to lend. Speaking for the joint-stock banks, Schuster believed that it was the Bank of England's duty to carry the main burden of increasing the size of the reserves. He suggested that the joint-stock banks need only make a modest contribution towards them by depositing a sum equivalent to 2 per cent of their liabilities with the Bank. This would create a second gold reserve which was only to be used in emergencies. The joint-stock banks did not want the Bank of England to use this money in peacetime to take some of their commercial business away from them. The Bank of England ought also to be permitted to issue more bank notes against securities in the event of a crisis. This last suggestion became increasingly popular amongst joint-stock bankers before the war. In January 1914 Sir Edward Holden, the chairman of the London City and Midland Bank, told his shareholders that the joint-stock bankers were preparing a scheme for an emergency currency based on securities and gold. In the event of a breakdown in credit they would deposit £20 million in gold and £40 million of securities with the Bank of England and ask them in return for £60 million of bank notes.[55] The idea of issuing bank notes without the backing of gold or at least securities was anathema to bankers. The French had done it during the revolution and the North had done it during the American Civil War, but Schuster believed: 'If you were to carry on your war with Greenbacks and Assignats I do not think you would get very far.'[56]

However, successive permanent secretaries to the Treasury claimed that any second gold reserve would merely establish a false sense of security. It would only make joint-stock bankers more careless than the Treasury already believed them to be in their lending policies. The Treasury refused to believe that it was any part of its job to save bankers from their own folly in not keeping adequate reserves to meet all emergencies. Sir John Bradbury was afraid that somehow the taxpayer might be called upon to meet the cost of this extra reserve and he wrote in February 1914:

> But whereas in this country banking is a commercial enterprise conducted for private profit there can be no reason why the general taxpayer should bear any part of the cost of the precautions necessary to the safe conduct of the business.[57]

He drew a sharp distinction between the proper spheres of activity of the government and of businessmen. In doing so he made explicit some of the assumptions which lay behind the Treasury's attitude towards government intervention in the business world even for the sake of national defence. He argued that

> It [the state] may properly prescribe the precautions (just as it prescribes the fencing of dangerous machinery) and by doing so safeguard the worthy trader from the unfair competition of a less scrupulous rival but this having been done and conditions having been equalised the banker should, like any other trader, be left to secure a proper return upon his capital by adjusting his charges to his customers.[58]

The government had neither a right nor a duty to interfere in the market to confer an unfair advantage on one trader as opposed to another. Furthermore, any conceivable second reserve would still be too small to meet all liabilities. Treasury officials remained wedded to the orthodoxy that the government's ultimate weapons were to raise the bank rate to attract gold from abroad and to increase the Bank of England's fiduciary issue to increase domestic credit. The Governor of the Bank of England agreed with them.[59]

The Desart Committee cautiously refrained from expressing an opinion on such a thorny question beyond recommending that a separate inquiry might be started. That effectively put an end to any further government action before 1914. Only two people could have instituted another inquiry: Asquith, or his successor as Chancellor, Lloyd George. Asquith believed that the gold reserve was quite large enough, and that the only reason that the French and German central banks hoarded large amounts of gold was that their credit system made this necessary because it was not so highly developed as Britain's. Lloyd George showed little interest in matters of international finance before 1914. In his Mansion House speech of 1913 he paid lip service to the financial dangers of a war, but he showed no immediate interest in that aspect of the Desart Committee's report.[60] Only in May 1914 was he prodded into acknowledging that a problem might even exist. Holden began to ask for a Royal Commission to be established on the gold reserves and the Chancellor felt compelled to ask the Treasury for its views, but nothing seems to have come from the paper it gave him. The criticism of one aggrieved banker, that the government had failed to consider the question seriously, was justified.[61] By the summer of 1914 the banking community viewed the prospect of war with pessimism.

Notes: Chapter 4

1   *Report of the Royal Commission on Supply of Food and Raw Materials in Time of War,* Cd 2643 (1905), see also B. McL. Ranft, 'The naval defence of British seaborne trade, 1860–1905' (D. Phil. thesis, University of Oxford, 1967), ch. 7 *passim.* I am indebted to Professor Ranft for allowing me to read his thesis and for indicating several other sources relating to the Royal Commission's work.

2   Cd 2643, op. cit., pp. 35–9; *Minutes of Evidence of the Royal Commission on Supply of Food and Raw Materials in Time of War,* Cd 2644 (1905), QQ. 2704, 1077, 1596, 1655.

3   Cd 2643, op. cit., pp. 42–3.

4   *Royal Commission on Supply of Food and Raw Materials in Time of War. Appendices,* Cd 2645 (1905), app. 49.

5   Sir G. Tryon, 'National Insurance: a practical proposal', *United Services Magazine* (May 1890), pp. 184–92; see also 'National Insurance – III', *United Services Magazine* (July 1890), p. 297.

6   D. E. W. Gibb, *Lloyd's of London. A Study in Individualism* (London, 1957), pp. 221–4.

7   Sir N. Hill, *War and Insurance* (London, 1927), p. 15; Cd 2644, op. cit., QQ. 6282, 10086, 10091–2, 5162, 5897–5900, 5912, 10134.

8   C. E. Fayle, *A History of the Great War. Seaborne Trade* (London, 1920), Vol. 1, p. 38.

9   Cd 2643, op. cit., pp. 53–5. For the Admiralty's views in favour of National

Guarantee see Cd 2644, op. cit., QQ. 6365–71, 6387, 6521, 7254, 10086, 10565; PRO Adm. 1/7661, Memorandum on National Guarantee, E. F. Inglefield, 1 Oct. 1903; see also PRO Cab. 17/80, Chamber of Shipping of the United Kingdom to A. J. Balfour, 31 Oct. 1905.

10   Cd 2643, op. cit., pp. 54–5. For a cogent expression of the underwriters' views see H. M. Hozier, 'Commerce in maritime war', Admiralty Library, confidential, January 1904. Hozier was the Secretary of Lloyd's.

11   PRO Cab. 4/1/46B, National indemnity or insurance of the war risks of shipping, G. S. Clarke, 5 Dec. 1904; PRO Cab. 4/2/69B, Remarks by the Board of Trade on CID 46B, F. J. S. Hopwood, 4 Apr. 1905. The Admiralty's evidence was not published in the minutes of the committee, but it is in PRO Cab. 16/24, Evidence by Sir A. K. Wilson to the Treasury Committee on National Insurance, 2 July 1907.

12   PRO Cab. 4/1/56B, National insurance of the war risks of shipping, 8 May 1905.

13   Sir A. Chamberlain, *Politics from Inside: An Epistolary Chronicle, 1906–1914* (London, 1936), p. 67. For remarks by Clarke in a similar vein see Lord Sydenham (Clarke), *My Working Life* (London, 1927), p. 215.

14   *Report by the Committee on a National Guarantee for the War Risks of Shipping to the Lord Commissioners of His Majesty's Treasury*, Cd 4161 (1908), paras 211, 217, 224; Hill, op. cit., pp. 16–17.

15   *The Times*, 6 Mar. 1903.

16   Slade mss (microfilm in the National Maritime Museum), The defence of commerce with proposals for its defence in peacetime, E. W. Slade, 16 Sept. 1908. The Germans had, in fact, abandoned plans to attack shipping at the mouth of the Thames on the outbreak of war as long ago as 1897; see also P. M. Kennedy, 'The development of German naval operations plans against England, 1896–1914', *English Historical Review*, vol. 89 (1974), pp. 51–5.

17   PRO WO 32/5270, Memorandum on the measures required for the protection of the capital in time of war, A. J. Murray, 11 Dec. 1908.

18   PRO Cab. 17/26/B27(1), F. Bolton to Asquith, 19 Jan. 1909; Lord Hankey, *The Supreme Command* (London, 1961), Vol. 1, p. 103.

19   PRO Cab. 2/1, Minutes of 105th meeting of the CID, 24 Feb. 1910.

20   PRO Cab. 37/107/70, The present unrest in the labour world, G. R. Askwith, 25 July 1911; minute by W. S. C[hurchill], 30 July 1911.

21   PRO HO 45/10654/file 82, Manifesto. Transport Workers' National Dispute, Ben Tillett, 21 July 1911.

22   PRO HO 45/10654/files 7, 25, 81, 123, of 4, 12, 15, 17 Aug. 1911.

23   Haldane mss 5986, Haldane to his mother, 11 Aug. 1911.

24   PRO HO 45/10655/file 208, Board of Trade statement to the press, 17 Aug. 1911; PRO Cab. 41/33/24, Asquith to the king, 17 Aug. 1911; see also C. J. Wrigley, *David Lloyd George and the British Labour Movement in Peace and War* (New York, 1976), pp. 62–5.

25   McKenna mss 3/21, Churchill to McKenna, 13 Sept. 1911; R. S. Churchill (ed.), *Winston S. Churchill*, Vol. 2: *Companion* (London, 1969), pp. 1296–7.

26   PRO Cab. 4/4/133B, Report of a sub-committee of the standing sub-committee of the CID on the local transportation and distribution of supplies in time of war, 1 Nov. 1911; Appendix I. See also J. E. B. Seely, *Adventure* (London, 1930), p. 139.

27   PRO Cab. 4/4/33/152B, Asquith to Seely, 15 Sept. 1911; Grant-Duff mss 2/1, diary entry, 13 Nov. 1911.

28   PRO Cab. 17/30, written information supplied by the Admiralty (n.d.); Grant-Duff mss 2/2, diary entry, 30 Jan. 1912.

29   PRO Cab. 4/4/33/152B, Report of a sub-committee on the internal distribution of supplies in time of war, 20 June 1912.

30   *Report of His Majesty's Commissioners Appointed to Inquire into the Military Preparations and Other Matters connected with the War in South Africa*, Cd 1789 (1903), para. 194; *Minutes of Evidence of the Royal Commission on the War in*

South Africa, Cd 1790 (1903), QQ. 219, 226–7; Mance mss, PRO 30/66/4, Army Order, Cape Town, 9 Nov. 1899; E. A. Pratt, *The Rise of Rail Power in War and Conquest* (London, 1915), pp. 230–60.

31 Cd 1790, op. cit., QQ. 2186–7; E. A. Pratt, *British Railways and the Great War* (London, 1921), Vol. 1, pp. 12–25.

32 PRO BT 13/52/E24695, Board of Trade to the General Manager of the REC, 5 Nov. 1912. The Acts in question were the Regulation of the Forces Act, 1870, and the National Defence Act, 1888.

33 A similar pattern of state control emerged in Germany after the war began. The first example was the Raw Materials Section of the War Ministry, the KRA. See G. Feldman, *Army, Industry and Labour in Germany* (Princeton, NJ 1966), pp. 45–52.

34 PRO Cab. 4/4/33/152B, Minutes of 2nd meeting of the sub-committee, op. cit., 23 Apr. 1912.

35 PRO Cab. 2/2/1, Minutes of 119th meeting of the CID, 1 Aug. 1912.

36 PRO Cab. 4/4/33/160B, Report of a sub-committee of the Committee of Imperial Defence on trading with the enemy, 30 July 1912.

37 PRO Cab. 16/30, Supplies in time of war. Minutes of 1st meeting, 5 Nov. 1912.

38 PRO Cab. 16/30, Supplies in time of war. Report of a sub-committee of the CID, 26 Jan. 1914.

39 ibid.

40 PRO Cab. 16/30, app. 4 (n.d.).

41 PRO Cab. 17/32, C. W. Gordon to Hankey, 29 Jan. 1913.

42 PRO Cab. 16/30, Supplies in time of war. Report . . ., op. cit.

43 ibid.

44 PRO Cab. 17/32, Hankey to Richard Holt MP, 20 Jan. 1914.

45 PRO Cab. 16/30, Dissent by C. W. Gordon, 24 Jan. 1914.

46 A. W. Kirkaldy, *British Shipping* (London, 1914, repr. 1974), pp. 255–6; Hill, op. cit., pp. 17–19; PRO Cab. 16/29, Report and proceedings of the standing sub-committee of the CID on the Insurance of British shipping in time of war, Q. 3379; PRO Cab. 16/24, app. 6, Rates of insurance against war risks, July–Dec. 1911.

47 McKenna mss 3/21, Churchill to McKenna, 13 Sept. 1911; PRO Cab. 17/82, Churchill to Asquith, 29 Nov. 1911.

48 PRO Cab. 16/24, Report of a sub-committee . . . on the maintenance of oversea commerce in time of war, 18 Feb. 1913; PRO Cab. 2/3, Minutes of 122nd meeting of the CID, 6 Feb. 1913.

49 PRO Cab. 16/24, Report of . . . , op. cit; PRO Cab. 17/82, Runciman to Hankey, 18 Dec. 1912.

50 PRO Cab. 16/24, Note by Sir H. Llewellyn Smith on the Insurance of shipping and cargoes in wartime, 1 Feb. 1913.

51 Grant-Duff mss 2/2, diary entry, 1 Mar. 1913.

52 PRO Cab. 2/3, Minutes of 122nd meeting of the CID, 6 Feb. 1913; Hankey, op. cit., Vol. 1, pp. 105–7; Fayle, op. cit., pp. 39–41; PRO Cab. 16/29, Report and proceedings of the standing sub-committee of the CID on the Insurance of British shipping in time of war, 12 May 1914.

53 PRO Cab. 2/3, Minutes of 127th meeting of the CID, 21 May 1914.

54 PRO Cab. 17/75, War finance in Germany. Report by Sir F. Oppenheimer, July 1912; Sir F. Oppenheimer, *Stranger Within* (London, 1960), pp. 204–6, 217.

55 PRO T 168/97, 'Our gold reserves', speech by Sir Felix Schuster, vice-president of the Institute of Bankers, 19 Dec. 1906; PRO T 171/53, Sir E. Holden, 'The world's money markets', 24 Jan. 1914; M. de Cecco, *Money and Empire. The International Gold Standard 1890–1914* (Oxford, 1974), pp. 132–3; R. A. Sayers, *The Bank of England* (London, 1976), Vol. 1, p. 64.

56 Schuster made this remark during the discussion of a lecture at the Royal United Services Institute in March 1908. See *Journal of the Royal United Services Institute, vol. 52 (1908), p. 1, 351.*

57 PRO T 171/53, Bradbury to Lloyd George, 28 Feb. 1914; de Cecco, op. cit., pp. 134–9.
58 PRO T 171/53, op. cit.; for the Treasury's lack of interest in managing the money market see H. Roseveare, *The Treasury. The Evolution of a British Institution.* (London, 1969), pp. 218–19.
59 PRO Cab. 4/4/33/160B, op. cit.; Sayers, *The Bank* p. 63.
60 *The Times,* 11 July 1913; PRO Cab. 17/81, Asquith to Clarke, 1906.
61 R. H. Brand, *War and National Finance* (London, 1921), p. 1.

5

The Limits of Prewar Planning

The phrase 'business as usual' was not actually coined until 4 August 1914. However, it was an apt summary of the government's strategy before the war. Its plans were based on two premisses. The first was that Britain's military effort would, at the very most, be confined to sending the existing Expeditionary Force to France, mobilising the Territorial Army and controlling the seas with the Royal Navy. These activities would place little direct strain on the economy, and there would only be a very limited need to mobilise even a small sector of the economy, in the shape of the armaments industry, to support the war effort. If the word strategy had any precise meaning before 1914 it did indeed connote a purely military concept implying little more than the operational conduct of war by naval and military forces.

A detailed examination of the Emergency Powers Bill shows the very limited extent the war was expected to impinge on the civilian population. (This Bill became law in 1914 as the Defence of the Realm Act.) By 1917–18 its scope had been so far extended that there were few areas of civilian life that it did not touch.[1] But when the General Staff first contemplated it before 1914 they had a much more restricted measure in mind, and this illustrates clearly the army's thinking about the role of the civilian population in wartime. In March 1905 the director of military operations and the director of military training were concerned that in the event of an invasion the army would have to take extraordinary measures which were bound to infringe the personal liberties and property rights of many citizens. Military officers did have some legal powers to do this but they were buried in a bewildering variety of statutes dating back as long ago as 1842. They had been brought together in a handbook in 1901 but it was 576 pages long. It was quite unreasonable to expect any officer to be able to master such long and detailed provisions.[2]

Since the 1880s the War Office had wanted a single Act which would codify all of these provisions. From its point of view this was important. The Governor Eyre case had shown that soldiers had no automatic legal protection from prosecution for excesses they were alleged to have committed during a period of martial law. In 1888 Sir John Ardagh, the director of military intelligence, had asked that a Bill should be prepared containing provisions to enable the executive, either just prior to or during a war, to take any measures necessary to ensure the defence of the realm. They should be permitted to use all roads, lands and water supplies, and take possession of all buildings. They should also be empowered to requisition anything they needed, including livestock, transport, food, fuel, mills, workshops, and bakeries, or order that they should be destroyed. They also wanted to be able to order local inhabitants to abandon their homes. Finally, they wanted to be able to prohibit the publication of naval and military news in the press, to censor private telegrams, to arrest spies and to refuse aliens entrance to or egress from the country.[3] Clearly the emergency Ardagh had in mind was an invasion and equally clearly the only help the army wanted from the civilian population was that they should surrender their goods and rights and suffer in silence. His Emergency Powers Bill was designed to facilitate military operations within Britain by defining exactly what the army's powers under a state of martial law were. It was not intended to facilitate the kinds of collectivist measures by the state which were actually adopted during the First World War to mobilise economic resources in support of the war effort.

These limits remained on War Office, and later Admiralty, thinking until 1914. In private the General Staff were even prepared to abandon the euphemism 'Emergency Powers' and say more explicitly what they wanted. In 1914 they informed the Committee of Imperial Defence that

> The General Staff have continued to think that it is essential that the whole question of emergency powers, or, expressed in other terms, of martial law, should be examined, and that martial law regulations, suitable for issue in the United Kingdom on an emergency should be prepared.[4]

The service departments had little success in pushing forward their ideas before 1914. In 1912 they did reach a gentlemen's agreement with the Newspaper Publishers' Association under which the press agreed not to publish naval and military news if the Admiralty or War Office asked them not to do so.[5] And in August 1911, at the height of the Agadir crisis, Parliament agreed to pass a new and drastic Official Secrets Act to make it easier for the authorities to apprehend and punish spies. By 1913 this had been supplemented by a secret and unofficial register containing the names, addresses and occupations of 11,000 Germans and Austro-Hungarians living in Britain.[6] Ministers were not necessarily unsympathetic towards what the service departments wanted, but they were acutely aware of the political difficulties of passing an Emergency Powers Bill in peacetime. They recognised that there was a very deep public aversion to martial law. In September 1906 the First Lord of the Admiralty minuted on a suggestion that an Emergency Powers Bill was needed as soon as possible that

> it is improbable that any Government would consent to initiate legislation with the object of placing in the hands of the Executive new and arbitrary powers in anticipation of possible emergencies or that Parliament could be easily brought to enter on the discussion of any such proposals.[7]

Haldane and Seely shared his opinion and after the new Official Secrets Bill had been drafted they carefully put it on one side until August 1911, when they were able to introduce it into Parliament as an emergency measure and rush it through both Houses with no serious debate.[8]

Paradoxically the Liberal government's Law Officers had fewer scruples about obeying the letter of the law than did naval and military officers. In 1914 a Committee of Imperial Defence subcommittee presided over by McKenna examined the case for an Emergency Powers Bill. The Attorney-General and the Solicitor-General told the subcommittee that an Act setting out exactly what the government could and could not do would only serve to curtail their freedom of action. The Common Law gave the government the powers to take any steps necessary to secure the defence of the realm, and they argued that it could be used to 'justify even an unprecedented course of action if it is fairly covered by the maxim *salus reipublicae (sic) suprema lex'.*[9]

Thus the government was not restrained from planning to interfere in the running of the economy by any philosophical or legal scruples. Rather, given the expected scope of Britain's war effort, it did not appear to be necessary or expedient to do more than it planned to do.

The second premiss upon which the government's prewar plans were based was that a European war would produce general disruption throughout the European economy as direct trade and financial links between the belligerents were severed. This possibility presented a particular danger to Britain because of its great dependence on overseas trade. It was regarded as being axiomatic that war would produce food shortages, high prices and unemployment. To mitigate these disasters the government planned to rely heavily on the enterprise of British businessmen to secure new markets and raw materials and on the might of the Royal Navy to keep open the sea lanes. But it was recognised that this might not be enough, and in order to ensure the safe delivery of imports it intended to place the railways under government control and plans were prepared to support the war risk insurance market with government money.

However, to speak of the government in this context is an over-simplification which requires qualification. Most officials and ministers who were concerned with preparing the government's plans adopted an essentially pragmatic view of what should be done, but, of course, their pragmatism was constrained by how they expected the war to be fought. Champions of *laissez-faire* did exist, as the cases of the railways and the war risk insurance market illustrate. Permanent officials from the two service departments, the Board of Trade and the Committee of Imperial Defence, supported the cause of state action. They recognised that it would be in the immediate interests of the community at large. Treasury officials, ever conscious of the need to keep expenditure down, took a different view, and this helps to explain their eagerness to reduce expenditure at the ordnance factories and their dislike of schemes which threatened to call for large and unpredictable expenditure on the railways and in the war risk insurance market. Hankey later described the Treasury as 'the least helpful of all the Government Departments'.[10] Its reluctance to sanction expenditure, to con-template future expenditure, or to depart from its traditional attitude towards currency management did impede prewar planning. But it is not fair to lay all the blame for the inadequacies of the government's plans at the feet of a handful of senior Treasury officials. Their obstructiveness could have been overcome if the political will to overcome it had existed. Biut often it did not exist.

Neither Campbell-Bannerman nor Asquith had the same enthusiasm for the Committee of Imperial Defence as its found-er, Balfour, had. Sir George Clarke believed that Campbell-Bannerman was only mildly interested in the committee's work. Ottley frequently had difficulty in gaining access to Asquith to discuss matters of business. Nor was Asquith a particularly effec-tive chairman of the Committee of Imperial Defence when he did preside over its meetings. He was frequently reluctant to reach a decision. He had great skills as a political mediator which proved to be very valuable in peacetime during a period of political strife, but in wartime his propensity for postponing decisions was to prove to be a liability.[11]

Ministers were too busy to attend frequent or regular Committee of Imperial Defence meetings. Their inability to attend meetings when they were called meant again that decisions had to be postponed until a later date.[12] In the spring of 1914, for example, the Irish question was such a pressing issue that the Prime Minister and his colleagues had little time to spare for committee meetings. The Liberal Party's interest in defence matters did not extend very much beyond a desire to keep the estimates as low as possible. Looking back to the prewar period in 1925, Haldane noted that the Cabinet took little interest in his army reforms, and the House of Commons, 'although at times it grumbled, did not interfere'.[13] Llewellyn Smith believed that the Cabinet was completely uninterested in economic preparations for war. The prewar Cabinet was made up of about twenty ministers, but Hankey thought that only five played an active role in the Committee of Imperial Defence's work.[14]

Thus it is difficult to determine where the Cabinet as a whole stood on the issue of whether or not it was right for the government to interfere in private business activities to protect the interests of the state in wartime. For a majority of ministers before 1914 it simply was not an issue. Of those remaining, Seely, Churchill and Buxton seem to have favoured government interference on the railways and in the war risk insurance market on the grounds of expediency. There is no evidence to suggest that they recognised that any issues of principle were at stake. Similarly Runciman and McKenna appear to have opposed government interference in the insurance market because they believed that the actual danger from German cruisers was being exaggerated and because they were afraid that what Churchill proposed would open the Treasury to fraud on a massive scale. Lloyd George, who was 'rather out of the picture in the detailed work of preparations for war', seems to have shared the general indifference of most of his colleagues to these issues.[15]

The failure to realise that in a great war Britain would have to mobilise its civilian economy alongside the army and navy, coupled with indifference and even hostility to the Committee of Imperial Defence as an institution, were responsible for one of the most serious ommissions in its plans. This was the government's failure to create a permanent and unified central planning staff to coordinate the work of the naval, military and civil departments. Hostility towards the Committee of Imperial Defence came from two sources. Ministers who were excluded from its deliberations were jealous of it. They believed that it was usurping the Cabinet's function to decide on naval and military matters.[16] Meetings like the one held on 23 August 1911 served only to confirm their suspicions. The second source of hostility came from officers of one or other of the two service departments. In 1903 the War Office Reconstitution Committee had planned that the Committee of Imperial Defence secretariat should become a joint General Staff to control the strategic policies of both services.[17] But the service departments were, by turns, very reluctant to allow the committee to interfere in their own strategic contingency planning. Until the end of 1905 the General Staff were hostile to the committee because it appeared to be dominated by the Admiralty. But early in 1906 the development of a military entente with the French undermined this community of interest between the Admiralty and the committee. Fisher, wrongly in fact, believed that the committee's secretariat had betrayed him by pioneering the military staff talks with the French, and from 1906 onwards he virtually boycotted the committee's deliberations.[18] Shortly afterwards Clarke antagonised him even further by questioning the need for the two-power standard. In July 1907 Sir George left the committee a disappointed man. It had failed to win the willing co-operation of the service departments. The Cabinet was unwilling to impose a single strategy on them, and Clarke was now convinced that the committee would never develop into the unified planning staff he had hoped for.[19]

His successors were only too well aware of the precarious position in which this left the secretariat. It had lost most of its original rationale, and it dared do nothing to excite the jealousy of other, more powerful, departments. Ottley supported the concept of the secretariat becoming an Imperial General Staff but he was concerned that 'the most serious danger that besets this Committee is the jealousy of the great Departments, if its members or secretariat seek (or unwittingly contrive) to trespass on their prerogatives'.[20] Hankey's assistant, Adrian Grant-Duff, reflected similar fears when he noted in his diary: 'There is much danger to the C.I.D. [sic] in trying to hurry its development. Few people in the least understand its position, and there is much risk of rousing violent jealousies'.[21]

Ottley's recipe for ultimate success was for the committee gradually to win supporters to its cause by dealing with non-controversial issues which were the responsibility of no department. He hoped that this would demonstrate that his secretariat did have a vital and independent function, and that it could operate without causing antagonisms.[22] The result of his initiative were the numerous subcommittees which prepared contingency plans for the war at home. Esher, who had been the chairman of the War Office Reconstitution Committee, disliked this cautious approach and remained eager that the committee should reassert its role as the General Staff of the whole empire. As a preliminary step he suggested to Asquith in January 1910 that he should allow the committee to establish a permanent standing subcommittee to investigate whether or not the Anglo-Japanese Treaty should be renewed.[23] Ottley was adament that other departments would regard this as poaching and would resent the committee because of it.[24] He wanted to proceed more stealthily by continuing the existing procedure of appointing *ad hoc* subcommittees to investigate particular questions. They could be made *de facto* permanent subcommittees by giving them tasks to do which required constant revision for at least two or three years. For example, they could examine the security of the Fleet's anchorages against surprise attack. They could determine whether or not it was in Britain's interests under the terms of the Hague Convention that German vessels caught in British harbours on the outbreak of war be granted 'Days of Grace' in which to sail. Many government departments would have special tasks to perform on the outbreak of war, but no one had ever told them exactly what these would entail. Similarly the government had no definite policy on how to treat enemy aliens. And, as Ottley explained, 'behind these questions of direct warlike activity, is the terrible question of the "feeding of the people" and of "employment" in war. – That [*sic*] alone will take the patience of angels and the strength of giants to unravel and provide for.'[25] Hankey in particular wanted to ensure that all of these tasks would be properly co-ordinated on the outbreak of war. With the help of all the other departments he wanted the committee to

> elaborate a common system for adoption by the various departments in order to ensure that the departmental war organisation shall work without a hitch when the emergency arises, and that all the Orders-in-Council, Regulations, telegrams, and other communications, which can reasonably be foreseen, are drafted ready for date and signature, so that action will not be delayed on an emergency by the mass of paper-work to be dealt with.[26]

Lest any of the departments feared that this process of coordinating their plans would encroach upon their planning prerogatives, he denied that the committee had any intention of interference in 'such questions as the policy, strategy, or plans of the Admiralty, War Office, and Foreign Office.'[27]

Asquith agreed with the secretariat's views of how the Committee of Imperial Defence should operate, and not with Esher's.[28] The Prime Minister disapproved of having a permanent standing subcommittee with a fixed membership and instead agreed to the setting-up of a standing subcommittee whose membership could be varied according to the questions under discussion. This was no more than a new form of words to describe the existing *ad hoc* committee structure. From 1910 onwards most of the government's plans to mitigate the economic dislocation of war were prepared under the auspices of this fictional subcommittee. Ottley and Hankey both realistically realised that they could not impose their own strategies on either of the service departments or on the Foreign Office or Cabinet. Both of them deprecated the General Staff's plans and favoured a navalist policy. They also recognised that the Cabinet was divided not only over whether or not to support France in the event of a war with Germany, but also on how to give that support. The committee's secretaries recognised that the most help the majority of Cabinet ministers would be prepared to give to the French, *if* they decided to give any help at all, would be in the shape of the existing army and navy. Thus their own inclinations combined with a sound grasp of domestic political realities to ensure that economic planning for war would be confined to mitigating the upheavals caused by the expected breakdown of the economy.

One of the first of the new subcommittees to report was on whether or not German merchant ships should be granted 'Days of Grace' to escape if they were caught in British harbours on the outbreak of war. In recommending that they should be granted this privilege if the Germans granted it to British ships in their ports, the subcommittee pointed out that the implementation of this policy would need a great deal of very detailed work by several departments. The secretariat took the opportunity of showing this recommendation to Asquith and putting before him their case to make the Committee of Imperial Defence into a co-ordinating body for policies which required simultaneous action by several departments. In January 1911 the Prime Minister agreed to let it proceed and it began to formulate its findings in the War Book.[29] This marked the final defeat of Esher's concept of the committee's secretariat as a central strategic planning staff for the whole empire. The essence of the War Book was that it co-ordinated all the administrative actions of the civilian departments with the mobilisation plans of the army and navy on the outbreak of war. It did not even attempt to co-ordinate naval, military and foreign policy. The ambiguities in these policies persisted.

The work of preparing the War Book devolved upon a small subcommittee presided over by Sir Arthur Nicholson, the permanent under-secretary of the Foreign Office. But the actual work of compiling the Book was left to two assistant secretaries of the committee, Grant-Duff and Longridge.[30] They produced three editions before the war. The final one, which was completed barely a month before the start of war, consisted of eleven chapters. Each chapter was devoted to a single department, and it listed that department's actions during the 'precautionary period' when diplomatic relations were strained, during mobilisation and on the outbreak of war. Each chapter also indicated parallel actions being taken by the other departments. Thus, for example, when war was declared the War Office was called on to submit a Bill to Parliament to give the army powers to control the movements of enemy aliens. Once the Bill had become law the War Book told the Home Office to obtain an Order in Council so that it could be enforced, and the Admiralty was told to suspend any pilots' tickets held by enemy aliens. Every department was told to prepare all the telegrams it had to send on the outbreak of war, and to place them in sealed envelopes ready for dating and dispatch when the emergeny came.[31]

The War Book represented a policy which fell a long way short of Esher's concept of the proper role of the committee, but he still had nothing but praise for the detailed administrative plans it embodied.[32] But it did have two major limitations. It ignored all considerations to do with the higher direction of the nation's war effort. The administrative measures set out in such meticulous detail in the War Book did not extend beyond the first few days of the war. The government's reluctance to face the need to pursue a single national strategy in wartime meant that it completely overlooked the need to establish some special administrative machinery to ensure that the naval, military and civilian war effort was coordinated during the war. Paradoxically, even Esher, the archapostle of the Committee of Imperial Defence in a strategic planning role, did not recognise that it ought to perform that function in war as well as in peace. In October 1907 he asserted that 'In *War* [*sic*] the Defence Committee possesses no function. It is a machine intended for the purpose of preparation and not of action.'[33] Thus the need to develop a permanent contingency planning staff to assist in the higher direction of the war was ignored and no steps were taken to preserve the committee's secretariat in its role as a *de facto* economic general staff. This proved to be extremely unfortunate when war came because there was no organised body of experts to warn the Cabinet that by Christmas 1914 its economic and military plans were getting increasingly out of step.

More fundamentally, the War Book ignored all questions of industrial mobilisation and manpower planning. This was because the British shared many of the illusions that the other Great Powers held in 1914. They believed that the war would be short because either their forces would win decisive victories on land or sea in the opening encounters of the war, or all the belligerents would perish as the world economy collapsed. In either event there would not be enough time to mobilise civilian resources to help in the war effort. The British, along with most of the other belligerents, did not realise how robust industrial societies were. Nor did they recognise that the very strength industrialisation had given nations would eventually compel them to fight a war of exhaustion in which governments would have to step in to control all aspects of national life for the sake of the war effort.[34] But in 1914 all this lay in the future. The British planned to fight a limited and a short war. The generals and admirals were to be left to get on with the fighting; the most that was to be asked of the civilian population was that they should stay calm and suffer in silence.

Notes: Chapter 5

1   A. Marwick, *The Deluge* (Harmondsworth, 1967), *passim.*
2   PRO Cab. 16/31/EP2, Emergency powers in war. Memorandum by the General Staff, 4 April 1914; PRO Cab. 16/3A, Report and proceedings of a sub-committee of the CID appointed by the Prime Minister to re-consider the question of oversea attack, Q. 658 (Brig.-Gen. A. J. Murray).
3   Edmonds mss IV/4, The powers possessed by the executive in times of emergency and war (lecture at the Staff College by J. E. E[dmonds]) (n.d.), pp. 13–16.
4   PRO Cab. 16/31/EP2, op. cit. For the Admiralty's views see PRO Adm. 116/3408, Powers required by the executive in times of emergency, 1906.
5   P. Towle, 'The Debate on wartime censorship in Britain, 1902–14', *passim,* in B. Bond and I. Roy (eds), *War and Society* (London, 1975), Vol. 1, pp. 103–13.
6   D. French, 'Spy-fever in Britain, 1900–15', *Historical Journal,* vol. 2 (1978), pp. 355–70.
7   PRO Adm. 116/3408, Minute by L[ord] T[weedmouth], Sept. 1906.
8   French, 'Spy-fever in Britain', pp. 360–1.
9   PRO Cab. 16/31/EP2, app. 2, Martial law in the United Kingdom. Opinion of the Law Officers, R. D. Isaacs and John Simon, 17 July 1914.
10 Hankey mss 8/24, memorandum by Hankey, 7 Nov. 1922.
11 Esher mss 10/38, G. S. Clarke to Esher, 3 Jan. 1906; ibid., 5/33, Ottley to Esher, (?) Mar. 1910; C. Hazlehurst, 'Asquith as Prime Minister, 1908–16', *English Historical Review,* vol. 85, (1970), p. 506; J. P. Mackintosh, 'The role of the Committee of Imperial Defence before 1914', *English Historical Review,* vol. 77 (1962), pp. 495–6; H. H. Asquith, *The Genesis of the War* (London, 1923), p.109.
12 See, for example, Esher mss 4/5, Esher to Col. à Court Repington, 20 July 1914.
13 Haldane mss 5921, 'Memories', 16 Jan. 1925.
14 Lord Hankey, *The Supreme Command* (London, 1961), Vol. 1, pp.147–8.
15 ibid.

16 Haldane mss 6109 (II), Memorandum of events between 1906–15, Lord Haldane, April 1916; Esher mss 2/11, journal entry, 11 Feb. 1908.
17 N. d'Ombrain, *War Machinery and High Policy* (London, 1973), pp. 39–41.
18 D'Ombrain, op. cit., chs 1 and 2, *passim*.
19 J. Gooch, 'Sir George Clarke's career at the Committee of Imperial Defence', *Historical Journal*, vol. 18 (1975), pp. 567–8.
20 Esher mss 5/32, Ottley to Esher, 16 Oct. 1909.
21 Grant-Duff mss 2/2, diary entry, 18 July 1912; see also S. Roskill, *Hankey, Man of Secrets* (London, 1970), Vol. 1, p. 119.
22 Esher mss 5/32, Ottley to Esher, 16 Oct. 1909.
23 PRO Cab. 4/3/1/112B, The functions of the sub-committees of the CID memorandum by Lord Esher, 21 Jan. 1910.
24 Esher mss 5/32, Ottley to Esher, 16 Oct. 1909 and 18 Oct. 1909; Haldane to Esher, 22 Oct. 1909.
25 Esher mss 5/32, Ottley to Esher, 18 Oct. 1909.
26 Hankey, op. cit., Vol. 1, p. 119.
27 ibid.
28 PRO Cab. 2/1, Minutes of 105th meeting of the CID, 24 Feb. 1910.
29 PRO Cab. 2/1, Minutes of 108th meeting of the CID, 26 Jan. 1911.
30 Grant-Duff mss 1/4, Hankey to Mrs Grant-Duff, 8 Sept. 1919; PRO Cab. 15/1/K4, Minutes of 1st meeting of the sub-committee of the CID on the co-ordination of departmental action on the outbreak of war, 5 Apr. 1911; Sokolov Grant, 'The origins of the War Book', *Journal of the Royal United Services Institute*, vol. 117 (1972), pp. 65*ff*.
31 PRO Cab. 15/5, War Book, 1914.
32 Esher mss 2/13, War Journals, entry 4 Aug. 1914.
33 M. V. Brett (ed.), *Journals and Letters of Reginald, Viscount Esher* (London, 1934–8), Vol. 2, p. 251.
34 Similar mistakes were made by most of the other great powers who became involved in the war. See, for example, G. Feldman, *Army, Industry and Labour in Germany* (Princeton, NJ, 1966), pp. 6–7, 52, 64, 98; R. D. Challener, *The French Theory of the Nation in Arms, 1866–1939* (New York, 1955), pp. 91–135; J. Whittam, *The Politics of the Italian Army* (London, 1976), pp. 191–3; N. Stone, *The Eastern Front* (London, 1975), pp. 48–9, 145.

6

The July Crisis

A deep pessimism pervaded the government's thinking about the likely domestic repercussions of the outbreak of war. Trade across the North Sea would collapse, the mechanisms of international finance would seize up, hundreds of thousands would be thrown out of work and hungry mobs would riot in the streets and perhaps try to force the government to make a premature peace. With the benefit of hindsight these fears can be seen to have been exaggerated but the government was not being alarmist when it believed this. The utterances of trade union and Labour Party leaders before the war appeared to give substance to its beliefs. The 1911 strikes had demonstrated the trade unions' industrial power and shown that talk of a general strike to avert a war might not just be idle gossip. As early as September 1910 Keir Hardie had proposed a resolution at a meeting of the Socialist International calling on the world's labour movement to declare a general strike if war seemed imminent. In January 1911 a group of Labour MPs took up the same call at a party conference. The idea also seems to have attracted certain trade unionists. In December 1913, after a speaker at the Royal United Services Institute had painted a particularly bleak picture of wartime Britain racked by famine and unemployment, a member of the London Trades Council warned the meeting that the workers he represented would seize food if they were hungry. He then asked the meeting: 'Who is to say that a general strike shall not be declared, and that we will refuse to work any goods whatever on behalf of the classes who proclaim war?'[1]

In reality, for every socialist like Hardie and Ramsay Mac-Donald who preached anti-war propaganda there were at least as many trade unionists who took their opinions from Will Thorne, H. M. Hyndman and Robert Blatchford and were as anti-German as many Unionists.[2] Nevertheless, perhaps because MacDonald was the leader of the Labour Party in Parliament, it was his views the government took note of before the war. In 1911 Seely's first subcommittee had examined what might happen if a general strike were declared on the outbreak of war. It believed that it would probably be possible to use 'black-leg' labour, drawn from amongst the many thousands of workers the war made unemployed, to break it, but they were certain that the government would have to provide troops and police to protect those willing to work, just as it did during the 1911 strikes.[3]

In January 1913 the government thought it would be prudent to take further precautionary measures in London. The commissioner of Metropolitan Police, the permanent undersecretary at the Home Office and the director of military training began to prepare a list of buildings and public utilities that ought to be guarded on the outbreak of war. These included grain stores, cold storage depots, flour mills and bakeries, 'in case there should be bread riots'. The War Office promised that 6,000 troops would be ready to assist the police if they were needed, and in case they had to be withdrawn suddenly, they also agreed to hold a stock of 5,000 rifles for the police.[4]

By 1914 the industrial scene hardly seemed propitious. According to the Board of Trade more working days were lost through strikes in the first half of 1914 than in any comparable period since 1909, with the exception of 1912, when the figures were distorted by the national coal strike. In January 1914 the War Office was afraid that the Triple Alliance of the railwaymen, the dockers and the transport workers, which was about to be formed, might cripple the ports and railways at the very moment when the army was mobilising. It asked the Treasury Solicitor whether the government had any powers to compel them to work in a national emergency. His reply was a confession of impotence. The government did have such powers, but during a strike there was no way it could implement them.[5]

The prospect of a general strike on the outbreak of war was bad enough, but to make matters worse, in March 1914 the Irish situation erupted into the Curragh Mutiny. Senior officers began to wonder whether the army could deal with the Irish situation and a war in Europe simultaneously. In July 1914 the military members of the Army Council prepared a paper for the Cabinet stating that given the existing state of unrest in India, Egypt and Europe, together with the fact that 200,000–300,000 men were illegally drilling in Ireland, the army was liable to be called upon to perform tasks beyond its abilities and numbers if two of these crises coincided.[6]

Against this background it is hardly to be wondered at that when the outbreak of war became probable at the end of July the Cabinet felt itself to be on the edge of a precipite. The crowds outside Downing Street may have cheered at the prospect of war, but the Cabinet inside felt only gloomy forebodings. On 2 August 1914 Keir Hardie addressed an anti-war rally in Trafalgar Square and called on the workers of the world 'to use their industrial and political power in order that the nations shall not be involved in war'.[7] The government's conviction that war would put an end to the status quo rather than strengthen it seemed to be about to come true. Sir Edward Grey believed that the war would be short because it would produce the collapse of the entire European economy. Both his thoughts, and those of John Morley, dwelt upon the revolutions of 1848. As the latter told the Cabinet: 'The atmosphere of war cannot be friendly to order, in a democratic system that is verging on the humour of [18]48.'[8]

Such considerations were one of the reasons why the Cabinet hesitated at the very end of July to give a firm promise to the French that it would stand by them. On 31 July Grey told the French ambassador that the commercial and financial situation looked exceedingly grave. The total collapse of world trade might only be averted if Britain remained neutral. But then Grey may have been given courage by Eyre Crowe who dismissed the commercial panic as something which had been whipped up by German commercial houses in London.[9] The Cabinet eventually decided to put commercial considerations to one side. If it had decided to remain neutral because of its fears for the economy it would have been tantamount to deciding that Britain could no longer afford to be a Great Power. In 1914 it was not prepared to make that decision, and the decision to go to war was taken on purely political and strategic grounds.[10] Britain had to stand by France and Russia because otherwise the Germans might dominate the continent.

In fact the possibility of a general strike was already more apparent than real. On 2 August the Liberal MP C. R. Buxton urged Ramsay MacDonald to call a general strike and to rally the entire Labour movement against the war.[11] MacDonald was not prepared to do anything so drastic, and he limited himself to making a speech against the war in the House of Commons.[12] But his decision not to call a strike was not known to the Cabinet, so on the same day the War Office began to deploy troops to protect vulnerable points. Its orders ended with the draconian pronouncement 'As the emergency will be great, armed guards will be given definite orders to fire to protect the premises they are watching or to prevent crime or riot.'[13]

The Cabinet's first concern was to preserve public order. On 6 August it finally agreed to dispatch the Expeditionary Force to France but for the time being it kept back two divisions. These were to be used to help the Territorial Army in the event of an invasion or raid but they were also needed to preserve public order. The public utterances of Hardie and MacDonald had alarmed the Cabinet, perhaps because they had been coupled with a sharp rise in food prices beginning on about 3 August, and this had awakened all their fears about bread riots.[14] Regular troops were, therefore, needed in Britain because, as Asquith told the War Council, 'the domestic situation might be grave and colonial troops or Territorials could not be called on to aid the civil power'.[15]

Territorials could not be trusted to fire on their own neighbours, and if Indian troops were used to fire on Englishmen it would damage the prestige of British rule in India. Only regulars could be relied on to act against rioters.

But the government did not confine itself to these purely defensive steps. It also began to take positive steps to remove possible causes of strikes or riots by restoring the conditions of trade to as near normal as possible. Its first measure was to put into practice the Huth-Jackson war risk insurance scheme. Since 31 July shipowners had been clamouring for it and Lloyd George introduced it into Parliament on 3 August with the explanation that 'unless there is some guarantee as to the war risks, we might not be able to get our ships to carry goods at all during the war'.[16] It is some measure of the Cabinet's concern that Runciman abandoned his opposition to the scheme without a struggle. Contemporaries thought that the Huth-Jackson scheme represented a major piece of state intervention in the economy. One Liberal MP called it 'the most socialistic measure, after [National] Insurance to which this Government has even been committed'.[17]

The government's next step was to establish a Cabinet Committee on Food Supplies. Its chairman was McKenna, the Home Secretary, and he was assisted by Runciman, Lord Lucas (the President of the Board of Agriculture) and E. S. Montagu, the Financial Secretary of the Treasury.[18] It was under the auspices of this committee that most of the emergency measures planned by the Committee of Imperial Defence were put into operation. The Railway Executive Committee took control of the railways on 4 August. An Admiralty Advisory Committee on TRade Diversions was set up to issue daily confidential bulletins on the safety of shipping routes and the ability of particular ports to load or unload ships. But the Cabinet Committee received little publicity and it left behind it no minutes of its deliberations. However, it is possible to reconstruct an outline of its work, and this affords a valuable glimpse of just how far the Cabinet was prepared to abandon *laissez-faire* principles on the altar of expediency in wartime.

McKenna told the House of Commons that the desire of the

committee 'has been not to interfere with ordinary trade at all, but to leave the traders to conduct their own business'.[19] This was little more than a vague statement of intent; it did not represent what the Cabinet Committee actually did. Its actions went a considerable way towards belying these mild assurances. In accordance with the Runciman Committee's recommendations it was prepared to allow food prices to rise to a certain extent because it believed that such a rise, by encouraging exporters to send their goods to Britain, would quickly increase supplies, and so eventually lower prices. But it did not place all its confidence in the blind operations of the market. When measures of more direct control seemed to be necessary and likely to be successful, it adopted them. On 8 August, as a warning against potential food-hoarders, Parliament passed the 'Unreasonable Withholding of Foodstuffs' Act, giving the Board of Trade powers to requisition any stocks of food speculators deliberately withheld from the public.[20] Before the war Britain had purchased most of its sugar from the Central Powers. This source had now completely dried up, and so from 12 August the Cabinet Committee stepped into the market directly. Within a week it had made four contracts in New York for sugar worth over £260,000. It then passed the business on to the newly established Royal Commission on Sugar Supplies.[21] The Admiralty also ordered all British vessels carrying foodstuffs destined for enemy ports to land their cargoes in Britain. This had a double purpose. It prevented the food from reaching the enemy and it enabled the government to build up a stock of food in Britain. The Cabinet Committee had been told by British grain merchants that American dealers were threatening to repudiate their contracts and withold supplies from Britain until prices and their profits rose.[22] The government's law officers had no scruples about adopting such high-handed methods even though they virtually amounted to the seizure of neutral property. They justified the Cabinet Committee's actions on the grounds that pre-emption of cargoes was an act of state, and foreign owners were not permitted under English law to sue the government for damages. Not surprisingly the American dealers did not quite see things this way, especially as by the end of August over a hundred vessels had been forced into English ports and their cargoes seized. In an attempt to placate the neutrals, the cargoes in question were not sent before a Prize Court and condemned but instead a Diverted Cargoes Committee was set up to sell them.[23] But still the American grain-dealers resented the government's actions, and for the first time in the war the Americans threatened trade sanctions against Britain. The grain merchants threatened to suspend all shipments unless the British government stopped seizing their property.[24] It was a threat the Cabinet Committee had to take seriously. Britain was too heavily dependent on United States supplies of grain, and too interested in winning American goodwill, to risk alienating the merchants. On 20 August it ordered the Admiralty to stop diversions. This episode was important because it indicated that the Cabinet was made aware that its freedom of action was severely limited from the very start of the war. As the Runciman Committee had foretold, the government dared do nothing to antagonise foreign food suppliers, because if it did they would simply refuse to sell to Britain.

This high-handed policy solved the immediate food problem but it was not a long-term solution to the much more serious problems facing the economy caused by the breakdown of the world's foreign exchanges, because that threatened to paralyse world trade. The crisis first reached London on 27 July, two days after the Austro-Hungarians and the Serbians had broken off diplomatic relations. By 29 July the fear of war had led to heavy sales of securities on the continental and New York stock exchanges. Trade had almost ceased because there were no buyers. On 31 July the London Stock Exchange closed as well. This breakdown was paralleled by a similar breakdown of the foreign exchange markets. This threatened the position of the London accepting houses. They were unwilling, and in many cases unable, to finance further international trade because they no longer had any bills coming forward to meet their immediate obligations to their own bankers.[25] The situation was then made infinitely worse by the actions of their bankers. On 29 July the joint-stock bankers had begun to fear that if a European war did break out their depositors would panic, and would rush to them to withdraw their money. A large proportion of the bankers' liquid assets were tied up in now unrealisable stock exchange loans, and the bankers felt that they had no alternative but to save themselves, and protect their depositors, by calling in their loans to the accepting houses. They also refused to make new loans available to anyone. As one of their representatives admitted to Lloyd George on 4 August: 'The bankers are going to keep the gold in their own safes and not hand it over.'[26]

Consequently the only way the accepting houses could ensure their own liquidity was to take their bills of exchange to the Bank of England. This had the effect of draining the Bank's own cash reserves to the ultimate benefit of the joint-stock banks. The latter also attacked the Bank of England's reserves in a second way by refusing to pay their customers in gold sovereigns but instead giving them Bank of England bank notes. They then immediately went to the Bank and demanded gold for their notes. It appears that the joint-stock banks were motivated by a combination of panic and self-preservation. But it is also possible that their motives were not quite as black as they may at first sight appear. They may have acted as they did to accumulate a large gold reserve because they hoped and expected that the plan for an emergency currency Holden had spoken of in January 1914 would be accepted by the government. If it was they would need all the gold they could lay their hands on so as to be able to deposit it with the Bank of England in exchange for an extra issue of bank notes.[27]

The Bank of England tried to stem the outward flow of its reserves by introducing a sharp rise in the bank rate, a step which had little relevance in the circumstances. Despite all previous predictions the threat to the Bank's reserves did not come from abroad, or even from private depositors in England; it came from the joint-stock bankers. On 30 July the rate was raised from 3 to 4 per cent and the next day, when the Stock Exchange closed, it was doubled to 8 per cent. Between 29 and 31 July the Bank lost £6 million, or about 16 per cent of its pre-crisis reserves.[28]

By 31 July Ministers were alarmed at the financial situation. Churchill told his wife that the City was in chaos, world credit was suspended, and that it was impossible to borrow money or to sell shares. The next day the cabinet delegated a Cabinet Committee of seven ministers to deal with the crisis.[29] It was presided over by Lloyd George and this was the start of a rescue organised by the government which saved the whole economy from ruin. The Cabinet Committee already had two lengthy memoranda before it. The first was by Sir George Paish, the editor of the *Statist*, and an unofficial adviser to the Chancellor. He argued that unless the government acted to re-establish normal financial conditions, foreign trade and industry would cease, and it would be impossible to finance a war. He told the Chancellor:

> It is obvious that unless the machinery of production and of distribution is kept in full working order, we shall neither be able to buy food and materials from abroad nor sell our own goods in return. Our income would thus be destroyed and we should not be able to finance the great loans which the country may be called upon to raise for its own defence and to provide the money which its allies and friends will need to ensure a successful issue in the struggle which seems to be so near and so threatening.[30]

Paish's emphasis on the need to continue to import and export if employment and food supplies were to be maintained, and if Britain was to be in a position to be the financial and economic powerhouse of the Entente, became official government policy. Indeed his memorandum did no more than reiterate the essential conclusions of the Runciman Committee, with its emphasis on the vital need to preserve Britain's economic strength as a way of winning the war. Lloyd George succinctly summarised this strategy when he explained to a group of businessmen and bankers on 4 August that the government's policy was 'to enable the traders of this country to carry on business as *usual*'.[31] (The italics were in the original minutes of the meeting.) 'Business as usual' was a highly successful slogan. The government's immediate aim was to restore business confidence, and the slogan helped to do just that, but it also gave a misleading impression of the measures the government actually took. These were anything but 'usual', and indeed once they had been taken they meant that for all the government's rhetoric business could never again continue quite as usual. Few observers realised the full scope of these steps in the midst of the crisis, so quickly did the government act, although one perceptive Liberal MP did note that they represented, 'experiments in state socialism which, in the ordinary course, would have led to months of controversy'.[32] In essence the government abandoned its olympian attitude towards the money market and intervened to support the whole edifice.

To save the situation Paish advised the Cabinet to do three things. He called for a moratorium on all debts because unless this was done the accepting houses, and all traders who were owed money from abroad and who now could not collect it, would be bankrupted. He also urged that the Bank of England should suspend specie payments and issue more paper money because he hoped that this would preserve the Bank's gold reserves. And finally he wanted the Bank, backed by a government guarantee against losses, to begin to discount bills of exchange drawn against imports. He hoped that this would be sufficient to restart the flow of food and raw material imports into Britian.

The second memorandum before the Cabinet Committee was a proposal by the Gold subcommittee of the London Clearing Banks similar to the one Holden had spoken of in January 1914. Its purpose was to increase the supply of money in circulation and thus enable business to continue. The bankers agreed with Paish that there should be a moratorium and that specie payments ought to be suspended, but their main concern was to save themselves from the expected internal drain on their own reserves. In fact they were afraid of a ghost which never appeared. Private depositors did not rush to the banks to hoard gold, but the bankers were too preoccupied with their own private nightmares to notice. As Lloyd George subsequently remarked, 'money [i.e. the bankers] was a frightened and trembling thing'.[33] In order to increase the cash they had to pay their own depositors, they were willing to deposit with the Bank of England up to £15 million of gold and £30 million of bills of exchange and securities. In return they wanted £45 million of bank notes. If this was done they were prepared to meet all demands by employers for money to pay wages and salaries, and to pay all their depositors up to 10 per cent of their net deposits, to a maximum of £3,000. They believed that this would be sufficient 'to permit of the carrying on of all industrial, commercial and financial business'.[34]

But it would have done nothing of the kind. The bankers' measures would have done nothing to help the foreign exchanges to restart or to encourage foreign trade. All they would have done was to save the bankers from their own fears.[35] The Cabinet, however, could take a wider view of what was necessary. The Cabinet Committee agreed to introduce a moratorium on all debts to last, in the first instance, for one month, and also to issue emergency paper currency. In order to arrange these measures the August bank holiday was extended for three days.[36] Initially the Chancellor was also prepared to contemplate suspending specie payments, but he was persuaded not to do so. The Governor of the Bank of England, Bradbury, and J. M. Keynes, who had been brought into the Treasury as an expert adviser, were united in opposing suspension. The Governor was not afraid of a run on his reserves. Bradbury and Keynes repeated the argument that if London ceased to be a free market in gold it would lose its dominant position as the financial centre of the world. Keynes, however, was prepared to see gold payments at home restricted or even suspended, because then all the gold in the country could be used for external transactions. Lloyd George eventually accepted their advice, and so, as Keynes wrote, 'specie payment by the Bank of England has now been saved by the skin of its teeth'.[37]

When these steps were put into practice and when the banks reopened on 7 August, they reported that business proceeded as usual. However, all the government had suceeded in doing was to save the accepting houses and foreign traders from immediate bankruptcy and ensure that employers could meet their wages bills. They had done nothing to restart foreign trade. The banks still refused to lend money to industrial borrowers, and unless they could raise money their factories would come to a standstill, and their workers would be without work. As the president of the United Kingdom Chamber of Commerce told the Cabinet Committee: 'The result may be riots and the wiping out of his [i.e. the factory owner's] means of production.'[38] On 24 August Lloyd George had actually to threaten the bankers with increased government controls if they did not advance more money to industry.

Between mid-August and the end of the year the government

undertook to pledge its credit behind almost the entire financial system so as to re-establish foreign trade. It worked through the Bank of England by guaranteeing the Bank against any losses it might make on lending money to commercial borrowers. On 12 August the Bank announced that it was prepared to discount pre-moratorium bills which could not be discounted in the normal way. Within three weeks it had bought £51 million worth of these bills.[39] But all the government had actually done was to change the accepting houses' creditors from the banks to the Bank of England. The accepting houses still had no funds with which to finance new trade on a large scale.[40] So on 5 September the government agreed to advance them money, again through the Bank of England, to finance new trade. On 3 November it also agreed to advance to merchants and manufacturers up to three-quarters of any losses they might suffer on debts due to them from enemy countries.[41] The banks agreed to advance the remaining 25 per cent. Thanks to these steps, by the time the moratorium was finally lifted on 4 November foreign trade had begun to revive. The legal position of debtors was also drastically altered. To ease the position of businessmen embarrassed by debts because they could not collect money owing to them due to the war, Parliament passed the Courts (Emergency Powers) Act on 31 August. It forebade actions to recover debts on prewar contracts without prior application to the courts. The courts were empowered to grant the debtor immunity from prosecution until after the war if his predicament was due to the outbreak of hostilities.[42]

The financial crisis on the outbreak of war was the first occasion on which the government was faced with the unavoidable fact that if it wanted the co-operation of businessmen, it would have to pay for it. Businessmen in general, and financiers in particular, had little or no sense that the power they possessed through manipulating money gave them a responsibility to safeguard the public good. They were only in business to make money.[43] If the government wanted to encroach on their business activities and needed their help to do so, they expected the government to pay a price for their co-operation. In the case of the accepting houses this presented no challenge to the Cabinet Committee. The accepting houses had either to accept the government's terms or face bankruptcy. But the joint-stock bankers were in a much stronger position. The attempt to buy their co-operation centred on the interest to be paid on the new emergency paper currency. Lloyd George and the Governor of the Bank of England – who was in the awkward position of representing not only the public interest, but those of the Bank's private shareholders as well – were reluctant to allow the banks to charge interest on the new notes at a rate above the bank rate. If they were permitted to charge interest at a higher rate their shareholders would, in effect, be making a profit out of the national emergency. But the bankers bitterly objected to any restrictions being placed on the interest they could charge their customers. The bankers won, by issuing veiled threats to increase their interest charges to their industrial borrowers.[44] The Cabinet Committee was forced to step down. In order to ensure that industry had enough cash with which to continue business the government provided the banks with more money to lend and to make profits with. But at the time the Cabinet Committee considered that this was a small price to pay to ensure that business could continue (almost) as usual.

The government's emergency measures to restore the nation's finances had two effects. The immediate likelihood of food riots, unemployment and famine seemed to have passed, and it secured the foundations for the strategy of 'business as usual'. But whether or not that strategy would be sufficient to bring victory remained to be seen.

Notes: Chapter 6

1   These remarks were made by Mr J. Williams, a member of the London Trades Council, at a meeting of the Royal United Services Institute on 13 Dec. 1913; see *Royal United Services Institute Journal*, vol. 57 (1913), p. 1,606.

2   A. J. A. Morris, *Radicalism against War, 1906–14* (London, 1972), pp. 203, 331; K. O. Morgan, *Keir Hardie, Radical and Socialist* (London, 1975), pp. 259–61; Zara Steiner, *Britain and the Origins of the First World War* (London, 1977), p. 134.

3   PRO Cab. 4/4/1/133B, Report of a sub-committee of the standing sub-committee of the Committee of Imperial Defence on the local transportation and distribution of supplies in time of war, 1 Nov. 1911.

4   PRO WO 32/5270, Civil trouble in London in time of war, minute by C. E. T[roup], 30 Jan. 1913; Troup to Sir E. Henry, 22 Aug. 1913; Minutes of conference at War Office to consider certain questions in connection with the prevention of civil disturbances in London, 30 Jan. 1914.

5   PRO Cab. 37/121/104, Memorandum on the position of Employment and Trade at the end of the second quarter of 1914 (n.d.); PRO WO 32/5290, Minute by R. H. Brade, 7 Jan. 1914; Brade to A. H. Dennis, 10 Feb. 1914; Dennis to Brade, 20 Feb. 1914.

6   PRO Cab. 37/120/81, Memorandum by the military members of the Army Council on the military situation in Ireland, 4 July 1914; Maj.-Gen. Sir C. E. Callwell, *Field Marshall Sir Henry Wilson, his Life and Diaries* (London, 1927), Vol. 1, p.148.

7   *The Times*, 3 Aug. 1914.

8   J. Morley, *Memorandum on Resignation* (London, 1928), pp. 5–6; G. P. Gooch and H. Temperley, (eds), *British Documents on the Origins of the War, 1898-1914* (London, 1926–38), Vol. 11, doc. no. 86; Sir E. Grey, *Twenty-Five Years, 1893–1916* (London, 1925), Vol. 2, p. 20.

9   Gooch and Temperley, op. cit., Vol. 11, doc. no. 367; *Ministère des Affairs*

Etrangères, Documents Diplomatiques Français, 1871–1914, 3 série (1911–1914) (Paris, 1936), Vol. 11, p. 375.

10 Steiner, op. cit., *passim;* T. Wilson, 'Britain's "moral commitment" to France in August 1914', *History*, vol. 64 (1979), pp. 380–91.

11 PRO 30/69/5/99, C. R. Buxton to MacDonald, 2 Aug. 1914.

12 65 HC Deb., 5s., col. 1829, 1841, 4 Aug. 1914.

13 PRO WO 32/5270, R. H. Brade to Sir E. Henry, 2 Aug. 1914.

14 PRO Cab. 17/102B, Report on the opening of the war by the CID Historical Section, 1 Nov. 1914.

15 PRO Cab. 22/1, Minutes of the War Council, 6 Aug. 1914.

16 65 HC Deb., 5s., col. 1855, 3 Aug. 1914; PRO Cab. 17/102B, op. cit.; PRO Cab. 37/120/93, W. S. C[hurchill] to Cabinet (and enc.), 31 July 1914; C. Wright and C. E. Fayle, *A History of Lloyd's* (London, 1928), pp. 400–1.

17 C. Addison, *Four and a Half Years. A Personal Diary from June 1914 to January 1919* (London, 1934), Vol. 1, p. 33; Runciman mss box 183/2, Runciman to [? McKenna] (n.d. but *c*. Aug. 1914).

18 PRO Cab. 17/102B, op. cit.

19 65 HC Deb., 5s., col. 2217, 8 Aug. 1914.

20 W. H. Beveridge, *British Food Control* (London, 1928), p. 7.

21 PRO T 114/1, T. L. Heath to the chairman of the Royal Commission on Sugar Supplies, 21 Aug. 1914.

22 PRO Cab. 17/102B, op. cit.

23 PRO BT 5/120, minute by W. R. Runciman, 7 Aug. 1914; Bonar Law mss 37/6/1, Runciman to Bonar Law, 21 Aug. 1914.

24 *Papers relating to the Foreign Relations of the United States, Supplement* (1914), pp. 304–6

25 M. De Cecco, *Money and Empire. The International Gold Standard, 1890–1914* (Oxford, 1974), ch. 7, *passim*; R. S. Sayers, *The Bank of England* (London, 1976), Vol. 1, pp.72–3, E. V. Morgan, *Studies in British Financial Policy, 1914–25* (London, 1952), pp. 3–9.

26 PRO T 170/55, Conference between the Chancellor of the Exchequer and representatives of the bankers and traders, 4 Aug. 1914.

27 Sayers, *The Bank*, Vol. 1, pp. 72–3.

28 PRO T 172/163, pt 2, The emergency financial measures of 1914, W. R. Fraser (n.d. but *c*. late 1914–early 1915).

29 R. S. Churchill (ed.), *Winston S. Churchill, Vol. 2: Companion, Part III* (London, 1969), p. 1,993; Samuel mss A/159/694, Samuel to his wife, 31 July 1914; Haldane mss 5992, Haldane to his mother, 1 Aug. 1914; Gainford mss, diary entry, 1 Aug. 1914.

30 PRO T 171/92, Sir G. Paish to Lloyd George, 1 Aug. 1914.

31 PRO T 170/55, op. cit.; see also D. Lloyd George, *War Memoirs* (London, 1934), Vol. 1, pp. 112–14.

32 Addison, op. cit., Vol. 1, p. 33.

33 Lloyd George, op. cit., Vol. 1, p. 74.

34 PRO T 170/14, recommendations of sub-committee re. Moratorium, and London Clearing Banks to Lloyd George, 2 Aug. 1914; PRO T 170/28, Memorandum, bankers' proposals, by Felix Schuster *et al.*, 1 Aug. 1914. The earliest suggestion by the bankers that the government should adopt their scheme appears to have been made on 31 July; see H. Llewellyn Smith mss, F. S[chuster] and E. H[olden] to Llewellyn Smith, 31 July 1914.

35 PRO T 172/163, op. cit.

36 PRO T 170/26, Sir John Bradbury to the Prime Minister (and enc.), 7 Nov. 1914.

37 PRO T 170/14, Bradbury to Bonham-Carter (n.d.), and memorandum by J. M. Keynes, 3 Aug. 1914; de Cecco, op. cit., pp. 146 *ff*; R. F. Harrod, *The Life of John Maynard Keynes* (London, 1951), p. 197; Elizabeth Johnson (ed.), *The Collected Writings*

of J. M. Keynes (London, 1971), Vol. 16, p. 15.

38 PRO T 172/133, Conference between the Chancellor of the Exchequer ... and representatives of the Chambers of Commerce and manufacturers, 11 Aug. 1914; PRO T 170/28, A. Chamberlain to Lloyd George, 11 Aug. 1914; PRO T 172/134, Conference between the Chancellor of the Exchequer, members of the Cabinet and representatives of the accepting houses, 12 Aug. 1914.

39 PRO T 172/133, op. cit.; PRO T 172/163, op. cit.

40 PRO T 170/28, Montagu to Lloyd George, 15 Aug. 1914; PRO T 172/129, Conference between the Chancellor of the Exchequer ... and representatives of traders and trade associations, 3 Sept. 1914.

41 David French, 'Some aspects of social and economic planning for war in Great Britain, *c.* 1905–15' (PhD thesis, University of London, 1978), p. 145.

42 PRO T 170/26, op. cit.

43 S. G. Checkland, 'The mind of the City, 1870–1914', *Oxford Economic Papers,* vol. 9 (1957), p. 265.

44 PRO T 170/57, Adjourned conference between the Chanellor of the Exchequer ... and representatives of the bankers, 6 Aug. 1914.

7

The Failure of 'Business as Usual'

In August 1914 it was only dimly apparent that the success of 'business as usual' rested on the government's pursuing four policies successfully. The direct impact of the war on the British economy had to be minimised, otherwise the economy would suffer from shortages and inflation and business would not be able to continue as usual. Secondly, British traders had to be given a free hand to 'capture' German trade. Thirdly, an effective economic blockade had to be imposed on Germany but, at the same time, because of Britain's dependence on the USA for supplies, it was critical that the blockade did not so irritate the Americans that they placed an embargo on trade with Britain. And finally, the government had to forbear from raising a large army. The French and Russians had to be prepared to contribute millions of soldiers to the allied war effort and if necessary to suffer very heavy casualties whilst Britain made only a token contribution to the land war and instead devoted itself to the war at sea and to providing its allies with money and munitions.

Ultimately all these policies failed or were reversed by the government. The blockade did not bring Germany to its knees. Conciliating the Americans became a major British preoccupation. And yet, because of the blockade, British traders could not be given a free hand to 'capture' German markets. The impact of the war on the British economy could not be minimised and there were price rises and shortages. And finally, in a fit of absent-mindedness, the Cabinet allowed Lord Kitchener to raise a continental-scale army.

It proved to be impossible to shelter the civilian population and the economy from the effects of the war. The international economy did not collapse in 1914 but the outbreak of war did severely disrupt it, and between 1 August 1914 and 1 June 1915 the Board of Trade's retail price index rose by 39 per cent.[1] The government was criticised for permitting this to happen. Critics argued that it should have introduced price-fixing for basic foodstuffs, that it should have bought up supplies of meat and wheat on its own account, and that it should have paid British farmers a bounty to grow more wheat. Its failure to do all these things led to McKenna and Runciman in particular being labelled as arch-exponents of *laissez-faire*, zealous supporters of private enterprise and determined opponents of state trading.[2] But these charges are only partially true. The government had good reasons for not setting maximum prices, or telling the public that they were in fact buying up meat and wheat on their own account. As the Runciman Committee had noted, Britain's heavy dependence on imported food made it very dangerous to fix food prices in Britain below those in the rest of the world. If the government had fixed either retail or wholesale prices it would simply have encouraged suppliers to seek better prices elsewhere, and Britain would have gone short of food. When the German government tried to fix the prices of domestically produced food in 1915 the main result was to create a thriving black market.[3]

Perhaps the only really effective policy would have been for the government to have purchased all the basic food imports the population needed at the prevailing world price and then to have distributed them to the consumer at less than cost price. But for two reasons the Treasury chose to subsidise food prices only to a very limited extent. Subsidies were expensive and the Treasury was determined to conserve funds. As the Financial Secretary to the Treasury remarked, 'the country will win in this war whose purse is the longest'.[4] Secondly, the government was determined to use hunger and want as a way of directing economic and human resources towards the war effort. In August and September 1914 the Runciman Committee's fears about unemployment in wartime seemed to be about to materialise.[5] By the end of August the Board of Trade estimated that nearly 480,000 workers had lost their jobs because of the war. Ministers were clearly worried about this situation. On 4 August Runciman had described the task of organising food supplies and relief as 'terrible work'. On the same day a government whip told MacDonald: 'The present situation makes it probable that acute distress may occur in many parts of the country before long.'[6] The government acted swiftly to deal with the problem. Asquith appointed an eight-man committee under Herbert Samuel, the President of the Local Government Board. Other members of the committee included the former Unionist President of the Local Government Board, Walter Long and MacDonald. This committee was the first example of cross-party co-operation in the emergency.[7] Two days later local authorities were ordered to set up similar local committees to survey the state of employment in their areas and, where necessary, to try to prevent or at least to alleviate war-induced unemployment. Local Government Board circulars told them to encourage employers to keep their workers on short time rather than to dismiss them because of lack of work. If this proved to be impossible, the committees were told to consult their local authorities to try to find employment on public works. Only as a very last resort were they to be given doles. A circular dated 20 August ended with the solemn warning that the likely demand for relief would probably be so great that it would only be possible to pay each applicant for relief a bare pittance.[8]

But Treasury Ministers and officials were not impressed by these well-meant attempts to provide relief for the unemployed. On 8 September a deputation from the local authorities called at the Treasury to ask for a loan to pay for public works to help the unemployed.[9] The Treasury was most reluctant to provide them with money. Sir John Bradbury had already prepared a reply in which he argued that it was vital for industry to adapt itself to the needs of war as soon as possible. He recognised that during this period of readjustment there was bound to be hardship, but

From the military and economic point of view it is an actual advantage that the pressure of distress should be applied to divert labour from economically useless to national and economically useful employment, and though for humanitarian and political reasons it is clearly necessary to give it relief should not be so great as to neutralise the pressure altogether.[10]

Capital works schemes should be abandoned in favour of 'poor relief pure and simple'.[11] This statement stood much of the government's prewar thinking on its head. Bradbury no longer shared the fear that civilian morale might collapse if the government did not bend every effort to bring them relief. Instead he sought to use the new opportunities opened up by the war to bring about a shift in economic resources from industries suffering from the outbreak of war to industries likely to be of benefit to the war effort. That in itself would cure the problem of distress. In essence, by pursuing a policy of masterly inactivity the Treasury had taken the first step towards mobilising the economy to support the war effort. For the time being the Treasury worked to reverse Samuel's policy. It only advanced money to particular local authorities if they could show real evidence of acute and pressing distress.[12]

Hence by early October many public works schemes were being

curtailed for lack of money. This caused serious concern amongst the labour movement and the War Emergency Workers' National Committee sent a deputation to see Lloyd George on 6 October to ask for a return to Samuel's policy. The Chancellor refused their request because he shared Bradbury's concern to save public money and to mobilise the economy through the operations of the market. He told the deputation:

As the war progresses it is clear that the demands on the industries of this country will be enormous; there will be industries where not merely the employment will be full, but there will be overtime and [a] shortage of men. You must remember that over a million men have been withdrawn from the ordinary industry [*sic*] for the purpose of war and it looks at the present moment as if that number might be increased by another half million, so that you will have one and a half million men training for war, the vast majority of whom would in ordinary conditions be engaged in some industry or other. At the same time you have this abnormal demand upon the manufacturing resources of this country which will be progressing simultaneously. We are receiving orders from other countries constantly, belligerent countries which are friendly to us, and in a short time I am not sure, far from distress and unemployment, that you will not have a condition of abnormal employment in this country.[13]

If the government did not interfere, recruiting and the export drive would solve the unemployment problem in a few weeks was the Chancellor's message. And within a month he had been proved correct. By mid-November unemployment in the trades covered by the 1911 National Insurance Act began to dip below the corresponding figure for 1913. The Board of Trade could find two reasons for this. As the Runciman Committee had hoped, the navy had kept open the sea lanes and so, as Llewellyn Smith noted: 'It also soon became apparent ... that the restriction of ordinary industrial activities by the war would be much less serious than had at first been feared, owing largely to the continuance of our oversea commerce.'[14] And the second reason was that the New Armies removed hundreds of thousands of young men from the labour market.

But if unemployment could be solved by a policy of masterly inactivity, the rising price of food could not, and the Cabinet Committee on Food Supplies did not remain idle. In November it ordered the Board of Trade to appoint Sir Thomas Robinson, an experienced meat trader, to purchase meat on the government's account in Argentina and later in Australia. And within a few days the committee also set up a Grain Supplies Committee to do the very thing the 1905 Royal Commission had rejected, to accumulate a reserve stock of one and a half million tons of wheat and half a million tons of flour.[15] The Cabinet Committee's intention was to release these stocks on to the market in case prices did begin to rise in the spring and summer of 1915. The Grain Supplies Committee used a firm of private contractors, Ross T. Smyth & Co., as its purchasing agents. By the end of March 1915 the Cabinet Committee had spent £12·5 million on buying and selling wheat, meat and sugar.[16] The government entered into these contracts to ensure sufficient supplies at reasonable prices for the rapidly expanding New Armies and for the civilian population. Although it tried wherever possible to keep open the normal channels of trade, it was quite ready to modify them if necessary. It entered into these large contracts in an effort to diminish excessive competition between middlemen and to restrain rising prices. This would obviously benefit the Treasury but the government also hoped to pass on the saving to the civilian population as well by releasing part of its stocks on to the open market at competitive prices. The principle behind this policy was similar to that behind the war risk insurance scheme. The government became a trader in an effort to persuade the trade to keep its own prices down.[17]

But if this policy was to be successful it had to be kept secret. The Cabinet Committee's policies appeared to be weak and muddled because neither Runciman nor McKenna was permitted to defend or explain his actions in public. When the House of Commons debated food prices in February 1915 Runciman and Asquith deliberately witheld from MPs the news of the government's meat and wheat purchases. They had good reasons for doing so. Mention of the meat contracts might embarrass the Argentine government which was afraid that the Germans might interpret them as an unneutral act, and if the Germans knew of the size of the contracts they might be able to estimate the size of the New Armies. Ministers were also afraid that the original contracts were illegal, because they had been entered into without prior parliamentary sanction: no one was in any hurry to face Parliament with the news.[18] The news that other governments were buying wheat had caused international dealers to raise their prices, and to announce publicly that the Cabinet Committee was planning deliberately to undercut private traders in the flour market if their prices rose too steeply would have been counter-productive. Merchants who bought goods at a time of rising prices did so in the expectation that prices would continue to rise and that they would be able to sell them when they were even higher. But if they knew that when prices did go higher the government would begin to undercut them, they would simply refuse to continue buying. Therefore, on 17 February, Runciman totally misled the Commons when he told it that the government had rejected any idea of buying wheat on its own account.[19]

The Cabinet Committee's fears that publicity would ruin its plans were not idle ones. In March they came true when information about the Grain Supplies Committee's activities leaked out. News of what the *London Corn Circular* called 'the incubus of Government dealing', combined with the expectation that the opening of the Dardanelles would release large quantities of Russian wheat on to the market and depress prices, led to an importers' strike which lasted for some weeks. All the government could do was to announce that it had withdrawn from the market and hope that the Dardanelles would indeed be opened. Its secret experiment had failed and, as J. M. Keynes, who at one time acted as secretary to the Cabinet Committee, wrote: 'In the realm of action the only thing worth doing is to storm the Dardanelles. That done, this particular problem would soon lower its crests.'[20]

The Cabinet Committee did not fail because it was too addicted to *laissez-faire* or averse to state trading. Given the Treasury's policy of spending as little as possible on relief measures, there was perhaps little more it could have done. Its real failure to help to check the rise in food prices lay in another direction, and one where it perhaps did have a greater freedom of action. This was in its failure to co-ordinate naval, military and civilian demands on the transport system and so prevent congestion, delays and shortages, some of which could have been avoided. The Seely Committee left the Cabinet Committee with the belief that on the outbreak of war naval and military demands on the transport system would be slight. Hence in August there seemed to be no need to set any list of priorities between the army, navy and civilian population for transport. They were all permitted to try to take what they wanted. On 8 August Asquith did tell the two services to co-ordinate their shipping demands with the Cabinet Committee, but as the August panic faded so did his concern, and the services were soon preying on civilian resources without hindrance.[21] The War Office only consulted the Admiralty Transport Department when it wanted ships, and the latter took little or no account of civil interests when it requisitioned them.[22]

It was not until January 1915 that the Cabinet Committee began, very slowly, to cast off the prewar assumptions that wars were fought by soldiers and sailors and the civilian population stood by passively. Until then, according to Montagu, the Cabinet Committee had been hampered by its own reluctance to interfere with the work of the service departments.[23] But by January it was so concerned about rising prices that it brought the matter to the Cabinet, who discussed it no less than three times. Then, prompted by Runciman, who was realistically aware just how little it could do to control the world supply situation, it decided that the only steps open to it were to curtail Admiralty requisitioning and to unblock congested ports.[24]

On 16 January the Admiralty's director of transports suggested a plan which amounted to a complete rejection of 'business as usual'. He proposed that the government should stop trying to influence market conditions to enable trade to continue approximately as usual and instead that it should take direct control of all the shipping and distributive industries of the United Kingdom.[25] Churchill did not want to go quite that far, but he did want to take control of all merchant ships. In its essentials this was the plan which was successfully adopted in 1917–18, so it is worth examining why it was turned down in 1915. The essential argument that Runciman and McKenna used to defeat the Admiralty's plan was that if all British merchant ships were placed under state control and then forbidden to trade between two neutral ports but were confined to bringing goods to and from Britain, Britain would lose the valuable foreign currency its merchant fleet earned, currency which was needed to support the balance of payments. Instead they argued that the tonnage problem could be eased if captured German vessels were released for government service and if the Admiralty also released a proportion of the transports it had taken up.[26]

Runciman and McKenna won the day. They were still intent on pursuing 'business as usual' and were convinced that a healthy balance of payments was vital to the success of the British war effort. On 10 February the Cabinet Committee told the Admiralty to release as many vessels as possible.[27] However, this did not mean that Runciman and the Admiralty were divided over the principle of state control, merely on how far that control should extend and to what uses the British merchant fleet should be put. Runciman was quite prepared for the Cabinet Committee to control some vessels to assist it in its trading ventures. For example, in 1915 the Board of Trade requisitioned ships to carry sugar for the Royal Commission.[28] Furthermore, requisitioning the entire merchant fleet in 1915 would not have been so easy as the Admiralty seemed to assume. In December 1914 meat importers had begun to complain about the lack of insulated tonnage, so on 9 December Runciman conferred with the ship-owners. He merely wanted them to form a committee to keep him informed of the tonnage available, so that he could advise them on how to make the best use of it. But even securing this minimal degree of co-operation was difficult. Five of the twenty firms involved refused to help, and without the willing co-operation of the owners concerned requisitioning could not succeed.[29] The insulated tonnage situation became worse in 1915 and two more conferences were held in February and March. The negotiations highlighted the government's difficulties. As the letter the Admiralty sent to every owner whose vessels were requisitioned made clear, the Admiralty depended on them to manage the day-to-day running of their ships. The staff of the Admiralty Transport Department was too small to do it itself. Thus, as in the case of the railways, the insurance market and the bankers, the government could not arbitrarily seize their assets. It had to strike an acceptable financial bargain with the owners to buy their co-operation. Hence the insulated tonnage owners were able to force the government to pay them rates well above the current Blue Book rates, and even then not all of them were satisfied.[30] Given this major constraint on what the government could do, there was no certainty that even if it had taken over the entire merchant fleet that freight rates would have fallen.

But if the government was divided over what to do about the shipping industry, it was in agreement about how to relieve congestion at the ports. In January 1915 the Advisory Committee on Shipping Diversion surveyed the major west coast ports to discover why they were congested. Its first recommendations simply repeated those of the Runciman Committee. Naval, military and civilian demands on the ports had to be co-ordinated and this required the establishment of a small management committee at each port to control all its facilities. But it also identified shortages of labour as a major problem. The ports had suffered heavily because of recruiting but the committee had few positive proposals to make. Instead, echoing the prejudices of the Runciman Committee, it accused those dockers remaining of laziness and excessive drinking. The evidence it found for this was biased; in all its investigations it did not question a single union official. It was content to accept the opinions of dock managers who contended that high wages encouraged casual working habits and absenteeism, and it ignored the obvious fact that the docks had always operated on the basis of casual labour. The committee would have done better to recommend an end to all further recruiting in the docks. An industry as labour-intensive as the docks could not afford to continue to lose fit young labourers to the army indefinitely.[31]

The prices of imported staple foods like meat and wheat had risen by over 20 per cent by February 1915 and the Cabinet Committee's failure to do more than marginally slow down this rise was one reason why by the spring of 1915 the government was faced by a series of demands for higher wages by workers in various sectors of the economy. The other reason was that the Treasury had financed the war through inflation. Lloyd George was aware of the Pittite tradition of financing war through sharp increases in current taxation, particularly income tax. On 21 August Basil Blackett of the Treasury had presented him with a series of memoranda reviewing British war finance since the late eighteenth century, and all of them deprecated relying too heavily on loans. They included one extract from a memorandum written by Bradbury during the Boer War which included the advice that 'the traditional policy of Great Britain has been to defray war expenditure as far as possible by increased taxation'.[32] He went on to note that in many past wars nearly half the cost involved had been met from taxes.

But Lloyd George deliberately chose not to follow this advice when he prepared his first war budget in November 1914. The domestic economic situation still seemed to be grave and he was reluctant to make still more serious the plight of existing income tax payers by doing more than doubling the rates of income and super tax. He did toy with the possibility of lowering the income tax threshold from £160 to £50 p.a. but he rejected it on the ground that the tax on small incomes would have to be collected by employers. The introduction of the national insurance scheme before the war had shown just how unpopular it was to use employers as tax-gatherers, and the sum involved, a few million pounds in a full financial year, was too small to make it worthwhile for the government to court unpopularity.[33] Instead he decided to tax the poor by raising the duties on beer, sugar, tobacco and tea. Just how much these new duties and taxes would yield was problematical. The Board of Inland Revenue could not provide the Chancellor with an accurate forecast because it had no way of knowing how long the war would last or how seriously it would continue to affect trade.[34] But the Treasury estimated that by the end of the financial year in March 1915 they would bring in £15.5 million.

By mid-November the war was already costing the Treasury £900,000 per day but even so the Chancellor seemed to be perfectly content with such a small increase in the tax revenue. He congratulated himself that his new taxes would bring in enough money to meet interest payments on the swollen national debt and he was determined to raise the rest of the money the government needed by borrowing. The government needed a minimum of about £330 million to pay for the war up until the end of the current financial year and the Chancellor determined to find the money by issuing a long-term loan.[35]

That in itself need not have been inflationary because, had the government chosen to, it could have issued the loan in small blocks of £5 in a deliberate effort to attract working-class savers and this would have had the effect of soaking up their excess purchasing power before it could have fuelled inflation. But the Treasury chose not to do so. The National Debt Office advised the Chancellor that if the war loan was made attractive to small investors they would invest in it by withdrawing their money from post office savings banks and the government would only lose money.[36] So the government had to turn to the investing public and the banks for its money. With the financial world still disrupted by the outbreak of war, it did not seem to be a propitious time to try to raise a war loan of £350 million as the government did try to do in November. Therefore, to ensure that the loan was fully subscribed to, the government issued it on very attractive terms. It was offered to the public in blocks of £100 at £95 and bearing a nominal interest rate of 3·5 per cent but in fact it promised a real return of 4 per cent. The bankers lapped it up, and even before it had been issued a consortium of the Bank of England and the larger clearing banks had taken up £100 million and promised to buy more if private subscribers were not eager to take the rest.[37]

But in the meantime the government had heavy immediate demands to meet and it did so by the almost daily sale of very large numbers of Treasury bills. By June 1915 £235 million had been raised in this way.[38] This was a highly inflationary way of raising money. Most of the bills were bought by bankers, and, as the director general of financial inquiries explained to the Cabinet

> as bankers, every time they buy a security increase *pro tanto* the volume of Banking Deposits, we are by this method of finance inflating banking credits and leaving the public in possession of more money than usual, so encouraging it to spend freely and put up prices against itself and the Government.[39]

Bradbury, too, recognised that the government must stop creating 'bankers money' through its financial policies and instead issue its next loan in small denominations in order to attract the small investor and so encourage the working class to save and not to spend.[40] But these facts did not become apparent to the Treasury until June 1915, and so in the spring the government was faced by a problem it had never before considered. The possibility that trade unions would demand higher wages in wartime had not been anticipated before 1914. Labour had been expected to be abundant and in no position to demand more money. But now there were actually labour shortages in key sectors of the economy.

Prices had risen faster than wages and although earnings may not have lagged quite so far behind, the trade unions were convinced that their members were becoming impoverished.[41]

If the government failed to hold down prices the trade unions were determined to secure higher wages. The result was a revival of industrial strife early in 1915, despite the industrial truce proclaimed by the unions on 24 August 1914. In February 1915 when the railwaymen demanded an increase in wages the companies conceded them a war bonus of 10 per cent. The first major strike in a strategic industry took place amongst the engineering workers on Clydeside who demanded a 2d per hour increase and struck for it on 16 February. The employers offered them only $\frac{3}{4}$d but the government realised that it could not afford a prolonged strike in such an important munitions manufacturing area, and so it set up a three-man committee under Sir George Askwith to arbitrate in the dispute. This committee, the Committee on Production in Engineering and Shipbuilding, persuaded the men to return to work in return for a war bonus of 1d per hour.[42] In succeeding weeks the committee dealt with a number of similar disputes involving civilian workers in Admiralty dockyards, and also boilermakers, shipbuilders and men at the Woolwich Arsenal. On each occasion the committee gave the workers a war bonus of approximately 10 per cent, and although this was well below the rise in the cost of food, the unions accepted it.

But the turning point came in March. By then the Cabinet recognised that if it went on like this, inflation would proceed unchecked. Unable to restrain prices and not yet aware that its own financial policies were inflating the currency, it decided to try to restrain wages instead. When the postal workers claimed a 10 per cent war bonus several ministers, including Lloyd George and Montagu, wanted to reject their claim. J. A. Pease summed up their sentiments thus:

A strong feeling was expressed that on grounds of rise in prices a case in war did not justify Govnt [*sic*] money – the more wages the worker had and the more [*sic*] to spend the more would prices rise and they must be content to make some sacrifice during war.[43]

They were particularly afraid that if they conceded this increase the growing numbers of workers on government contracts would also demand more money. The arguments in favour of not granting the increases were explained fully in two memoranda by Montagu and Bradbury. The government was confronted by the problem of inflation. Large numbers of workers had left industry to join the army, and much of industry was in the process of being converted to war production. Hence fewer consumer goods, and fewer goods for export, were being produced, and so if the government continued to pay war bonuses, more money would be chasing fewer goods. The result would be still more inflation, and a further dangerous drop in the foreign exchange rate of sterling. Since December 1914 the exchange rate in New York had been going against Britain, and by mid-February it had fallen from $4·86 to the pound sterling to $4.·79½. Bradbury was afraid that if the Cabinet did not act soon, specie payments might eventually have to be suspended.[44] Montagu recommended that as a first step the Cabinet should reject the postal workers' claim.[45] On 17 March Bradbury elaborated his ideas in what amounted to a new austerity programme. Inflation could be checked, and internal consumption reduced, if the government simply refused to sanction large wage increases. Prices would then be stabilised, because the consumer would simply be unable to pay more for goods and services. In return for, as he admitted, 'going short of goods and clothing', the working classes were to be persuaded to 'submit to the necessary sacrifices', by the government taking steps 'to secure that no government contractor could make out of his country's necessities more than a decent remuneration for his personal services and a decent return on the capital he had himself put into the business'.[46]

The Treasury's analysis completely ignored the part played by external factors, such as rising world demand coupled with falling world supplies, in raising prices, nor did it yet have anything to say about its own financial policies and the part they played in driving up prices. The bargain it wanted to strike was a very one-sided one. The working class was to be asked to make real sacrifices in its standard of living, whilst the worst that might happen to its employers was that their excessive profits might be taxed. That the Treasury could suggest this policy, and the very next day Lloyd George could begin to negotiate on these lines with the trade unions, indicates that two things had changed since the war began. The Cabinet recognised that its attempts to hold down retail prices had failed. In a world war 'business as usual' was just not possible. The civilian population could not be sheltered from the impact of war. And secondly, the Cabinet no longer believed that it was so important to shelter them. Its lurid fears of anti-war strikes and bread riots had, for the time being at least, evaporated. By March 1915 'business as usual' at home was not finished, but it was obsolete. The British economy, and the British people, had proved themselves to be far more resilient than their rulers had thought possible.

The second facet of 'business as usual', the attempt to 'capture'

German trade, also failed. Within two weeks of the war starting the Cabinet was busy trying to put into practice the Runciman Committee's policy of strengthening the British economy by encouraging British traders to take the place of German traders all over the world. On 18 August the Cabinet told the Board of Trade and the Home and Colonial Offices to ensure that British manufacturers produced and exported 'the class of goods which Germany has up to now been supplying to overseas markets'. The press also quickly came to the government's aid in promoting this campaign. The *Spectator* remarked that because German commerce had been swept from the seas by the Royal Navy the opportunity awaiting British exporters was 'extraordinarily good'.[47] Arguments of this kind would not have been surprising in journals committed to protection before the war, but the *Spectator* was one of the few Unionist free trade papers. And Liberals too, like Leo Chiozza Money and E. D. Morel (a bitter critic of Grey's prewar foreign policy) also saw the war as an opportunity to overtake German commerce in the world markets.[48] Writing in the *African Mail* in October 1914, Morel urged the merchants of Liverpool to win back the markets in Africa they had lost to the Germans. Money was quite explicit:

> Never before in the world's history has such an opportunity been offered the British trader. Secure at home, and possessing free access to the world's materials, he is presented with the markets of his greatest competitor. At one and the same time he enjoys Free Trade with the greater part of the world, and absolute Protection in his own home market and all other markets from German and Austrian competition.[49]

In Money's opinion the world was waiting for Britain to supply it with everything 'from drugs to toys'.[50] Germanophobia was rife in Britain after August 1914 and British manufacturers were quick to sense the opportunity the war gave them. On 9 October the Sheffield Chamber of Commerce asked the Home Office to close all branches of enemy companies in Britain. Two weeks later the Employers' Parliamentary Association passed a similar motion, and also asked the government to close the businesses of naturalised Germans as well. Representatives of the toy industry asked the government to promise them protection after the war, fearing that the capital they hoped to sink in new factories would be wasted if the Germans were allowed to compete with them again in the future.[51] As a senior Home Office official remarked after reading some of these requests

The movement in favour of further measures against German firms in [the] United Kingdom seems to be growing, and it may be expected that as British traders come to realise more clearly what is involved in the 'war on German trade' they will demand more loudly further restrictions on the branches here.[52]

The Home Office was unwilling to agree to such requests because to have done so would have thrown considerable numbers of British people out of work, but that particular consideration did not weigh very heavily with British manufacturers eager to supplant German goods in the British market. For many of them the war was an excuse to introduce protectionism under the guise of patriotism, and in some cases the Board of Trade was happy to assist them. In December 1914 the British Laboratory Ware Association was anxious that the Board should revoke an import licence on German chemical glassware. They wanted to be protected from German competition while they built up their own strength in the home market. The Board, recognising the chemical industry was of strategic importance because of its close connection with the manufacture of explosives, was happy to oblige them.[53] Furthermore, the budget of November 1914 contained a grant of 1 million pounds which was to cover 'expenditure for the purpose of setting up an aniline dye industry in this country to rival or oust the German trade'.[54]

The Board also helped British manufacturers fill the gap left by the ending of trade with Germany by suspending patents granted to enemy subjects so that British manufacturers could break into German monopolies, and it also took active steps to encourage British traders to take full advantage of their new freedom. By October 1914 the Board's Commercial Intelligence Branch had taken on 100 new staff and rented extra offices in Cheapside in the heart of London's business district. From there it prepared a series of booklets on the various branches of German trade showing manufacturers where their opportunities lay. It organised a series of 'exchange meetings' in Cheapside to show industrialists who were thought to have suffered most from German competition the types of goods they should now manufacture.[55] Buyers who had hitherto bought from the Central Powers where also encouraged to attend so they could see what British industry had to offer them.

By December Runciman had high hopes that his policy was well on the way to being a success. He informed the Cabinet that thanks to these measures, 'there are several indications that a doll-making industry may soon be firmly established in the Potteries'. Between 10 and 23 May 1915 the Board sponsored an international trade fair in London as a direct rival to the prewar fairs that had been held in Leipzig. The object of the fair was to encourage the manufacturer and export of goods formerly imported from Germany. British consuls issued over 10,000 invitations to potential foreign buyers asking them to attend.[56]

But despite the undoubted enthusiasm with which interested parties tried to 'capture' German trade, the attempt failed. By April 1915 exports of manufactured goods were nearly £7 million less than in April 1914.[57] The failure to 'capture' German trade had several causes. The industries the government singled out for particular encouragement were toy and games manufacturers, and fancy goods, earthenware, glassware, paper, clocks and jewellery manufacturers. But the government did nothing to exempt them from the attentions of the recruiting officer. Thus, at a time when more men ought to have been available to fulfil growing order books, the numbers of men employed in all these industries actually fell.[58]

Secondly, the requirements of the blockade made it impossible for British manufacturers to occupy former German markets at will. The blockade, and the restrictions on the export of a growing list of strategic goods which were needed in Britain or which it was vital to deny to the Germans, made an all-out export drive impossible. On 4 August the Treasury established a committee to enforce the proclamation forbidding trade with the enemy.[59] The purpose of the proclamation was to assist the naval blockade by preventing the import of German goods into Britain, either directly or through neutral countries, and to stop British manufacturers exporting to Germany. Exporters were forbidden to send goods directly to Germany or to any European ports except those of France, Russia, or the Iberian Peninsula unless they had a government export licence.[60] The Treasury Committee was anxious that its work should hamper exporters as little as possible.

But the government's two aims of increasing British exports and ensuring that no goods reached Germany were in many ways incompatible. The Treasury Committee frequently erred on the side of caution when granting licences. Delays in granting them were often prolonged as each application had to pass through a labyrinth of government offices. An exporter had first to acquire an application form for a licence from the Board of Customs. When he had comleted it he had to return it to the Board, which then sent it to the Treasury Committee. It sent it to the War Office, the Admiralty and the Board of Trade, which between them compiled lists of prohibited exports. If they all approved of the exporter and did not think he was surreptitiously trading with the enemy, he was given his licence by yet another government department, the Privy Council's Office.[61]

By January 1915 this cumbersome system was trying and failing to deal with 900 applications each day. Every formality slowed down the very export drive the Board of Trade was trying to promote. Delays only harmed the reputation of British exporters in neutral eyes, and in some cases it meant that potential buyers of British goods looked elsewhere.[62] And despite all these elaborate precautions the Treasury Committee still issued licences without considering the need either to conserve stocks of a particular raw material in Britain or the value of a particular article to Germany if it should eventually reach it. It is not to be wondered at that one trader, who had asked for a licence in October 1914 and had still not received it in January 1915, remarked bitterly to the Board:

> we would ask you to consider whether this is treatment British manufacturers should expect from the government who are impressing on the one side upon the manufacturer to capture German trade and on the other hand are throwing obstacles in the way of the manufacturers so doing.[63]

Thus the Germans hardly had to lift a finger to defeat the British attack on their trade. The needs of the New Armies for men, the need to maintain the blockade and a mountain of red tape all combined to defeat British attempts to 'capture' German trade.

The blockade proved to be ineffective for quite different reasons. As soon as war broke out the Royal Navy began to take steps to interrupt German trade. German ships in British ports were prevented from sailing and the movement of enemy ships at sea was quickly paralysed. Those which escaped capture hastened into neutral ports. On 5 August a Royal Proclamation was issued containing a list of contraband goods corresponding largely to those laid down under Articles 22 and 24 of the Declaration of London. When the navy began to act against German trade it was legally bound to abide by the terms of the Declaration of Paris signed in 1856. Thus, with the exception of contraband, the navy could not seize enemy property in neutral vessels, or neutral property in enemy vessels. And it could only blockade the coast of an enemy, not that of any contiguous neutral. It was also morally bound by the Declaration of London which defined three types of contraband. Absolute contraband was goods like munitions clearly intended for military use which could be captured. Free goods were goods which were only for civilian use, and in between these two categories there was a third, conditional contraband, which could be for either civilian or military use.[64] If Britain stuck rigorously to the letter of the law the blockade would be ineffective on at least two counts. Many goods, including foodstuffs, were only conditional contraband, so before the navy could seize them it had to be shown that they were destined for the enemy's army. The list of free goods also included things like cotton, copper, wool, silk, jute and rubber and many metallic ores, all of which were vital in the manufacture of munitions. Moreover, Germany was surrounded by a number of neutral states, Holland, Denmark, Norway and Sweden, any one of which could act as an entrepôt for German trade: thus if the blockade was to be effective some way of plugging the gaps in it would have to be found.

Mention has already been made of the government's policy in August of seizing neutral cargoes of foodstuffs and landing them in Britain. Neutral reaction made it clear to the government very quickly that it could not ride roughshod over neutral opinion in such a fashion. On 13 August Churchill set up the Restriction of Enemy Supplies Committee under Sir Francis Hopwood. Its purpose was 'to examine and watch continually all means or routes by which supplies of food or raw materials may reach Germany and Austria'; and it was ordered to recommend financial, commercial, diplomatic and military methods by which this trade could be stopped.[65] The committee first turned its attention to Scandinavia and Holland, and in particular to the port of Rotterdam. On 12 August Lloyd George had pointed to the fact that large quantities of wheat were probably reaching Germany through the port, but the Cabinet was divided on what to do. Grey, supported by Haldane, wanted to declare a blockade across the whole of the North Sea and declare wheat to be conditional contraband. But Asquith, Simon, Harcourt and Emmott were afraid that such a policy would antagonise neutral, and in particular American, opinion. A Cabinet Committee was set up to examine Grey's idea, and Simon repeated that under the Declaration of London, food could not be stopped unless it could be proved that it was intended for the enemy's army.[66] Eventually on 14 August a compromise was reached; the Dutch government was to be invited to prohibit the export of food to Germany and in return Britain would allow the export of British coal to Holland sufficient to meet its own needs but insufficient to permit it to export any.[67] This tool of denying neutrals access to British-controlled raw materials unless they fell in with British wishes became widely used as the war progressed. It was, in fact, little short of blackmail, something the Committee of Imperial Defence's report on the opening of the war tacitly admitted when it said: 'Generally speaking the trend of the policy has been to keep the neutral countries rather short of supplies in order that they may have no temptation to supply the enemy.'[68]

But of course, as American reaction to the navy's seizure of American grain cargoes showed, two could play at this game. Almost as soon as the war had begun the American government had demanded to know whether or not the allies would adhere to the Declaration of London. Although Britain had helped to draft the declaration it had never ratified it. After the American warning about grain shipments the Cabinet felt it necessary to clarify its position. It was helped to do this by the fact that the German government had just taken control of all foodstuffs in Germany, so henceforth all such cargoes destined for Germany could be presumed to be contraband. On 20 August the British government issued the first of a series of Orders in Council defining its policy. It proclaimed its intention to act in accordance with the Declaration of London, but retained the right to modify it in future.[69] To clothe its policy towards the smaller neutrals in some semblence of legality it revived the doctrine of continuous voyage, so it could seize cargoes whose ultimate destination was Germany even if they were initially consigned to a neutral. It took its first step towards modifying the declaration on 21 September when it extended the list of conditional contraband to include copper, rubber, iron ore, hides and skins, which were all materials used to make munitions or military accoutrements.[70]

The United States State Department was angy at this. It was very reluctant to recognise Britain's right to pick and choose which bits of the declaration it would or would not obey.[71] The copper-mining states believed that the blockade would ruin them, and they had the ear of the Secretary of State. In the face of this pressure Grey lost his former truculence. He still believed that the blockade was a vital weapon in Britain's armoury but the rapid German advance in the west towards Paris made him recognise that the war would not be over quickly. For the time being France and Britain could hold their own but they would not be able to do so if they quarrelled seriously with America over the blockade. It could, if it chose, cut off supplies to them and they could not do without American food and raw materials or the munitions they hoped to get from American industry. Hence from September onwards the object of Grey's diplomacy was to secure the tightest possible blockade that could be enforced without a rupture with the Americans, and in the final analysis he was even prepared to abandon the blockade rather than lose American friendship.[72]

Continued American discontent led the Cabinet to reconsider its policy yet again in the autumn. The Restriction of Enemy Supplies Committee was asked to discover just how much trade was reaching Germany through neutrals. It reported that it could not come up with an exact answer but the quantities were probably so small that it might be better to abandon the doctrine of continuous voyage rather than alienate the Americans.[73] The Cabinet was still divided. Asquith was willing to go a long way to conciliate the Americans but Runciman wished 'to impede Germany in every way possible and effective short of a quarrel with America'.[74] His attitude was shared by Lloyd George on the ground that even if the blockade was interfering with American commerce the large orders Britain was placing in the United States more than compensated for that, and if the American government did place an embargo on trade with the Entente it would cripple its own economy.[75] Eventually caution triumphed. A new Order in Council intended to pacify the Americans was issued on 29 October. It gave effective immunity to conditional contraband provided it was to be delivered to a specified consignee in a neutral country, but at the same time articles such as iron ore, nickel, chrome, rubber and petroleum were raised from the status of conditional to absolute contraband.[76] But the government carefully refrained from doing the same to cotton. Grey believed that to have prohibited the export of American cotton to Europe would have done little to harm the Germans, who were thought to have extensive stockpiles, but it would have infuriated the southern states of the United States, and they might have driven President Wilson into placing an embargo on arms sales to the Entente.[77]

But the October Order in Council was a failure. Cargoes of cotton and food continued to reach Germany through neutral countries and at the same time British efforts to stop and search American ships only served to continue to antagonise the United States. Clearly the British needed to adopt a subtler and more effective policy. Grey began to search for one in November by setting up a Contraband Committee at the Foreign Office. Its purpose was to devise diplomatic measures to cripple German trade, but Grey specifically told his chairman that on no account was he to do anything to antagonise the Americans.[78] And in the meantime it was the French who suggested the next step forward. In mid-October the British ambassador in Paris noted in his diary a conversation he had had with the chief economic adviser to the French War Ministry. The latter had suggested that the allies should try systematically to ration imports into neutrals bordering Germany to their prewar levels. The Americans could be placated if the Entente arranged to buy up any cargoes which would increase neutral supplies above that level. The British had already begun to do something of the sort in mid-September. The Cabinet had set aside £400,000 to subsidise British firms to charter all available neutral oil tankers in an effort to stop them carrying cargoes to Germany. Now in early November an agent was sent to New York with a million pounds at his disposal to try to buy up all available stocks of copper. He failed, but in January 1915 a second attempt was made through the merchant bankers Morgan Grenfell and J. P. Morgan. Unknown to all but a handful of Cabinet ministers they succeeded in buying 95 per cent of the American export surplus.[79]

In the meantime the Foreign Office was busy trying to conclude rationing agreements with the European neutrals. Grey's policy was to enforce the Orders in Council in such a way that they could 'be readily harmonised with the legitimate interests of neutral countries whose territories lie in proximity to the enemy States'.[80] Hence on 17 November he suggested that if the neutrals would prohibit the export of contraband the Royal Navy would not insist on searching every ship making for its ports but would confine itself to simply inspecting their papers. The Dutch government was reluctant to accept these proposals on the ground that they would infringe its neutrality, but a committee of Dutch traders and ship-owners, calling itself the Dutch Commerce Commission, was more amenable. The Dutch were naturally anxious that the war should disrupt their own trade as little as possible, and it was they who suggested that they should constitute themselves into a trust company through which all imports into Holland could be channelled. The company was established on 23 November as the Netherlands Oversea Trust and it promised to ensure that no contraband reached Germany through Holland. Similar agreements were signed with other neutrals in the winter of 1914–15.[81]

However, the blockade was still very far from being watertight. The Entente's adherence to something which still resembled the Declaration of London meant that neutrals could still export free goods to Germany. But from February onwards this began to change. On 4 February Germany declared unrestricted U-boat warfare against merchant vessels around the British Isles. Two days later Wilson's personal representative, Colonel E. M. House, arrived in London on a mission to discuss the possibility of a negotiated peace.[82] The Cabinet now faced a dilemma. Given the Entente's growing dependence on American supplies, it could not afford to reject Wilson's overtures, but it was opposed to a negotiated peace and the Admiralty was eager to use the German declaration as an excuse for tightening the blockade.[83].

House began his talks with Grey on 9 February. In the course of their discussions they spoke of a possible covenant governing the rules of war. House suggested that it should include a clause setting down certain sea lanes in which merchant vessels were to be completely free from attack. Without consulting the Cabinet, the War Council, or the Admiralty, Grey quickly grasped at this idea and suggested that in future all belligerent and neutral merchant vessels should be immune from attack. House was surprised and pleased to see that Grey was prepared to go so far to meet American wishes.[84]

Had they known of these talks, Grey's colleagues would not have shared House's pleasure. They were in the midst of discussing a plan to retaliate in the face of the U-boat blockade. On 16 February the Cabinet decided to detain all ships carrying cargoes whose ultimate destination was Germany. Grey argued that if they did this the Americans would convoy their merchant ships to Germany under armed escort, but his colleagues were prepared to overcome that problem if and when it arose.[85] Fortunately for Anglo-American relations the Germans provided an escape from what could have become an impasse by rejecting the American declaration on the freedom of the seas. The British used that as an excuse to enforce their retaliation policy. On 11 March a third Order in Council was issued announcing that all cargoes destined for Germany would in future be detained.[86] This amounted to the declaration of an unrestricted blockade and a clear break with the Declaration of London. For the first time the Entente were trying to stop all trade with the enemy. However, in practice the British still bowed to American pressure and an effective embargo on American-German trade was not enforced for several months. Neutral goods going to Germany were not necessarily confiscated, and at first only certain American vessels were stopped. The purpose of this was 'so that the Yankees might be let down lightly'.[87] But the Americans did not entirely appreciate this consideration and on 7 May it seemed as if the thing Grey most dreaded might be about to happen. House told him that Wilson was looking with increasing favour on 'an embargo upon shipments of arms and war supplies'.[88]

By May 1915 reality was beginning to undermine many of the navalists' and radicals' hopes that maritime pressure would bring Germany to its knees. 'Business as usual' had prevented the British economy from collapsing in the first weeks of the war, but the effort to build up the export industries would not win the war. Nor, for two very good reasons, would the blockade. The need to take account of neutral opinion meant that there were large gaps in the blockade. And secondly, Germany's European hinterland was too extensive and rich to make it vulnerable to a blockade in anything but the long run. In cases where it had been dependent on overseas supplies for strategic raw materials it was often able to use its own scientific ingenuity to overcome shortages.

Early reports reaching Britain about stringent economic conditions in Germany had given the British an overly optimistic picture.

In October the Cabinet was informed that the Germans were beset by serious unemployment problems. In November it was told that the strain on the German economy was steadily increasing, that its industries were suffering from a severe depression, and that the wheat harvest had been so poor that the government had been compelled to fix the price of grain. In December, despite all the German government's efforts, its economy was supposed to be almost paralysed. But the same report admitted of one note of surprise. It seemed incredible that such a highly developed economy as that of Germany, which allegedly had been heavily dependent on foreign trade, could have survived for so long the dislocation of the war. Germany seemed to have confounded all past precedents, at least as far as they were understood in Britian.

In fact the German economy was far more robust than it had been given credit for being. This gradually became clearer in the new year. Even though the blockade was tightened, the possibility that it would swiftly cripple Germany receded. In March even the news that bread rationing had been introduced was not taken as signifying that it was in serious straits.[89] It was assumed that if the situation was serious the German government would not have announced the fact in such a public manner. By May the Restrictions of Enemy Supplies Committee admitted that reports coming from Germany were too confused to enable it to estimate exactly how serious the state of the German economy was, but it was apparent that the blockade would not bring a swift end to the war.[90]

Indeed, by May 1915 it was becoming apparent that the whole strategy of 'business as usual' would not produce a quick decision, far less one which favoured the Entente. No end to the war seemed to be in sight, and the allies were becoming increasingly restive about the fact that Britain was not bearing its fair share of the fighting. Lord Esher, who fulfilled the role of roving ambassador to France, sent back a gloomy report about French morale at the end of January 1915 which included the observation:

The universal instinct, therefore, of soldiers and civilians appears to be that it is essential to bring about a rapid decision. The urgent enquiries about the forces available, or likely to be soon available, in England are largely the outcome of a moral weakness, which has become apparent among many sections of French people.[91]

Clearly the French, and for that matter the Russians too, were not prepared to do all the fighting whilst British industry waxed rich. They demanded that the British do their fair share of the fighting and suffering, and at the same time they also wanted British economic aid and munitions. But, as subsequent chapters will demonstrate, they could not have all these things at once. Men recruited into the British army could not produce munitions for the allies, and anyway, if the British were to try to raise a huge new army it would need equipment as well. The fundamental problem facing the British in the early months of 1915 was that they had to work out what their strategic priorities were and then decide how to apply their resources to meet them. Their basic failure was that they did not do this.

Notes: Chapter 7

1 David French, 'Some aspects of social and economic planning for war in Great Britain, *c.* 1905–15 (PhD thesis, University of London, 1978), pp. 164–73.
2 W. H. Beveridge, *British Food Control* (London, 1928), p. 6. The contemporary outcry against the government's policies was led by the War Emergency Workers National Committee. See R. Harrison, 'The war emergency workers national committee', in A. Briggs and J. Saville (eds), *Essays in Labour History 1886–1923* (London, 1971), pp. 227, 231.
3 PRO Cab. 37/123/51, Wheat prices, 26 Jan. 1915; for the German experience see G. Feldman, *Army, Industry and Labour in Germany* (Princeton, NJ, 1966), pp. 97 *ff.*
4 Lloyd George mss C/1/1/29, Montagu to Samuel, 1 Oct. 1914.
5 PRO Cab. 37/120/100, Unemployment due to the war, 28 Aug. 1914; David French, 'Some aspects of social and economic planning' pp. 197–200.
6 C. P. Trevelyan mss box 30, Runciman to Trevelyan, 4 Aug. 1914; PRO 30/69/5/98, Wedgewood Benn to MacDonald, 4 Aug. 1914.
7 *Memorandum of the Steps taken for the Prevention and Relief of Distress due to the War*, Cd 7603 (1914).
8 ibid.
9 PRO T 171/93, Deputation to the Chancellor of the Exchequer and the President of the Local Government Board, 8 Sept. 1914.
10 PRO T 171/93, The relief of distress in relation to finance [Bradbury], 7 Sept. 1914.
11 ibid.
12 PRO T 172/94, H. C. Dale to H. P. Hamilton, 5 Oct. 1914; Lloyd George mss C/1/1/29, Montagu to Samuel, 1 Oct. 1914.
13 PRO T 172/142, Deputation by the War Emergency Workers National Committee to the Rt Hon. David Lloyd George, MP, 6 Oct. 1914.
14 *Report of the Board of Trade on the State of Employment in the United Kingdom in October 1914*, Cd 7703 (1914–16).
15 PRO Cab. 15/6/28, Board of Agriculture and Fisheries, General outline of the special war activities of the Board of Agriculture and Fisheries (n.d. but *c.*1919); Runciman mss. box 92, note by Lord Lucas, 10 April 1915.
16 PRO T 171/109, First Budget, 1915, Treasury I (n.d.).
17 David French, 'Some aspects of social and economic planning', pp. 158–63.
18 Montagu mss as. 1–4, Runciman to Montagu, 11 Nov. 1914; Montagu to Runciman, 12 Nov. 1914.
19 69 HC Deb., 5s., col. 1178, 17 Feb. 1915.
20 PRO Cab. 37/123/51, op. cit.; see also PRO Cab. 17/118, Note on the wheat position, R. H. R.[ew], 26 Apr. 1915.

21 Asquith mss, Vol. 46, ff. 93–4, Asquith to the War Office and Admiralty, 8 Aug. 1914.

22 PRO Cab. 1/11/9, Report by the Director of Transports, Admiralty, on the memorandum on the shortage of merchant shipping tonnage prepared by the Board of Trade, G. Thompson, 16 Jan. 1915; PRO Cab. 19/30, Dardanelles Commission, Minutes of evidence, QQ. 975–6 (Hankey) and 1373 (Churchill).

23 Montagu mss 217(1)–(6), Montagu to Asquith, 21 Jan. 1915.

24 Runciman mss box 303, Runciman to his wife, 21 Jan. 1915; PRO Cab. 37/123/23, Asquith to HM the King, 3 Jan. 1915.

25 PRO Cab. 1/11/9, op. cit.

26 PRO Cab. 1/11/7, Shortage of merchant tonnage, 11 Jan. 1915.

27 Asquith mss, Vol. 27, f. 28, Directions from the Cabinet Committee on food prices to the Transport Department, Admiralty, 10 Feb. 1915.

28 C. E. Fayle, *The War and the Shipping Industry* (London, 1927), pp. 139–41.

29 PRO BT 13/60/E27152, minute by G. S. Barnes, 9 Dec. 1914; Committee of owners of refrigerated tonnage, H. W. M [acrosty], 16 Dec. 1914.

30 71 HC Deb., 5s., cols 203–4, 20 Apr. 1915; Fayle, *The War and the Shipping Industry*, pp. 73–82; PRO BT 13/62/E27579, Memorandum of rates and conditions agreed for the use under requisition by the government of the insulated space of all steamers in the Australian trade, 10 Mar. 1915; PRO BT 13/62/E2765, minute by H. W. Macrosty, 1 Apr. 1915; PRO BT 13/63/E27987, Owen Phillips to Runciman, 6 May 1915.

31 PRO Adm. 1/8415/79, Congestion in ports of the UK, 25 Mar. 1915.

32 PRO T 171/106, The financing of naval and military operations, 1793–1886, Sir John Bradbury, 12 Feb. 1900.

33 PRO T 171/97, E. E. Nott-Brown to Lloyd George, 3 Nov. 1914; D. Shackleton to Masterman, 3 Nov. 1914; Masterman to Lloyd George, 3 Nov. 1914; PRO T 170/12, M. Nathan to H. P. Hamilton (and enc.), 9 Sept. 1914.

34 PRO T 171/96, Board of Inland Revenue to the Chancellor of the Exchequer, 10 Nov. 1914.

35 PRO T 171/95, War Budget, 1914, Expenditure, 1914/15. Forecast (n.d.).

36 PRO T 171/106, War loans – confidential print, W. G. Turpin, National Debt Office, 31 Aug. 1914.

37 PRO T 171/106, Treasury to Lloyd George, (n.d., but *c.* Nov. 1914); J. H. Tritton to Lloyd George, 16 Nov. 1914.

38 W. Ashworth, *An Economic History of England, 1870–1939* (London, 1972), pp. 271–2; F. W. Hirst, *The Political Economy of War* (London, 1915), p. 307.

39 PRO Cab. 37/129/29, The financial position in May – Report by the Director of Financial Enquiries, 8 June 1915; S. Pollard, *The Development of the British Economy, 1914–67* (London, 1969), pp. 67–8.

40 PRO Cab. 37/129/19, War Loan, John Bradbury, 7 June 1915.

41 A. Clinton, 'Trades councils during the First World War', *International Review of Social History,* vol. 15 (1970), p. 221.

42 M. B. Hammond, *British Labour Conditions and Legislation during the War* (New York, 1919), p. 66.

43 Gainford mss, diary entry, 26 Mar. 1915; PRO Cab. 37/126/3, Asquith to HM the King, 27 Mar. 1915.

44 Kathleen M. Burk, 'British war missions to the United States, 1914–18' (D. Phil. thesis, University of Oxford, 1976), pp. 12–16.

45 PRO Cab. 37/126/24, Postal servants: proposal for war bonus, E. S. Montagu, 24 Mar. 1915.

46 PRO Cab. 37/126/12, The war and finance, J. B[radbury], 17 Mar. 1915.

47 'Commercial possibilities of the war', *Spectator,* 22 Aug, 1914.

48 M. Swartz, 'A study in futility: the British radicals and the outbreak of the First World War', in A. J. A. Morris (ed.), *Edwardian Radicalism, 1900–14* (London, 1974), p. 259.

49 L. G. Chiozza Money, 'British trade and the war', *Contemporary Review*, vol. 106 (Oct. 1914), p. 475.
50 ibid., p. 479.
51 PRO HO 45/10750/265402/4, Sheffield Chamber of Commerce to McKenna, 9 Oct. 1914, and J. Harworth (the Employers Parliamentary Association) to the Home Office, 30 Oct. 1914; Bonar Law mss 35/4/13, E. Hamley to Bonar Law, 7 Dec. 1914.
52 PRO HO 45/10750/265402/4, memorandum by H. B. B[utler], 19 Oct. 1914.
53 PRO BT 12/98, C. A. Mercer to the President of the Board of Trade, 24 Dec. 1914; PRO BT 12/98, M. Muspratt to W. Runciman, 10 Dec. 1914, and Whitmore & Co. to the Intelligence Department of the Board of Trade, 12 Jan. 1915.
54 PRO T 171/95, Expenditure, 1914–15 (n.d.).
55 Money, op. cit., p. 481.
56 PRO Cab. 37/122/198, The capture of enemey trade, exchange exhibitions and Leipzig fair, W. R[unciman], 31 Dec. 1914; *The Times*, 14 Jan., 11 Feb., 8 Apr., 8 and 11 May 1915; *The Economist*, 1 May 1915.
57 *The Economist*, 15 May 1915.
58 Runciman mss box 141, Estimate of the condition of the people with regard to enlistments, state of employment on government and other works in various occupations in April 1915.
59 PRO HO 45/10728/245895/2, Treasury minute, 4 Aug. 1914.
60 PRO HO 45/10769/274473/1 contains copies of the proclamations; see also PRO Cab. 15/6/24, War Trade Department, Full record of the department, Sir N. Highmore (n.d. but *c.* 1919).
61 PRO HO 45/10728/254895/94, minute by H. B. Butler, the Home Office representative on the committee, 14 Aug. 1914; PRO Cab. 42/1/15, The co-ordination of the war arrangements for trade restrictions, [M. P. A. Hankey], 13 Jan. 1915.
62 PRO Cab. 42/1/34, Trading with the enemy, CID paper 211B Note by the Board of Trade, 10 Feb. 1915.
63 PRO BT 12/104, Boardman Bros to the Assistant Secretary of the Board of Trade (Commercial Department), 11 Feb. 1915.
64 A. Marsden, 'The blockade', in F. H. Hinsley (ed.), *British Foreign Policy under Sir Edward Grey* (London, 1977), pp. 488–90.
65 Marion C. Siney, *The Allied Blockade of Germany, 1914–16* (Ann Arbor, Mich., 1957), p. 30; PRO Adm. 1/8480/1, Neutral and enemy trade index, 1 Jan. 1915.
66 PRO FO 800/89, Sir John Simon to Grey, 14 Aug. 1914; Emmott mss, diary entries, 17 and 19 Aug. 1914; E. David (ed.), *Inside Asquith's Cabinet – from the Diaries of Charles Hobhouse* (London, 1977), p. 182; PRO Cab. 41/35/28, 29 and 30, Asquith to HM the King, 12, 13, and 15 Aug. 1914.
67 PRO Cab. 41/35/34, Asquith to HM the King, 20 Aug. 1914.
68 PRO Cab. 17/102B, op. cit.
69 Marsden, op. cit., pp. 491–2; Bonar Law mss 37/6/11, Minute of a meeting of the co-ordinating committee held in the Home Secretary's room on Thursday, August 27, M. P. A. Hankey, 1 Sept. 1914.
70 Marsden, op. cit., p. 492.
71 B. J. Hendrick, *The Life and Times of Walter Hines Page* (London, 1930), Vol. 1, pp. 368–90.
72 Sir E. Grey, *Twenty-Five Years, 1893–1916* (London, 1925), Vol. 2, pp. 103–4.
73 Siney, op. cit., p. 25.
74 PRO FO 800/89, Runciman to Grey, 27 Oct. 1914.
75 D. Lloyd George, *War Memoirs* (London, 1934), Vol. 1, p. 397.
76 Marsden, op. cit., p. 494; PRO Adm. 1/8400/397, Declaration of London, Order-in-Council (no. 2), 29 Oct. 1914.
77 Grey, op. cit., Vol. 2, pp. 110–12; Runciman mss box 14, Grey to the Cabinet (?) Aug. 1915.

78 G. M. Trevelyan, *Grey of Fallodon* (London, 1937), p. 306.
79 David (ed.), op. cit., p. 216; H. N. Scheiber, 'World War One as entreprenurial opportunity: Willard Straight and the American international corporation', *Political Science Quarterly*, vol. 84 (1969), pp. 494–5.
80 PRO BT 11/8, Grey to Sir A. Johnstone, 3 Nov. 1914.
81 ibid.; see also BT 11/8, Johnstone to Grey, 14 Dec. 1914 (and enc.); Siney, op. cit., pp. 34–44.
82 C. J. Lowe and M. L. Dockrill, *The Mirage of Power* (London, 1972), Vol. 2, pp. 236–8.
83 W. S. Churchill, *The World Crisis, 1915* (London, 1923), p. 296.
84 C. Seymour (ed.), *The Intimate Papers of Colonel House* (London, 1926), Vol. 1, p. 376.
85 David (ed.), op. cit., p. 222.
86 PRO Adm. 1/8414/65, Order-in-Council, 11 Mar. 1915.
87 David (ed.), op. cit., p. 226; PRO Cab. 37/131/50, memorandum by Mr Leverton Harris, c. 30 July 1915.
88 Runciman mss box 144, memorandum, E. G[rey], 7 May 1915.
89 PRO Cab. 37/122/157, Sir A. Johnstone to Grey, 26 Oct. 1914; PRO Cab. 37/122/155, The economic situation in Germany in the third month of the war, Sir V. Chirol, 13 Nov. 1914; PRO Cab. 37/122/180, The economic situation in Germany and Austria-Hungary (n.d. but c. Dec. 1914); PRO Cab. 37/125/25, The economic situation in Germany and Austria-Hungary, M. Muller, 8 Mar. 1915; G. Hardach, *The First World War, 1914–18* (London, 1977), ch. 2 *passim*.
90 PRO Cab. 17/118, Restriction of enemy supplies committee. Shortage of foodstuffs in Germany, May 1915.
91 PRO Cab. 42/1/28, The war after six months, Lord Esher, 29 Jan. 1915.

8

Kitchener and the Creation of the 'Nation in Arms', August–December 1914

Within a few days of becoming Secretary of State for War, Lord Kitchener was responsible for one of the most complete and far-reaching reversals of policy of the whole war. In place of what had passed for a manpower policy before the war, Kitchener substituted one of his own, and it almost completely undermined or simply ignored every precept of 'business as usual'.

When Kitchener became Secretary of State for War on 5 August 1914 the total strength of the regular and Territorial armies stood at 707,466 men.[1] On 6 August Parliament was asked to sanction an increase in the size of the army of 500,000 men, and the next day this was granted.[2] It was the first of several increases. Kitchener's reasons for expanding the army, and doing so by creating the New Armies rather than relying on the Territorials, are obscure. But from the scattered evidence available it is possible to piece together at least some of his reasons. He did not underestimate the task facing Britain. Two men who worked closely with him, his friend and confident, Lord Esher, and Sir George Arthur, his personal secretary at the War Office, both recalled that he expressed similar sentiments on entering the War Office. 'I am put here to conduct a great war, and I have no army.'[3] He disagreed with the tentative and vague estimates about the likely duration of the war which had been in vogue before its outbreak, and were still common currency in August. Sir Archibald Murray, Sir John French's chief of staff, believed that the war would last between three and eight months.[4] On 8 August Churchill told the Admiralty to assume that the war would last for one year.[5] Kitchener thought that these estimates were far too short. On 13 August he told Esher that the war might go on for as long as three years. He told the Cabinet a few days later that, although the first big battles would be fought by the end of August, the war could last for two more years. He was, therefore, the first minister who contemplated anything other than a short war. His prediction also had the effect of removing one barrier to raising more troops; he was convinced that the war would last long enough for them to be trained and put into the field, and he thought that with a strong army Britain could dictate to the other powers at the peace conference.[6]

Kitchener also firmly embraced the continental strategy and was determined to fight the Germans to a standstill in France. On 14 August he gave Murray some last-minute instructions. He counselled him against taking too many risks with the Expeditionary Force, and above all he warned him against being shut up in a fortress as the French had been at Sedan in 1870. Rather than let that happen the army should make its way to the coast. But, Murray recorded, 'he [Kitchener] did not intend that we should leave the Continent. We should hang on until he sent reinforcements. He did not intend to leave the Continent until the Germans were utterly crushed.'[7] Among the reinforcements he promised were three more regular divisions, two colonial divisions, six New Army divisions and even six Territorial divisions.

Kitchener did not disband the Territorial Army, or even stop it from recruiting, but his attitude towards it was one of neglect compared to the care and attention he lavished on the New Armies.[8] Why he adopted this attitude towards the Territorials requires some explanation. Many senior officers and civilian officials within the War Office would rather have seen the Territorials expanded than have been forced to embark on the creation of the New Armies from scratch.[9] And outside the War Office Hankey and Haldane gave him similar advice. However, as almost everyone who worked with him was unanimous in recording, Kitchener was by experience and temperament an autocrat, unaccustomed to either seeking or taking advice.[10] Hankey wrote of him in November 1914 that he was someone 'who liked to do things in his own peculiar way and ignore all existing machinery'.[11] Hence he ignored all their advice. He was also ignorant of Britain's existing military organisation, and in particular he was doubtful about the military value of Territorial units.[12] They had enlisted for home services only. They were under no obligation to serve abroad, and he was most reluctant to put pressure on the men to serve overseas.[13] He was so reluctant to send married men to the continent that he told Esher that he would punish any officers who tried to force their men to go abroad.[14] He was uncertain, too, of their military qualities. Possibly prompted by memories of the failures of French Territorials which he had witnessed in the Franco-Prussian War, and misunderstanding exactly what the County Associations were, he told Lord Midleton that they were administered by mayors in their parlours.[15] Far better, therefore, to start from scratch, and enlist men for general service for three years or the duration of the war.

The Cabinet accepted his decision with astonishing meekness, even though it completely reversed its existing policy. This may be accounted for by the fact that those ministers most likely to have opposed the raising of a massive new force of troops were bewildered and dazed by the outbreak of war. Runciman admitted that by 4 August he and colleagues like Pease, Harcourt and Lloyd George, had already endured 'ten days of anxiety and torturing thought', and that he was 'miserable beyond measure'.[16] When the War Councils of 5 and 6 August recommended that the Expeditionary Force should be sent to the continent, there seems to have been little or no opposition from within the Cabinet to their advice. For many ministers their world seemed to be dissolving into a bad dream. Lloyd George told his wife that he was living in a 'nightmare world'.[17] Perhaps they were prepared to accept the advice of the military experts because it represented the only policy which was put to them at a moment of crisis. Nor can Kitchener's own personal ascendency over the Cabinet be neglected in the early months of the war. His advice was that of the military expert *par excellence*. With the exception of Roberts he was the empire's most distinguished soldier. Ministers were very reluctant to question anything he wanted done. Grey expressed this view some years later when he wrote of a conversation with a Cabinet colleague just after Kitchener had asked for the first increase in the size of the army:

> I believed the war would be over before a million new men could be trained and equipped, but that, if this expectation were wrong, the million men should of course be sent abroad to take part in the war. It was, therefore, clear that we should all agree to what Kitchener wanted.[18]

Churchill was also only guilty of some slight exaggeration when he told the Dardanelles Commission that Kitchener, 'dominated absolutely our counsels at this time'.[19] The only minister with sufficient stature to question his policies was Asquith, and he deliberately refrained from doing so, because he had a high opinion of his colleague. On 3 November he wrote: 'My opinion of K's capacity increases daily. I think he is a really fine soldier and he keeps his head and temper wonderfully considering how he is tried.'[20]

Although the Cabinet did not realise it, by permitting Kitchener to raise the New Armies it was allowing him to drag the British army into the second half of the nineteenth century. Kitchener was intent on aping the prewar military organisation of the major European powers. He wanted to transform Britain's small army into a 'nation in arms' in which every able-bodied citizen became a soldier. But one difference was to remain between the British army and those of its European neighbours. Their armies were manned by conscripts; Britain was to continue to recruit its troops from volunteers.

The raising of the New Armies was one of the most important and far-reaching decisions taken by the British throughout the war. Kitchener's advocacy of raising a continental-scale force must remain his major claim to fame. It ensured that by 1916 Britain was able to assume a major share of the fighting on the western front at a time when the French were reaching the point of exhaustion. But the New Armies also created new, and unprecedented, problems for the British. Until January 1915 they were raised with little or no thought being given to the effect that taking over 1 million men from their normal occupations would have on the economy. The New Armies deprived industry, commerce and agriculture of much of the manpower they needed to carry on their normal peacetime functions. They also created a huge new demand for different types of goods and services, as they had to be fed, equipped and transported. They probably did as much to disrupt the peacetime pattern of the economy as the outbreak of war had done. Consequently they were a major factor in their own right in undermining the strategy of 'business as usual'. By the spring of 1915 manpower was so scarce in many industries and munitions were thought to be so vital that many people no longer considered that 'business as usual' was viable. The raising of the New Armies in the closing months of 1914 was haphazard and done with little thought for the future. The Cabinet made no attempt to draft a manpower budget or to apportion labour between the competing demands of industry and army. Writing in 1935 and with the benefit of hindsight, Hankey highlighted most of the government's omissions when he wrote:

> The Government had no national plan for an expansion of the army, or for its armament. None of the problems had been worked out or thought of at all – exemption from military service of skilled or unskilled labour, machine tools, raw materials, and national

industrial mobilisation generally. Consequently, and in particular there was no basis for programme making or for estimating future requirements and supplies, no warning was given to the armament firms of what would be expected of them.[21]

As Hankey indicated, the economic repercussions of raising the New Armies could only have been minimised if the government had taken firm control of the situation from the very start of the war and had been quite clear about the size of army it wanted and how it wanted to equip it. But it was not. The Cabinet lurched from one leap in the size of the army to the next. And if the government had wanted to regulate the economic dislocation caused by the New Armies it would have had to do two things. Conscription would have had to have been introduced so that workers in economically non-essential occupations could have been taken into the army, and workers in essential occupations could have been left where they were. And the government would also have had to take control of the armaments and engineering industries to ensure that their resources were put to the best possible use. But in 1914 it did neither of these things. Conscription was politically impossible and the Cabinet was late in recognising that private enterprise would be slow in developing the capacity to produce all the munitions needed in good time.

The Liberals were often unfairly criticised for their failure to introduce conscription in 1914. Churchill later argued that if Kitchener had insisted on conscription in August 1914 the Cabinet would have followed him. This was not true. On 25 August Churchill told the Cabinet that he believed that the voluntary principle exploited the patriotism of married men in the Territorials by placing moral pressure on them to serve abroad, whilst allowing unmarried unenlisted men to remain at home. In place of this he argued that conscription should be introduced. He was alone in this recommendation. His colleagues thought that such a move would be impractical, impolitic and unnecessary. Lloyd George still believed that 'the people would not listen to such proposals'. Asquith was very doubtful about the support such a step would receive from Liberal MPs, and both he and Grey argued that 'such a proposal would divide the country from one end to the other'. Lord Emmott described Churchill's ideas as premature and a waste of time.[22] But it was Kitchener who delivered the *coup de grâce*. He told the Cabinet that although conscription might be necessary at some unspecified date in the future, it was not at the moment. He was already getting more recruits than he could equip.[23] Three days later the Cabinet settled the question for the foreseeable future, at least as far as it was concerned. As long as men continued to volunteer in sufficient numbers there was no need to introduce compulsion.

The Cabinet's collective judgement that conscription was impractical because the public would not agree to it was probably correct. If conscription was to be introduced then the most important part of the public who would have had to be won over to it was the organised working-class movement. Although in August 1914 the trade unions and most sections of the Labour Party quickly rallied to support the government, their prewar prejudices against conscription were far from dead.[24] This was vividly, if rather forcibly, expressed by Robert Williams, the secretary of the National Transport Workers' Federation, in a letter he wrote to Ramsay MacDonald on 6 August 1914. He told MacDonald:

> We ought to be fully prepared to counter the machinations of the yellow press with defiant working class pronouncements. Personally, if I am compelled to shoot, I would much prefer to blaze away at the enemies I know inside our own country than attempt to murder members of my own class at the behest of blood-drunken maniacs like Churchill and others. We must be prepared to organise forcible revolt against Conscription, come in what form it may.[25]

It is doubtful whether many trade unionists would have been prepared to go to quite the lengths Williams advocated, but it is more than probable that they would have resisted conscription. Given that fact, the government had no real choice but to rely on voluntary methods of recruiting. Whatever mistakes were made under the voluntary system, and it will be argued here that there were major ones, Asquith's Cabinet was forced to rely on voluntary recruiting not because of any ideological commitment to it, but because its grasp of political reality indicated that conscription was beyond the bounds of practical politics in 1914. Indeed, there was literally no alternative to voluntary recruiting in 1914 because there was no alternative government prepared to take office and implement conscription. Both the Liberal and the Unionist Party leaders wanted to fight the war on the basis of the normal party system.[26] The Unionist leaders were, however, prepared to support the Cabinet in prosecuting the war, as Bonar Law and Lansdowne indicated to Asquith on 2 August.[27] But they were not prepared to coalesce with the Liberals in 1914, and only a coalition would have secured enough popular support for conscription. Bonar Law explained to Lord Curzon at the end of January that the Unionists had two options facing them. 'One is to go on as we are doing, without responsibility, and with a limited amount of criticism, such as was at the meeting of your House; or to face a coalition. The latter proposal I should certainly be against.'[28]

The government's manpower policy between August and December 1914 was anarchic. Kitchener made his first call for 100,000 men on 8 August, but he did not explain his plan for creating the New Armies to the Cabinet until 24 August. Its reaction was to listen to him 'in silence'.[29] The gravity of the situation may have been brought home to it by the fact that it had just received the first bad news from the front in Belgium, so he was given a free hand to proceed as he thought best. Exactly how many men he told the Cabinet he would need is far from clear. Pease noted a figure of thirty divisions by April 1915, which would mean about 550,000 men. Grey, in writing his memoirs, gave a figure of 1 million men. Churchill, writing in *World Crisis*, though that Kitchener had asked for twenty-four divisions, or rather more than 433,000 men.[30] The last two sets of figures may have been distorted by the fallible memories of the writers who were noting down their impressions some years after the event. But the different figures they give may also indicate that even Kitchener himself had no very clear idea of what the ultimate size of the army he was creating would be. Addressing the House of Lords for the first time as Secretary of State for War, he made a passing reference to a figure of thirty divisions, but he then told his audience: 'I cannot at this stage say what will be the limits of the forces required or what measures may eventually become necessary to supply and maintain them.'[31] Thus it is apparent that the expansion of the army was very largely unplanned. Kitchener set out to recruit as many men as he could, and he opened the way for a period of anarchic recruiting which lasted until the end of 1914.

The public response to Kitchener's call for men was immediate. In August 298,923 men enlisted in the New Armies and the Territorial Army. In the next month a further 462,901 men came forward, making a total of 761,824 new recruits by the end of September, more than enough to fill any figure Kitchener may have spoken of, and more than doubling the size of the prewar army. By the end of October the total number of new recruits came to 898,635, of whom 656,965 enlisted in the New Armies, an eloquent testimony to the popularity of Kitchener's creation.[32] The army as a whole was receiving in one week over three times as many recruits as the regular army had received in a year before 1914.

Herbert Samuel told his wife that he thought that this response was 'wonderful', but he doubted whether the War Office would be able to cope with such numbers.[33] His doubts were justified. The recruiting machinery had never been intended to cope with anything like such a sudden and enormous influx of recruits, and it soon broke down. The director of recruiting, Sir Henry Rawlinson, was at his desk from 9 a.m. to 11 p.m. daily in August and early September. Long queues formed outside recruiting offices and men sometimes had to wait all night to enlist. Once they had enlisted there were soon not enough barracks, arms, or even uniforms for them. At the start of the war there was only enough barrack space in the country for 175,000 men. As soon as the Expeditionary Force had vacated this it was filled by new recruits. To make room for another 349,000 men the space allocated to each man was reduced and soldiers' families were evicted from the barracks.[34]

It was soon apparent that the War Office had come to the end of its own resources. Prompted by Leopold Amery, the director of civilian recruiting for southern command, on 4 September Kitchener reluctantly gave the task of helping to organise the next batches of recruits to a committee presided over by a former Unionist Secretary of State for War, Lord Midleton. Midleton described his task as one of 'making bricks without straw, trying to provide for 200,000 or 300,000 men who have no officers, non-commissioned officers, rifles or places to live'.[35] Midleton's task was to harness the resources of the ninety-three Territorial County Associations to house and undertake the preliminary training of the New Armies.[36] His committee worked day and night until 10 September, conferring with the Associations and preparing a circular setting out their new duties. But on 11 September Kitchener suddenly relieved the committee of its duties, saying that the military authorities would now take them over. The reasons for this abrupt reversal of policy are not entirely clear. On 8 September Kitchener had denied that recruits were being badly treated,[37] but a few days later he reversed his opinion. Both Sir Charles Hobhouse and Midleton believed that Kitchener had been deeply angered by criticisms made in the House of Commons by Sir Ivor Herbert, criticisms which Rawlinson believed at least in part to be justified. They thought that he wanted to protect his reputation by shifting the blame for any shortcomings on to the Midleton Committee. But if blame was to be placed anywhere it did not rest with Midleton or even Kitchener. It must be more widely apportioned. It rested on the government's inability and unwillingness to face the necessity of a full commitment to a continental strategy before 1914, and on the unwillingness of the country at large to accept that strategy and its logical corollary, a conscript army, raised, trained and equipped before war was declared.

Once the War Office assumed the work of the Midleton Committee it began to requisition schools and government buildings to house troops, and large numbers of men found themselves living in crude tent camps or billeted in private houses.[38] But organising this took time, and to gain it, on 11 September the physical standards for recruits were raised without any prior warning. This had the immediate effect of doing what Kitchener intended, that is, stemming the number of recruits. But it also had the effect that about 10,000 men who had been accepted just before 11 September and who had in the meantime left their jobs prior to joining their units were now turned away as being undersized when they arrived.[39] The number of recruits plummeted from its wartime high in September to 135,811 in October. This episode taught the War Office an important lesson whose implications became clear in January 1915. It was imposible to run a voluntary recruiting system in wartime on a 'stop-go' basis. Enthusiasm to enlist could not be turned on and off like a tap. If men were willing to enlist, the army had to accept them at that moment. Men who were turned away because there was no room to accommodate them were reluctant to return in a few months simply because, after their first rejection, they had come to doubt whether they were really needed. Many instead sought work in industries which they thought were of national importance, and it was very difficult for the government to rekindle their martial enthusiasm.[40]

However, these problems did not dissuade the government from trying to raise more troops. It did so in a completely haphazard manner. On 10 September the government asked Parliament for permission to raise another 500,000 men. A month later the Cabinet, after some 'desultory conversation', agreed to let Kitchener raise still more men. From their own accounts ministers differed on exactly how many men were to be raised. Pease thought that the Cabinet had agreed to another 500,000 men. Hobhouse thought it had settled on twice as many. When Asquith presented its request to Parliament, he asked for 1 million.[41] The response to this call was still satisfactory, although far below that of August and September. Between October and December another 424,533 men were enlisted, bringing the total number of new recruits to well over 1 million by the end of December.

The government's policy in the early months of the war, if something so ill-thought-out as what it did can be dignified with the name policy, represented a complete reversal of what it had intended to do before the outbreak of war. Without thinking through any of the implicatioins, the Cabinet lamely agreed to Kitchener's drive to create the largest possible army. On 16 January Lord Crewe, who was both the Secretary of State for India and one of the government's main spokesmen in the House of Lords, told their Lordships that the number of men the government wanted to put into the field 'can only be limited by the possibility of equipping them, arming them, supplying them with the requisite drafts, and keeping going the regular supplies of ammunition and other warlike stores'.[42] But it was just these problems, the need to clothe, arm, equip, move and feed the men they were raising, that the government had all but ignored in its headlong rush to get recruits.

Three days after Parliament had consented to raising the first new 500,000 men the director of army contracts placed the first orders for their equipment. In August and September he ordered, from the regular arms manufacturers and the ordnance factories, enough shells and guns to replace those issued to the troops in France and to equip seven new divisions.[43] But the war soon revealed a fundamental weakness in the War Office's purchasing organisation. It was not designed to meet the needs of an army whose size went on increasing by huge and erratic leaps and bounds solely at the behest of the secretary of state. In peacetime the master-general of the ordnance estimated the army's requirements for munitions and the contracts department actually negotiated contracts with particular suppliers. Although it seemed cumbersome, this system of dual responsibility worked well enough before 1914, when manufacturers' capabilities were not taxed by War Office demands, and the quantities of munitions needed were small and easily calculated. But by the end of September 1914 this was no longer the case. There was no organisation at the War Office with the responsibility for predicting all the army's needs for equipment. Such needs now ultimately depended on the willingness of hundreds of thousands of individuals to leave their jobs and enlist, and on the almost equally erratic but growing demands of Sir John French and the Expeditionary Force in France for shells. Kitchener did not consult Sir Stanley von Donop, the master-general of the ordnance, about the possibility of equipping new recruits before he accepted them because supplies were only a secondary consideration in his plans. Kitchener recognised that voluntary recruiting was the only way open to him to increase the size of the army, so he was compelled to accept men as and when they were ready to come forward, not when he was ready to equip them. This meant that supplying the New Armies had to proceed on a hand-to-mouth basis, and contracts and deliveries always lagged behind recruits.

In this situation the prewar practice of placing orders and then expecting the manufacturers to fulfil them out of their own resources was not enough. Their plant was now so overtaxed that it was recognised that without government help they would not be able to complete their contracts. Kitchener was slow to react and when he did his initial response was somewhat irrational. He placed all the blame for delays in deliveries on the director of army contracts and sacked him. He replaced him with a Board of Trade official, U. F. Wintour. That was in October, but it was not until January 1915 that he began to recognise what was really wrong with the system. He then tried to improve it by subordinating the contracts branch to von Donop, thus making one department responsible for estimating future needs and placing contracts to meet them.[44]

The Cabinet also began to intervene in the autumn of 1914, because by October it was anxious that the New Armies should be ready to take the field by the spring of 1915. When it became apparent to it that existing contracts were not large enough to do that, it was seriously disturbed.[45] On 9 October Asquith, Lloyd George and Grey combined to force Kitchener to accept the establishment of a Cabinet Committee on Munitions to speed the delivery of supplies. The driving force behind the committee was Lloyd George, and its inception marked the end of munitions production organised on the basis of 'business as usual'.

Just as Kitchener thought that he could create whole armies by calling for volunteers, Lloyd George thought that he could arm them simply by spending lavish sums of money. He reasoned that the larger the orders the government placed with the trade, the more money manufacturers would be prepared to invest in new plant and machinery to fulfil them, and the sooner the guns and shells would be delivered.[46] Before the war the Treasury had been blind to the adverse effects its parsimony had on the ability of the munitions industry to increase its production rapidly in wartime. Now Lloyd George naively expected that by loosening the Treasury's purse-strings he would be able to call into being almost overnight all of the equipment the New Armies required. On 29 January 1915 he issued a formal Treasury minute explaining the Treasury's new philosophy:

> The first interest of the taxpayer is that the supplies should be secured. With this object it may be to the public advantage to con-clude contracts in the negotiations of which the prime necessity of securing expeditious and satisfactory delivery has been regarded as of more urgent importance than the actual terms of the bargain.[47]

Whether the Chancellor's recipe of injecting large amounts of cash into the industry would make up for the years of neglect before the war remained to be seen. By mid-October the director of army contracts had placed orders for 892 18-pounder guns, enough to equip the eighteen divisions of the first three New Armies by June 1915. But there were already enough recruits available for fifty-two new divisions, so on 12 October the Cabinet Committee arbitrarily decided to raise existing contracts to 3,000 guns, enough to equip sixty-two divisions. But it gave no thought to the practical problems of actually producing the guns, beyond agreeing that the arms manufacturers would have to subcontract much of the work. Lloyd George had almost unlimited faith in the ability of private enterprise to overcome practical obstacles.[48] The next day the Cabinet Committee actually put these new orders to representatives of the ordnance factories and the trade. It wanted Vickers and Armstrongs to promise to deliver 1,000 18-pounder guns each by 1 June instead of the 360 and 450 they had already contracted for. Both firms flatly refused to agree, and it was only with considerable reluctance that they agreed to *try* to deliver 640 and 850 guns respectively. Similar pressure was placed on the ordnance factories, Coventry Ordnance, Beardmores and the rifle manufacturers to increase their production.[49]

Thus by the end of October 1914 Britain seemed to be well on the way towards adopting a new strategic policy. In a fit of absentmindedness the Cabinet had allowed Kitchener to begin recruiting a continental-scale army, and by December over 1 million men had enlisted. It was widely assumed in the Cabinet that the arms to equip this force would soon be ready now that the Treasury had loosened its purse-strings. But very soon events in France and at home were to persuade some ministers and generals that Kitchener's attempt to create a 'nation in arms' would not be enough to ensure victory. In France Sir John French was beginning to believe that the Cabinet was not completely behind him and that unless he could provide it with a clear-cut victory it would starve him of resources. And even more important than that, the British were soon to be made aware that their allies were not convinced that they were bearing their fair share of the war effort in the field. By the spring of 1915 Lloyd George had crystallised these growing doubts about the adequacy of Britian's contribution to the Entente and was arguing that Britain should prepare itself to wage a total war.

Notes: Chapter 8

1   *The General Annual Report on the British Army for the Year ending 30 Sept. 1913* Cd 7252 (1914).

2 65 HC Deb., 5s., cols 2100, 2164, 6 and 7 Aug. 1914.
3 Lord Esher, *The Tragedy of Lord Kitchener* (London, 1921), p. 35; Sir G. Arthur, *Life of Lord Kitchener* (London, 1920), Vol. 3, p. 7.
4 Esher mss 2/13, diary entry, 13 Aug. 1914.
5 PRO Adm. 1/8388/235, Duration of the war, W. S. Churchill, 11 Aug. 1914.
6 Esher mss 2/13, diary entry, 13 Aug. 1914; Beaverbrook mss box 3, folder 7, Memorandum supplied by Mr McKenna on 20 Mar. 1927; Lt Col. Repington, *The First World War, 1914–18* (London, 1920), Vol. 1, p. 21.
7 PRO WO 79/62, Murray mss, Note of conversation with Lord Kitchener, Wellesley House, Aldershot, 14 Aug. 1914, by A. J. Murray.
8 Brig.-Gen. Sir John Dunlop, 'The Territorial Army – the early years', *Army Quarterly and Defence Journal*, vol. 84 (1967), pp. 57–8.
9 Esher mss 7/27, Esher to M. V. Brett, 12 Aug. 1914; PRO Cab. 17/106, Esher to Hankey (and enc.), 11 Aug. 1914; Maj.-Gen. Sir C. E. Callwell, *Experiences of a Dug-out* (London, 1920), pp. 49–50; L. Amery, *My Political Life: War and Peace* (London, 1953), Vol. 2, pp. 24–5.
10 Callwell, op. cit., pp. 49–50; PRO Cab. 19/33, Minutes of the Dardanelles Commission, QQ. 3560, 3563.
11 Hankey mss 4/5, Hankey to Esher, 20 Nov. 1914.
12 Esher mss 2/13, diary entry, 13 Aug. 1914.
13 ibid.
14 Esher mss 7/27, Esher to M. V. Brett, 13 Aug. 1914.
15 Earl of Midleton, *Records and Reactions, 1859–1939* (London, 1939), p. 278; Churchill, *World Crisis*, p. 150: Amery, op. cit., Vol. 2, p. 25.
16 C. P. Trevelyan mss box 33, Runciman to Trevelyan, 4 Aug. 1914.
17 K. O. Morgan (ed.), *Lloyd George. Family Letters, 1885–1936* (London, 1973), p. 167.
18 Sir E. Grey, *Twenty-Five Years, 1893–1916* (London, 1925), Vol. 2, p. 69.
19 PRO Cab. 19/33, op. cit., Q.1195.
20 Earl of Oxford and Asquith, *Memories and Reflections* (London, 1928), Vol. 2, p. 48.
21 PRO T 181/50, Royal Commission on the private manufacture of, and trading in, arms, Annex II, Prewar orders, Sir M. Hankey, May 1935.
22 Churchill, *World Crisis*, pp. 149–50: Grey, op. cit., Vol. 2, p. 70; Gainsford mss, diary entry, 25 Aug. 1914; Emmott mss, diary entry, 25 Aug. 1914; E. David, (ed.), *Inside Asquith's Cabinet – from the Diaries of Charles Hobhouse* (London, 1977), p. 184.
23 Gainford mss, diary entry, 25 Aug. 1914.
24 David French, 'Some aspects of social and economic planning for war in Great Britain, c. 1905–15' (PhD thesis, University of London, 1978), pp. 193–4.
25 PRO 30/69/98, Robert Williams to J. R. MacDonald, 6 Aug. 1914.
26 B. McGill, 'Asquith's predicament, 1914–18', *Journal of Modern History*, vol. 39 (1967), p. 285.
27 R. Blake, *The Unknown Prime Minister. The Life and Times of Andrew Bonar Law, 1858–1923* (London, 1955), pp. 220–3.
28 Bonar Law mss, 37/5/6, Bonar Law to Curzon, 29 Jan. 1915.
29 *General Annual Reports on the British Army (including the Territorial Forces from the Date of Embodiment) for the Period from 1 October 1913 to September 1919*, Cmd 1193 (1921); Beaverbrook mss box 3, folder 7, op. cit.
30 These figures are calculated on the basis that each infantry division contained 18,073 officers and men. See General Staff, War Office, *Field Service Pocket Book, 1914* (London, 1914, repr. Newton Abbot, 1971), p. 6.
31 17 HL Deb., 5s., col. 504, 25 Aug. 1914.
32 HMSO, *Statistics of the Military Effort of the British Empire* (London, 1922), p. 364.
33 Samuel mss A/157/733, Samuel to his wife, 30 Aug. 1914.

34 *Statistics,* op. cit., 'Supply services during the war; Note by the Quartermaster-General to the Forces (the late Gen. Sir J. S. Cowans)', p. 833; PRO WO 159/1, The war (August 1914 to May 1915). Note by the Secretary of State for War, 31 May 1915.
35 St Loe Strachey mss S/24/2/18, Midleton to St Loe Strachey, 10 Sept. 1914; see also Amery, op. cit., Vol. 2, p. 29.
36 Bonar Law mss 34/6/44, Midleton to Bonar Law, 14 Sept. 1914; PRO WO 159/18, telegrams from A. G. 2B, 4 Sept. 1914.
37 Oxford and Asquith, op. cit., Vol. 2, p. 32.
38 Cmd 1193, op. cit.
39 St Loe Strachey mss S/24/2/11, Sir Henry Sclater to St Loe Strachey, 5 Dec. 1914; Amery op. cit., Vol. 2, p. 30–1; *Statistics,* op. cit., p. 364.
40 Arthur, op. cit., Vol. 3, p. 311.
41 Gainford mss, 'War Reminiscences' (unpublished), p. 82; PRO Cab. 41/35/58, Asquith to HM the King, 11 Nov. 1914; David (ed.), op. cit., p. 206.
42 18 HL Deb., 5s., col. 259, 16 Jan. 1915.
43 PRO T 181/112, Minutes of evidence taken before the Royal Commission on the private manufacture of, and trading in, arms, Q. 1256 (Sir S. von Donop); PRO MUN 5/6/170/28, Notes on the supply of certain types of shell prior to the formation of the Ministry of Munitions, August 1914–June 1915; PRO MUN 5/6/170/30, Notes on the supply of guns prior to the formation of the Ministry of Munitions, August 1914–May 1915.
44 PRO Cab. 19/33, op. cit., QQ. 197990–1 (Sir S. von Donop).
45 David (ed.), op. cit., pp. 196–7; PRO Cab. 41/35/51, Asquith to HM the King, 9 Oct. 1914; Lord Hankey, *The Supreme Command* (London, 1961), Vol. 1, pp. 308–9.
46 PRO MUN 9/2, Lloyd George to Gen. Sir Ivor Philips, 15 Nov. 1915; PRO Cab. 19/33, op. cit., Q. 19810 (Sir S. von Donop).
47 Treasury minute date 29 Jan. 1915, *Parliamentary Papers,* Vol. 38 (1914–16).
48 C. J. Wrigley, *David Lloyd George and the British Labour Movement in Peace and War* (New York, 1976), pp. 83–4, 89.
49 PRO Cab. 41/35/53, Asquith to HM the King, 16 Oct. 1915; PRO MUN 5/6/170/30, op. cit.; PRO T 181/65, Notes by Maj.-Gen. Sir S. von Donop, 6 July 1935.

9

The War in France, 1914–15

When the Expeditionary Force went to France in August 1914 its commanders were confident that they were amply supplied with all the guns and shells they would require. In his early letters home the commander of the army, Sir John French, had nothing but praise for his gunners and their equipment. He informed Kitchener that, although his men were outnumbered by the enemy

> I firmly believe with our splendid gun detachments, our magnificent artillery officers, our heavy eighteen pounder shell, and our five inch heavy gun, they will hold their own with a superior German artillery in front of them.[1]

But within a few months of the start of the war several senior commanders began to believe that the emphasis prewar doctrine had placed on predominantly light, shrapnel-firing artillery, was misplaced on a modern battlefield. By the end of 1914 senior commanders in France believed that they required three vital ingredients if they were to beat the Germans; more men, more heavy guns and more ammunition, especially high explosive shells. On 22 January 1915 Sir Douglas Haig, the commander of the First Army, told Lieutenant Colonel à Court Repington, the military correspondent of *The Times*, that with enough high explosive ammunition his troops could walk through the German lines.[2] Sir John French considered that without more heavy guns, howitzers and ammunition a successful attack on the German line would be impossible. During a visit to General Headquarters Lord Midleton recorded that French 'considers that anything in the nature of assaults turns on big gun preparation'.[3] Sir John officially passed on the essence of this change of heart to the War Office on 31 December 1914. It amounted to a request that the army completely abandon its prewar artillery doctrines. He wanted stocks of ammunition to be trebled or quadrupled and he wanted half of all field gun shells to be filled with high explosives. (This request was soon cut down to a quarter.) Finally, he demanded a large increase in the number of heavy guns in France.[4]

It says much for the performance of the armaments industry that it was able to go even some way towards meeting these demands. Before 1914 it had been planned that in the first six months of the war it should provide the army with 162,000 new shells, enough to equip the Expeditionary Force's 18-pounder guns with 500 rounds each. In fact, by the end of February 1915 the manufacturers had produced 409,000 18-pounder shells.[5] This was nearly twice the number of shells of all kinds that had been fired in two and a half years in the Boer War. And despite the fact that the number of field guns in France nearly doubled between August 1914 and February 1915, the manufacturers were actually able to increase the average number of rounds per gun stockpiled in France.[6] Stocks only failed to reach establishment levels because the number of guns in France rose sharply and they were firing much more rapidly than had been anticipated before 1914. The supply of rounds per gun would have been much better had it not been that the War Office, at Sir John's express insistence, sent men and guns to the front irrespective of whether or not it could supply them with all the ammunition he asked for. The field marshall was anxious to control as many divisions as he could. He told Kitchener, with massive disregard for logistical considerations, that he should send him as many reinforcements as he could as soon as he could, and that it would be time enough to worry about their supply problems when they were in France.[7] So, for example, on 6 February the military members of the Army Council agreed to send two batteries of 6-inch howitzers to France, 'as soon as possible, independently of any question of ammunition supply'.[8] French took an essentially short-term view of the situation, and the result was that supplies were diverted away from the New Armies training in Britain to meet his needs.[9] The real munitions shortage was in Britain, not in France. By March and April 1915 the ammunition stocks of the new divisions coming out from home were below establishment levels even before they went into the line because of Sir John's insistence that every available round should be given to troops already in France.[10]

Thus the munitions industry did more than fulfil all the requirements of the prewar Expeditionary Force and it could have met the needs of the much larger army that had assembled in France by the spring of 1915 if they had been measured by prewar standards. But it could not supply the new, and much larger, stocks of shells demanded by Sir John and the New Armies simultaneously. In his memorandum of 31 December Sir John had asked for fifty rounds per field gun each day.[11] The War Office knew that it could not supply such quantities but it promised that it would give him everything that the armaments industry could supply. The French army believed that twenty rounds per day was sufficient, and initially the War Office promised to supply him with that. Sir John's insistence on having more shells and his exaggerated worries that if he did not get them his line might be endangered made the War Office reluctant to agree to his request that half of the country's shell-producing machinery should immediately be turned over to making high explosive shells. It knew that at least ten weeks would elapse before the machinery could be converted and in the meantime shell production would fall by half.[12] Kitchener believed that to agree to Sir John's request would endanger the lives of his troops because they would be bereft of ammunition for some time until the new type was being produced in quantity. So instead of telling existing suppliers to cease producing shrapnel and ordering them to make high explosive shells, he began to look elsewhere for completely new sources of supply for the Expeditionary Force.[13]

But the production of a new type of shell, often by completely inexperienced suppliers, took time, and so it was some time before the Expeditionary Force began to receive all the high explosive shells it wanted. But by May 1915 the War Office had begun to deliver the twenty rounds per gun it had promised.[14] The number of heavy siege guns in France also increased. On 20 August von Donop could only muster twenty-nine seige guns in Britain, and all but one of them were obsolescent.[15] In September an expert committee was formed to consider how best to equip the army with modern heavy artillery. Working with commendable dispatch, within four days it recommended that two basic types of weapon were needed. It wanted a very heavy long-range howitzer able to destroy German frontier fortifications. (It was optimistic enough to believe that the British army would eventually advance to within range of them.) To supplement this it wanted a medium howitzer able to demolish enemy guns even if they were protected by field entrenchments. It recommended that the government should immediately purchase over eighty new howitzers of 9-inch calibre and above, and that in the meantime it should make the best use of the sixty 6-inch howitzers then in England. By the end of May 1915 sixty-eight siege guns had been sent to France.[16]

Thus by May 1915 most of Sir John's demands for heavy guns and ammunition were at least some way towards being met. But French was an impatient man, made even more impatient by conflicting pressures placed on him by his own government in London and his French allies in the field. Sir John wanted these supplies because, despite some momentary doubts, he was a convinced 'westerner'. French and his senior commanders had been educated to believe that a decisive attack was the solution to all military problems. They believed that the Entente could only win the war if the German army were defeated in France and Flanders, and that if the Germans were allowed to defeat the French Britain would soon face a similar fate.[17] Large-scale operations outside France would only serve to weaken the Entente in the decisive theatre. But by January 1915 some Cabinet ministers were beginning to doubt whether placing so much emphasis on operations across the Channel was a sound course to follow. Lloyd George, impatient with the stalemate in France, asked Churchill: 'Are we really bound to hand over the ordering of our troops to France as if we were her vassal?'[18] On 2 January Kitchener sent French a letter which reflected these growing doubts. 'The feeling here [he wrote] is gaining that although it is essential to defend the line we hold, troops over and above what is necessary for that service could be better employed elsewhere.'[19]

Sir John found that suggestion anathema, and so he swiftly sent his own proposals for future operations to the War Council. He refused to admit that the western front was permanently stalemated and that a breakthrough could not be achieved. He blamed past failures on the lack of shells. More ammunition was the key to everything. He did not want it for a lengthy battle of attrition because he did not think that the German line was so strong that it needed to be worn down by a prolonged siege operation. With enough shells he was convinced that he could achieve a swift breakthrough in one operation. 'If the attempt fails,' he went on to tell the War Council, 'it shows, provided that the work of the infantry and artillery has been properly co-ordinated, that insufficient ammunition has been expended.'[20] This was a tacit confession that the army had been wrong before the war to assume that attacking infantry would be able to rely mainly on its own determination to advance and that it would need only minimal artillery support. Sir John was beginning to recognise that unsupported infantry was no match for defenders who were dug in armed with machine guns and protected by barbed wire entanglements. To overcome this formidable combination he grasped at the artillery as the one weapon which was immediately available and seemed to offer a prospect of success.

The army was moving from one extreme to the other. Hitherto it had been considered that fire power would play a subordinate and supporting role on the battlefield, merely paving the way for a successful bayonet charge. 'To drive an enemy from the field', *Field Service Regulations, Part 1 (Operations) 1909* told its readers, 'assault, or the immediate threat of it, is almost always necessary.'[21] Now Sir John was prepared to abandon all surprise and tactical finesse in favour of massive artillery bombardments. If after these the infantry failed to walk through the enemy's line it was because the preceding bombardment had been too short. The answer was to make it even heavier before the next attack.

Although French's new policy went some way towards recognising that good morale and a willingness to advance across open ground to deliver a bayonet charge were no match for well-sited machine guns, it was in its own way no more realistic as a solution to the tactical problems of the western front. It never occurred to French that the rigid plan of attack which heavy bombardments imposed on his own infantry might actually prevent it from exploiting the advantages the gunners had won for it. Nor did he foresee that the Germans might learn to deploy their defending troops in depth so that most of them were out of reach of the initial British bombardment.

Sir John urged the War Council to concentrate all Britain's efforts in France. To send troops elsewhere would be to waste them and to play into the Germans' hands. The Germans had induced Turkey to join the war, 'to draw off troops from the decisive spot which is Germany herself'. French was anxious to attack in the west as soon as posible. By the spring the Germans might have begun to reinforce their armies by recalling men sent to the east and so it was 'of the utmost importance that we should take the offensive and strike at the earliest possible moment *with all our available strength'*.[22] The War Council was very reluctant to let him proceed on the basis of these considerations. On 13 January 1915 ministers agreed to allow planning to proceed for three possible alternative attacks, at Salonika, Alexandretta on the Syrian coast and at the Dardanelles. No final decision to send troops to any of these places was taken. But if by the spring the western front was still stalemated men would be sent to another theatre of operations. Henceforth Sir John was faced with the choice of demonstrating to the War Council that the enemy line in France could be broken or of seeing men and munitions diverted elsewhere.

But much more was at stake than Sir John's belief that the war could only be won in France. The French were loathe to see their ally even contemplating sending troops outside France. General Joffre, the French commander in chief, was intent on attacking in the west to drive the enemy from French soil and to relieve his hard-pressed Russian allies. Sir John, therefore, had two reasons for launching an attack at Neuve Chapelle in March 1915. He wanted to prove to the French that the British were reliable allies and he wanted to prove to the War Council that the Germans in France were not unbeatable. The offensive had no wider strategic purpose. Joffre declined to participate in it because the British refused to relieve his men near Ypres. The staff of Haig's First Army who actually planned the attack recognised that without French participation their own troops were too few to do more than make a small hole in the German line. The most they expected the attack to accomplish was the capture of Aubers Ridge, from where at a later date, they might be able to go on to capture Lille.[23]

Before the battle Sir John was confident of success, despite the fact that none of his demands for heavy guns and a lavish supply of ammunition had yet been met in full. Even though he estimated that he had only enough artillery ammunition for one week's heavy fighting he still told the Prime Minister that he would soon be able to make 'good progress'.[24] When he wrote that he really meant it. He was not simply trying once again to convince Asquith and his colleagues that the western front was not deadlocked. He repeated exactly the same confident sentiments in a private letter to a personal friend.[25] In neither letter did he complain of a lack of sufficient artillery ammunition or heavy guns. Sir Henry Rawlinson, who commanded the Fourth Corps at Neuve Chapelle, was equally confident. He believed that for the first time the British would enjoy a superiority in artillery and infantry and so would 'be able to force a big hole in the enemy's line'.[26] However, after some initial success the attack quickly broke down. On 10 March 30,000 men, supported by 240 field guns, three dozen howitzers and sixty-four siege guns, attacked on a narrow front of only 2,000 yards. The British had seriously underestimated the strength of the German defences and the tactical flexibility that would be needed to overcome them. The Germans had no intention of sitting down in a thin and brittle line of trenches and waiting to be slaughtered by the British gunners. The German front, support and reserve troops occupied a position that was approximately 6,000–7,000 yards deep. Only the front companies holding the foremost positions were within observation distance and range of the British field guns. A thousand yards behind the front line was a thin line of machine gun posts. In the event of a British attack the Germans intended that these would form the backbone of their defences.[27]

The opening bombardment so stunned the German troops holding their front line that within twenty minutes of the attack starting the British infantry had occupied 1,600 yards of their line. But from then onwards the British reliance on artillery to clear away all obstacles began to tell in the Germans' favour. It inhibited the initiative of local commanders. The advance halted for fifteen minutes to allow the gunners to bombard the village of Neuve Chapelle. This gave the Germans enough time to man their line of machine gun posts which, incidentally, had not been a target of the initial British bombardment. The British advance was then held up for a further seven hours whilst attempts were made to eliminate stubborn German garrisons still holding out in their front-line positions on both flanks of the penetration. The British insistence on proceeding strictly according to plan meant that it was almost dark before the attack was resumed. When the British tried again the next day the Germans had little difficulty in halting them in front of their machine gun posts. The First Army had driven a salient into the enemy's line, but it was no more than 1,200 yards wide and 4,000 yards deep and it cost them over 12,500 casualties.

By 16 March the Expeditionary Force's supplies of field gun ammunition were almost exhausted. In his telegrams to Kitchener Sir John seized on this shortage as the reason why the offensive had failed to break the German line. On 18 March he informed the War Office: 'If the supply of ammunition cannot be maintained on a considerably increased scale it follows that the offensive efforts of the Army must be spasmodic and separated by a considerable interval of time. They cannot, therefore lead to decisive results.'[28]

For Sir John the shell shortage was the perfect excuse for failure. It shifted the responsibility from his shoulders on to those of Kitchener and his political colleagues who, French argued, had failed to provide him with the tools he needed to do the job. Before the War Council could claim that Neuve Chapelle had proved that the western front was still deadlocked, Sir John had claimed that the line was impenetrable only because it had not supplied him with enough ammunition.

But there were numerous other reasons why the attack had failed which could not be laid at the door of the War Council. This is borne out by the private testimonies of some of the senior commanders who took part in the battle. Sir John had completely failed to co-ordinate his attack with the French. The result was that from the second day of the offensive the Germans had been able to concentrate all their reserves against the First Army. On the first morning of the attack Rawlinson's infantry spent too long occupying the village of Neuve Chapelle and so the Germans were given enough time to man their support line of machine guns. On the second day of the offensive the British front-line infantry was too tired to attack properly because no plans had been made to replace it with fresh troops during the night. In private even Sir John recognised that these were important and real reasons why the attack had failed, but he was never prepared to admit as much to the War Council.[29]

Neuve Chapelle had done nothing to shake the belief of Sir John or of his senior commanders in the importance of the western front. In May they were ready to attack again. Sir John still had every reason to prove that victory was possible on the western front. On 31 March Kitchener had warned French that he would only send the New Armies to France if the troops already there first broke the German line.[30] Sir John's new plan seemed to offer more hope than his previous one. This time the British advance would be co-ordinated with Joffre's operations. Indeed it was intended to draw German reserves away from the French so that they could break the German front. General Headquarters were confident that this time they would capture Aubers Ridge. When Sir John met Kitchener on 29 March he again asked for more ammunition. But even though supplies fell some way short of what he had asked for, he did not think that this was any excuse for postponing the attack. On 14 April he confidently told Kitchener that his stocks of ammunition were sufficient for the forthcoming attack. Even the heavy fighting during the Second Battle of Ypres, which began on 22 April, did not dismay him. On 29 April he telegraphed to the War Office that current ammunition expenditure was not excessive and would not hamper future operations.[31] Once again he was determined to prove that the German line could be broken in France.

The attack against Aubers Ridge began on 9 May. Although it was launched on a wider front than the Neuve Chapelle operation, the same inflexible tactics were used again. The result was much the same. The British suffered 9,500 casualties on the first day and still failed to break through. Five days later the War Council met and Kitchener declared that Sir John's policy of attacking on the western front had failed. But Sir John did not agree. Having failed in his assault against the Germans, he tried to protect his rear by preparing an assault on his political masters instead.

On 20 April 1915 Asquith paid a visit to Newcastle to make a speech on behalf of the North East Coast Armaments Subcommittee. This body consisted of representatives of local employers and trade unions engaged in munitions production, and War Office and Admiralty representatives. It was presided over by a naval officer, Captain L. E. Powers. In theory its purpose was to increase production for both services but Powers did not like playing the role of a neutral chairman. He was determined that production for the navy should not suffer just because the War Office wanted more shells. Before the Prime Minister's visit he told the Admiralty:

> It would be a pity if the Prime Minister's speech dealt only with the
> necessity for getting shell [*sic*] and guns, as that would tend to make
> men try to leave their present employment in favour of Elswick
> which would be fatal to us.[32]

This message, together with Sir John's telegram of 14 April saying that he had enough shells for his next attack, was passed on to
Asquith before he spoke and led him to say that whilst the government recognised the need for more munitions, there was no truth in
the rumours that British attacks had failed through lack of
ammunition.[33] But after the failure of 9 May the speech read very
differently to Sir John French. It seemed to him that the Prime
Minister himself doubted the truth of the excuse that attacks failed
due to lack of ammunition.[34] The attack had been witnessed by
Repington, who was staying at Sir John's headquarters. Repington
later claimed that he sent his famous telegram of 12 May, attribut-
ing the failure of the attack solely to the absence of enough heavy
guns and high explosive shells, entirely on his own responsibility.
This is very doubtful. Just after the first assault Sir John was told
by the War Office to send 20,000 rounds of field gun ammunition
to Marseilles for despatch to the Dardanelles.[35] This was the last
straw. To Sir John it seemed as if his own forces were about to be
run down in favour of the Dardanelles operation. He therefore
ordered that Repington should be told that the lack of high explosive ammunition had been a 'fatal bar to our Army [*sic*] success'.
Repington used almost the same phrase in his telegram. He stated:
'The want of an unlimited supply of high explosive was a fatal bar
to our success.'[36] On 19 May *The Times* followed this up with a
leading article laying all the blame for the want of high explosive on
Kitchener.

Repington's telegram concealed more of the truth than it
revealed. After Neuve Chapelle the Germans had gone to considerable pains to learn the lessons of the battle and to strengthen their
defences. In January 1915 the British had carried out trials to
ascertain whether 18-pounder shrapnel or high explosive was more
effective in cutting wire entanglements. The shrapnel shells proved
to be marginally more effective and they were used with success at
Neuve Chapelle. The Germans noted this, and henceforth concealed their main entanglements in trenches. This protected them
from anything but a direct hit. This simple precaution took the
British completely by surprise on 9 May. Similarly they were also
surprised at the new positions in which the Germans chose to place
their machine guns. They were now positioned underneath their

parapets, and sited to fire just above ground level. On the opening day of the operation the First Army's diary noted with satisfaction that 'the wire entanglements had been almost entirely swept away by our shrapnel fire'.[37] In fact the concealed wire and machine guns were not seen until it was too late. Better intelligence work might have revealed both of these innovations sooner. But as Rawlinson noted, being wise after the event, the root cause of the failure was 'a misconception of the strength and resisting power of the enemy bred of a persistent optimism at GHQ'.[38] Even Sir John recognised that lack of shells was not the only reason why the assault failed. After the failure of the first assault on 9 May he wrote in a private letter that the German trenches 'bristle with machine guns'. But rather than cancel an attack he now described as 'simple murder', he preferred to berate Kitchener for his supposed shortcomings and to intrigue to place the blame for failure on his shoulders.[39]

On 21 May French told a close friend that 'I doubly wish that we could get rid of Kitchener from the War Office. I'm sure nothing will go right whilst he's there.'[40] He was helped in his intrigue by Repington, who went to great pains to put his case before Lloyd George and several Unionist leaders, including Bonar Law. French had personal reasons for disliking Kitchener but he may have been prompted to take these steps by members of his staff, and in particular by Lieutenant-Colonel Brinsley Fitzgerald.[41] Both Repington and Fitzgerald were in regular communication with several prominent Unionists, who themselves were becoming increasingly critical of the way in which the Cabinet seemed to be mishandling the conduct of the war. On 4 January one of them, Walter Long, told Fitzgerald he had discussed the situation with his colleagues and that 'I am in a position to say that if any doubt exists as to the support given to the C-in-C there is nothing which we will not do, in or out of Parliament, to secure the removal of any obstacles which may exist to his unfettered control of the campaign'.[42] In February the Unionist chief whip twice asked whether the army had enough shells, and after Neuve Chapelle Fitzgerald was quick to tell another Tory lord that the attack had failed because of a lack of ammunition.[43] On the eve of the Aubers Ridge attack Lord Midleton sent a secret letter to Fitzgerald and French asking whether the army was in fact hampered by want of ammunition and reinforcements which had been sent to the Dardanelles.[44] So when Sir John decided to send confidential military information to opposition leaders he was almost certain of a sympathetic hearing.

Thus the 'shell scandal' was, if not totally imaginary, at least exaggerated by Sir John for his own purposes. It only provided the occasion for the collapse of Asquith's Liberal government, it did not cause it. Its repercussions in France were more serious. Senior commanders still believed that a breakthrough was possible if only more shells and a heavier bombardment could be used. The way was beginning to open for the lengthy bombardment which preceded the Battle of the Somme. The origins of the 'shell scandal' were much more complicated than Sir John's hunt for a scapegoat amongst the politicians in London implied. Before 1914 all planning had assumed a war of movement, not one of trenches, barbed wire and massed machine guns. Enormous quantities of shells and heavy guns were thought to be unnecessary. It was not anticipated that the artillery would have to maintain a high rate of fire for any real length of time. When they were confronted by the problems of trench warfare Sir John and his senior commanders were nonplussed. They abandoned all tactical finesse in favour of the brute force of even heavier and longer bombardments. When political and strategic considerations plus his eagerness to take the offensive led French into launching two unsuccessful assaults, he fell back upon the cry of a shortage of shells as a way of shifting responsibility on to the politicians at home. He especially wanted to blacken Kitchener, a man he intensely disliked. But the army did not suffer heavy losses and defeats in the spring of 1915 simply because it was short of shells. The French attacked to the south with many times more guns and shells but they were no more successful than their allies. Sir John was correct to insist that victory or defeat for the Entente would rest on what happened on the western front. But his execution of operations in France can be faulted. He launched Neuve Chapelle prematurely and without French support, in his over-eagerness to impress them with his reliability as an ally. It was carried out on too narrow a front to achieve any really important success. It showed that much more was required than just more shells if the British were to win success in France. But Sir John ignored many of the lessons of the battle and repeated the same faulty tactics in May. This was doubly unfortunate, because the Germans had learnt some of the lessons of March and they had spent the ensuing weeks strengthening their defences.

However, the most important effect of the 'shell scandal' was the significance it had for the future development of the British war economy. It brought to a head a debate which had been going on in the Cabinet since January 1915 concerning the correct way in which the British economy ought to be organised to support the British and allied war effort. By May 1915 ministers were faced with three economic strategies. Runciman and McKenna still wanted to continue with 'business as usual'; Kitchener was eager to continue to create his 'nation in arms'; and Lloyd George had become the leading exponent of the creation of a total war economy. The significance of the 'shell scandal' was that it offered the Chancellor the opportunity he needed to begin to break this deadlock and to put his plans into operation by creating the new Ministry of Munitions.

Notes: Chapter 9

1   PRO 30/57/49, French to Kitchener, 30 Aug. 1914.
2   R. Blake (ed.), *The Private Papers of Douglas Haig* (London, 1952), p. 84.
3   PRO 30/67/25, Diary of a visit to the front, Lord Midleton, 30 Dec. 1914; see also Spears mss 2/3/83, Lt.-Gen. A. Murray to First and Second Army, 28 Dec. 1914.
4   PRO WO 32/5152, French to the Secretary of the Army Council, 31 Dec. 1914.
5   HMSO *Statistics of the Military Effort of the British Empire* (London, 1922), pp. 470–1; von Donop mss, The supply of munitions to the army. Notes by Maj.-Gen. Sir S. von Donop (n.d. but *c.* Aug. 1915).
6   David French, 'Some aspects of social and economic planning for war in Great Britain, *c.* 1905–15' (PhD thesis, University of London, 1978), p. 213.
7   PRO 30/57/49, French to Kitchener, 25 Nov. 1914.
8   PRO WO 163/45, Minutes of 105th meeting of the military members of the Army Council, 6 Feb. 1915.
9   PRO WO 95/58, War diary, Director of Ordnance Services.
10 ibid., entries for 10 Mar. and 23 Apr. 1915.
11 PRO WO 32/5152, French to R. H. Brade (and enc.), 31 Dec. 1914.
12 PRO WO 32/5152, Cubbit to French, 15 Jan. 1915.
13 PRO WO 159/1, The War (August 1914 to 31 May 1915), Note by the Secretary of State, Lord Kitchener, 31 May 1915.
14 *Statistics*, op. cit., p. 471; PRO MUN 5/6/170/29, Statistics relating to the supply of shells before the formation of the Ministry of Munitions. Stock of gun ammunition in France [Nov. 1914–April 1915].
15 PRO WO 163/44, Minutes of 36th meeting of the military members of the Army Council, 20 Aug. 1914.
16 PRO WO 161/32, Interim report of Maj.-Gen. Hickman's siege committee, 19 Sept. 1914; PRO WO 159/1, The War . . ., op. cit.
17 J. Gooch, 'Soldiers, strategy and war aims in Britain, 1914–18', in B. Hunt and A. Preston (eds.), *War Aims and Strategic Policy in the Great War, 1914–18* (London, 1977), p. 25; T. H. E. Travers, 'The offensive and the problem of innovation in British military thought, 1870–1915', *Journal of Contemporary History,* Vol. 13 (1978), pp. 540–1.
18 Lloyd George mss C/3/16/17, Lloyd George to Churchill, 2 Jan. 1915.
19 PRO WO 79/63, Kitchener to French, 2 Jan. 1915.
20 PRO WO 79/62, memorandum by French (n.d. but *c.* 2 Jan. 1915); see also PRO Cab. 42/1/12, Minutes of the War Council, 8 Jan. 1915.
21 General Staff, War Office, *Field Service Regulations* (London, 1909), p. 20.
22 PRO Cab. 37/123/9, memorandum by Sir John French, 3 Jan. 1915.
23 J. Terraine, *Douglas Haig, the Educated Soldier* (London, 1963), pp. 138–9.
24 Asquith mss, Vol. 26, French to Asquith, 7 Mar. 1915.
25 French mss, French to Mrs Bennett, 2 Mar. 1915.
26 PRO 30/57/51, Rawlinson to Kitchener, 6 Mar. 1915.

27 G. C. Wynne, *If Germany Attacks* (London, 1940), pp. 19–42.

28 PRO WO 32/5152, French to R. H. Brade, 18 Mar. 1915.

29 See, for example, Lord Hankey, *The Supreme Command* (London, 1961), Vol. 1, p. 297; PRO 30/57/51, Rawlinson to Kitchener, 15 Mar. 1915; Wilson mss (microfilm reel vi), 11 Mar. 1915; French to Mrs Bennett, 11 and 13 Mar. 1915.

30 G. H. Cassar, *Kitchener: Architect of Victory* (London, 1977), pp. 352–3.

31 Asquith mss, Vol. 14, Kitchener to Asquith, 14 April 1915; PRO WO 159/13, French to Kitchener, 29 Apr. 1915.

32 Asquith mss, Vol. 14, P. Creed to Bonham-Carter (and enc.), 18 Apr. 1915.

33 *The Times*, 21 Apr. 1915.

34 Viscount French, *1914* (London, 1919), p. 356; Maj. G. French, *The Life of Field Marshal Sir John French* (London, 1931), p. 287.

35 PRO WO 32/5155, (Part I) Artillery ammunition – past and future supply requirements, Sir John French, 14 June 1915.

36 Viscount French, op. cit., p. 357; *The Times*, 14 May 1915.

37 PRO WO 95/2, GHQ diary. First Army weekly report of operations, 9 May 1915; Wynne, op. cit., pp. 43–6.

38 PRO WO 30/57/51, Rawlinson to Col. Fitzgerald, 24 May 1915.

39 French mss, French to Mrs Bennett, 9, 10 and 11 May 1915.

40 French mss, French to Mrs Bennett, 21 May 1915.

41 David French, 'Some aspects of social and economic planning' pp. 230–2.

42 Fitzgerald mss (microfilm), Walter Long to Fitzgerald, 4 Jan. 1915.

43 Fitzgerald mss, Lord Edmund Talbot to Fitzgerald, 14 Feb. 1915; Fitzgerald to Lord Selborne, 16 Mar. 1915.

44 Fitzgerald mss, Lord Midleton to Fitzgerald, 4 May 1915.

10

Lloyd George and Total War

In August 1914 Lloyd George was immediately plunged into the problem of overcoming the financial panic which accompanied the outbreak of war. He did so successfully and within a few weeks he was able to begin to consider the next problem the allies faced. Within the framework of 'business as usual' Britain had to find money to finance its allies. In the autumn and winter of 1914–15 he busied himself doing just that. But his fertile imagination, coupled with his contacts with allied finance ministers and his own growing sense of frustration at the slow progress of the war, conspired to turn him into a bitter critic of both 'business as usual' and Kitchener and the War Office. By the spring of 1915 he was vehemently arguing that Britain was simply not doing enough to win the war, and that if it did not mobilise all its financial, industrial and human resources the Entente would lose the war.

On 2 September the Cabinet made its first effort to supply Britain's allies with money. It initially agreed to supply a loan of £800,000 to the Serbs, and a week later it discussed a loan of £10 million to Belgium. On 23 September it agreed to help Russia finance a £20 million loan in Britain to enable it to purchase British munitions and to meet the interest payments on existing Russian debts. In return for this help the Russian government very reluctantly agreed to ship £8 million of gold to Britian.[1] This was no more than the British had always expected to do, but at the end of November they were dismayed when the French came to them asking for a loan of £8–10 million. Hitherto the Cabinet had assumed that because the French had a large gold reserve French government credit was still good. But now it appeared that the French government was so uncertain of its own credit that it wanted a British guarantee of support for a loan in London. It believed that if it could raise £8 million in London it would encourage its own investors to lend it money in France.[2] Lloyd George was downcast by this revelation of France's weakness, and was afraid that it indicated that the French might not be able to go on fighting beyond June 1915.[3] This, coupled with his conviction that the western front was stalemated, led him to two conclusions. Britain should deploy its New Armies outside France in operations against Austria-Hungary. It was materially weaker than Germany and success against it would have the effect of encouraging Italy, Greece and Romania to throw in their lot with the Entente. This would enable the Russians to break through on the Carpathian front and advance towards Budapest and Vienna. Such a victory would give an emormous boost to allied morale. But he was aware that this would not be possible unless Britain bent every effort to bring material support to its allies.[4]

This became doubly important in January 1915. The Russians were clearly not winning the war for the Entente in the east and reports were beginning to reach the Treasury in London that the Russians felt that the British were not doing their fair share of the fighting but were prepared to sacrifice Russia for the sake of British interests. In mid-December the Russians had asked for a loan of £100 million. The British Cabinet only agreed to advance them £40 million. That was bad enough but what really angered the Russians was the fact that the British not only demanded that one-quarter of the money spent outside Britain should be covered by the Russians sending gold to the Bank of England but on top of that they demanded 5 per cent interest on the loan.[5] It was in order to gain a better understanding of the allies' financial problems, and to persuade the Russians that the British were not really intent on fighting to the last Russian, that Lloyd George attended the first allied financial conference in Paris between 2 and 5 February 1915.

The ostensible purpose of the conference was to discuss how best the Entente could mobilise their financial resources to support their war efforts. Lloyd George was anxious to explain to the Russians why the British needed Russian gold. If Britain advanced money to Russia to enable it to buy munitions in Britain and the USA it would reach a point when its balance of payments would be affected and it would have to export gold to support the sterling exchange rate in New York.[6] Aware of Russian reluctance to part with its gold, J. M. Keynes, who was advising the Chancellor, suggested that for the time being Russia should be permitted to keep its gold. Only if the British exchange rate did begin to deteriorate would Britain actually ask for it to be shipped.[7]

The conference was only a partial success. The finance ministers of the three powers agreed in principle to pool their financial resources. Lloyd George believed that he had persuaded the

French to release £160 million of gold they had been hoarding so that they could make a joint loan to Belgium, Greece, Romania and Montenegro, and also advance £25 million each to help Russia with its foreign purchases. But this last part of the agreement quickly became a dead letter. France was only prepared to finance Russian purchases in France, and so Britain found itself with responsibility for financing Russian expenditure in the rest of the world.[8]

But the real significance of the conference was that it persuaded Lloyd George that Britain was simply not doing enough to win the war. He explained what he meant to the House of Commons on 15 February. 'An alliance in a great war, to be effective, means that every country must bring all its resources, whatever they are, into the common stock. An alliance of war cannot be conducted on limited liability principles'.[9]

Hitherto Britain had believed that it could run the war on limited liability principles. Only now was it becoming apparent, at least to Lloyd George, that neither 'business as usual' nor Kitchener's quest for a 'nation in arms' would be enough to hold the alliance together. The allies needed visible proof that Britain was as totally committed to the war as they were. Lloyd George was determined to give them that proof in the shape of enormous quantities of men and munitions. But before he could do that two obstacles had to be overcome. The Cabinet had to be persuaded to abandon the pursuit of 'business as usual' and the creation of a 'nation in arms' and the entire engineering industry had to be turned over to producing munitions. If this were done Britain would be on the road to total war.

The War Office had already begun to take steps to use outside engineering firms to make munitions. On 24 August it had suggested to its regular suppliers that they should subcontract part of their work to civilian engineering firms, and by October its regular suppliers were surrounded by a group of 2,500–3,000 subcontractors.[10] But the War Office was reluctant to place whole orders with these newcomers to manufacture complete guns and shells. Such work required considerable expertise and trained machine operatives. The newcomers (sometimes) had the ability to make particular components, but normally only the established manufacturers had the experience and the facilities to produce complete rounds and shells. But Lloyd George had acquired an exaggerated faith in the ability of outside firms to make all types of munitions on a visit he paid to France between 16 and 20 October. French experts described to him the steps they had taken to bring in outside firms to make munitions. The Chancellor was over-impressed with their success, because what no one yet knew was that the shells these newcomers made were often of such poor quality that they exploded in the breech. Kitchener and von Donop did have the foresight to recognise that this might happen, and so whilst they were happy to see subcontractors making simple items like casings, they were reluctant to let them supply delicate items like fuses. Such caution was justified, because despite precautions faulty fuses destroyed five of the Expeditionary Forces' precious heavy guns in February and March. Even so Lloyd George persisted in believing that 'the high explosive is a simple shell and any engineering firm could easily produce it'.[11]

Lloyd George also frequently overlooked the practical problems standing in the way of increasing munitions production. He expected the orders given out by the Cabinet Committee in October to bear fruit almost overnight, but many of the problems the manufacturers first had to overcome could not be tackled overnight and anyway the solutions to them lay outside their control. Their first need was to erect more buildings, but the winter of 1914–15 was very wet and this delayed construction work.[12] It was then difficult to equip the new buildings with machine tools, gauges and blueprints. Some firms were trying to multiply their plant as much as fiftyfold and as British firms could not supply them with the necessary tools and gauges they had to be imported from the USA. But by January 1915 the French and Russians were doing exactly the same thing and the result was to drive up prices and slow down deliveries.[13] And once the tools had been put on board ship at New York, the voyage to Liverpool could take up to three times as long as normal, and thanks to port congestion at Liverpool they might be held up at the docks for another five weeks. Thus, for example, the production of high explosive shells at Vickers was delayed by five months because of lack of machine tools. Certain raw materials, like brass, manganese and bronze rods, also in short supply in Britain, had to be imported from America, which also added to delays in starting production.

Labour was also a major problem because recruiting had bitten deeply into the engineering workforce, and by June 1915 it was estimated that another 12,000 men were needed in the munitions industry.[14] As Sir Trevor Dawson of Vickers explained, 'whereas we can spend money in buying machines, land, shops, they are of no National [*sic*] use without men, and if we don't obtain the necessary men all our endeavours will be of no use'.[15] Even the regular suppliers with all their experience found it difficult to overcome these problems. But the legion of inexperienced subcontractors who had gathered around them often found them insurmountable. By the end of 1914 experienced suppliers were discovering that the failure of just one subcontractor to deliver even a small quantity of parts could delay the completion of whole orders. Yet Lloyd George seemed to be oblivious to many of these practical problems. He believed that the suppliers had promised to deliver the October orders on time. The suppliers, however, had left the Cabinet Committee meeting believing that all they had done was to promise to do their best. When production fell below what he had imperiously demanded, he placed all the blame on the War Office for its supposed incompetence, stoutly denying that the Treasury's prewar parsimony had hamstrung the manufacturers in their efforts to increase supplies quickly.[16] It never occurred to him that the targets he had set the manufacturers just could not be met in the time he had allocated to them.

The result was that by the end of December 1914 the 'nation in arms' was very slow to arm itself. All the shortcomings of the government's prewar plans had been exposed. Shell deliveries were enough to keep the expanding Expeditionary Force supplied with ammunition at the expected prewar rate of expenditure, but the industry could not supply Sir John French *and* the New Armies. By 31 December not enough 18-pounder guns to equip one division had been delivered. This failure was due to an almost complete lack of realistic planning both before the war and in the first few months of the conflict. Many of the lessons of the Boer War about the need to stockpile gauges, blueprints and machine tools had been forgotten.[17] Private enterprise assisted by the ordnance factories was expected to suffice in wartime. Kitchener began to raise the New Armies with hardly a thought about how they were to be equipped. This has been characterised as a policy of *laissez-faire*, but it seems better to regard it as no policy at all.

On 21 December the Cabinet Committee and the shell manu-facturers met to consider the reasons for the shortfalls in shell deliveries. The main one the industrialists could point to was the lack of labour.[18] Runciman agreed that the Labour Exchange Department of the Board of Trade should co-operate with the War Office in securing the transfer of as many skilled workers as possible from private engineering firms to the munitions manu-facturers. But this decision raised the whole question of the proper relationship between economic organisation and strategy. Britain could not survive simply by creating the New Armies and making munitions. It had to manufacture exports to pay for its growing list of imports of food, raw materials and munitions. While it was fighting it had to maintain a tolerable level of existence for its civilian population, and it also had to find the money with which to subsidise its allies. This posed a fundamental problem about how the economy ought to be organised. Manpower was now becoming increasingly scarce, and some decision had to be made about how to allocate it between these different priorities. The first politician to recognise this stategic and economic dilemma was A. J. Balfour, who raised it briefly at the War Council on 16 December and again in a paper he wrote for the Council at the end of the year. The very success of Kitchener's call for men meant that soon a point would be reached at which enlistments should cease. Some industries, like the mines, railways, merchant marine and munitions production, were of such immediate value to the war effort that not a man more should be taken from them. But there were other classes of men who should not be recruited. To keep its industries going and its population fed, Britain had to import large quantities of food and raw materials. It now also had to subsidise its allies. To find the money to do this it had either to borrow abroad, sell securities held abroad, or export manufactured goods. Balfour dismissed the first two alternatives as undesirable, and decided on the third.

> If so, it follows that anything in the way of enlistment that cripples those industries which either produce commodities for our export trade, or produce commodities at home (such as foodstuffs) which, if not made by ourselves, must be purchased abroad, may, and indeed must, diminish our fighting efficiency.[19]

The Board of Trade should look at the question 'from the point of view of national production considered merely as an instrument of military success'.[20] Industries necessary for the war effort or for exports should be closed to the recruiting officer, but men like gamekeepers, lawyers and teachers, who were worthless in an economy geared to war, should still be recruited. The Board agreed with his analysis. It had already received numerous complaints from industrialists claiming that if recruiting in a particular industry was not stopped they would be unable to support the war effort. At the end of December it had already begun to divide occupations into three categories: those in which there should be no more recruiting, those in which there should be as much recruiting as the War Office wanted, and an intermediate class in which the Labour Exchange Department, which was conversant with local conditions, should be consulted before more recruiting was permitted.[21] Its list was ready on 23 January, and its author, Llewellyn Smith, told his counterpart at the War Office:

> I am more and more convinced that the only hope of extending recruiting to the large extend [*sic*] which Lord Kitchener desires

without at the same time crippling our industrial and financial power, depends on a careful discrimination between industries in which it is desirable or undesirable to encourage recruiting for the time being.[22]

The coupling together by Balfour and Llewellyn Smith of the need to create a large army and to preserve Britain's economic power was significant. It indicated that they recognised that 'business as usual' and Kitchener's drive to create a 'nation in arms' were incompatible. The former would deprive Britain of the army it needed to support the French and meet the Germans on something like equal terms; the latter would give it an army, but it might bankrupt it. The time was fast approaching when the Cabinet would have to confront these choices and decide to pursue a single strategy.

Llewellyn Smith presented some of the practical problems to the Cabinet in his memorandum of 23 January. Working on the assumption that the age limit for recruits was between 17 and 45, and that two-thirds of the men in that age-group would be fit for military service, he calculated that a theoretical maximum of 6 million men could be enlisted. Two million men had already joined the army, 1 million were working in industries vital to the war effort, and of the remaining 3 million he calculated that only a further 1,100,000 could be taken without crippling industry. If the economy was not to suffer fatal damage a maximum limit of 3 million men should be put on the size of the army.[23] This was the first time anyone had looked into the future and tried to set a finite limit to recruiting for the New Armies. The temporarily resurrected Committee of Imperial Defence examined his memorandum on 27 January. This was the first time ministers had really considered an alternative economic policy to 'business as usual'. Runciman and McKenna were not convinced that it should be abandoned. They recognised that unchecked recruiting for the New Armies was a threat to their preferred policy and they were anxious to limit their further expansion. They argued that men would be better employed in producing war material, coal, food and supplies for the allies, rather than in joining the army. But Kitchener brushed their arguments aside. He remained convinced that if Britain was to be victorious it had to become a great land power, and he wanted at least another 1½ million recruits by the end of 1915. With memories of how recruiting had slumped after September 1914 when the War Office had tried to set limits on it because of lack of accommodation, he rejected any attempts to limit it now for the sake of the economy. He believed that 'it would be a dreadful thing at this stage to put a limit on recruiting'.[24] Implicit in this statement was the conviction, which no one present questioned, that if voluntary recruiting were restricted and an insufficient number of men came forward, then conscription would have to be introduced.

The opponents of further recruiting lost the first round of the fight; Kitchener was not told to curb recruiting. The meeting then turned its attention to a related issue, for if recruiting was to continue, then the most efficient use possible had to be made of the plant and labour that was available. Kitchener saw this problem in very stark terms, arguing that

> the whole question depends on the organisation of labour. Men who could not fight must work, and *vice versa*. Employees must eventually be replaced by women and others. If we had an organisation of labour such as Germany has, we should have no difficulty in getting 3,800,000 men. We should be able to organise to get that number.[25]

This proposal achieved a wider measure of agreement, although many of those present were quick to point out the difficulties there would be in substituting unskilled, semi-skilled and female labour for skilled labour in factories. It meant that the government would have to undertake the delicate task of persuading the trade unions to relax many of their normal practices. The meeting also formally decided to end government-sponsored relief works for the unemployed and to encourage labour engaged on them to enlist. They also decided to appeal to trade unionists and employers alike to release fit men for the army and to replace them with women and men who were too old or infirm to enlist.[26]

However, this amounted to little more than a policy of exhortation, not compulsion. It did not stop the drain of skilled labour from the economy at a time when more, not fewer, skilled men were needed. In the winter and spring of 1915 conscription was still not believed to be politically possible. Voluntary enlistment was still supplying more men than could immediately be trained or equipped, and so it still appeared to the public at large to be a success. Only a few senior civil servants and ministers recognised that it was creating as many problems as it solved. Even the Unionist leader Bonar Law believed that the voluntary system had not yet failed and that nothing could be done to replace it until its failure became manifest. The dilemma facing the government was this. In theory, although not in practice, it was simple to discourage recruiting in key industries, but it was much more difficult to discriminate between men in essential and non-essential occupations. If the army refused to accept the former, the latter believed that either they were not needed or that they were being unfairly exploited. In April the Board of Trade carried out another survey of the state of employment. It showed that the government's attempts at persuasion were not working. By May the Board recognised that it was engaged in a farcical situation. As fast as it was encouraging men to enter engineering and munitions factories, the army was recruiting them.[27]

The spring of 1915 was not a propitious time to begin to organise the industrial workforce. Skilled trade unionists in the engineering industry were jealous of their comparatively privileged position in the labour world. In December 1914 and January 1915 trade unionists in the shipyards and engineering works of Clydeside threatened to strike if their employers did not grant them wage increases.[28] The Board of Trade recognised that the unions had to be persuaded to accept the dilution of skilled labour and at the same time forgo the right to strike for the duration of the war, and that there was little possibility of the employers and unions reaching such an agreement on their own initiative. Neither of them trusted the other, and Sir George Askwith, the Board's chief industrial conciliator, was convinced that the government would have to step in to engineer an agreement. He wanted the government to call a conference of all the trade unions involved and to persuade them to agree to send any future disputes to a committee of government arbiters without any stoppage of work.[29] Askwith's board of arbiters, the Committee on Production in Engineering and Shipbuilding, was set up when the Clydesiders declared an overtime ban on 3 February. But on 16 February, before the committee could act, the overtime ban became a strike, and it was not until 3 March that Askwith could persuade both sides to accept a compromise and return to work.

The strike seriously alarmed the Cabinet and on 24 February it spent an hour hotly debating what should be done. This gave Lloyd George the opportunity he wanted to put a new set of strategic proposals to the Cabinet. He set these out in an epoch-making Cabinet paper. He wanted the government to enact legislation to give itself power to commandeer all engineering factories capable of producing munitions. He also wanted the government to arbitrate in all trade disputes and to punish any workers who refused to abide by its rulings.[30]

These steps may at first seem to have gone some way beyond what was immediately demanded by the Clydeside strike but the Chancellor was concerned with more than the immediate problem in Scotland. He went even further than Balfour and Llewellyn Smith had done in January in calling for a greater concentration of economic resources behind the war effort. Unless the government acted firmly and swiftly the war might end 'in irretrievable disaster for the cause of the Allies and for the future of the British Empire'. The Germans occupied most of Belgium and northern France, and they were rapidly driving the Russians eastwards. The Russians had no armed reserves to stop them and they were losing men faster than they could equip their replacements. The Central Powers could put a maximum of 9,200,000 men into the field, compared with the Entente's 7,200,000 men. Britain at the moment barely contributed 2 million men. He was convinced that every effort had to be made to help the Russians and to increase the number of armed men the Entente could field. Britain's contribution to the Entente's war effort should be twofold. He did not believe that Britain should be just the paymaster of the allies. It had to put its own troops into the field alongside those of its allies, and so, in line with Llewellyn Smith's calculations, he was prepared to raise another $1-1\frac{1}{2}$ million men if this could be done without restricting war production. But just as important as raising more men was the need to outproduce the Germans. This could only be done if the entire British engineering industry were turned over to war production, and that could only be achieved if the civilian population were persuaded to undergo considerable hardships. He told the Cabinet:

> I do not believe that Great Britain has even yet done anything like what she could do in the matter of increasing her war equipment. Great things have been accomplished in the last few months, but I sincerely believe that we could double our effective energies if we organised our factories thoroughly. All the engineering works of the country ought to be turned on to the production of war material. The population ought to be prepared to suffer all sorts of deprivations and even hardships whilst this is going on.[31]

This was a manifesto for total war. All human and economic resources were to be directed towards the immediate tasks of increasing the size of the army and the production of war materials. The barest minimum of resources was to be left over to secure the comfort of the civilian population.

Asquith described his suggestion as being 'of a very strong character', but Lloyd George was allowed to draft a Bill to take over the munitions manufacturers and the engineering industry.[32] But Kitchener was not enthusiastic about the Chancellor's proposals because he was afraid that they would only serve to upset the War Office's own plans. Kitchener was convinced that these were just about to come to fruition. What really set him apart from Lloyd George was that he did not share the Chancellor's concern with Russia. Kitchener's first priorities were to supply Sir John French and the New Armies. He recognised that if Britain sent supplies to Russia the British army would probably have to make do with less.[33] As von Donop explained to the Chancellor, 'As you can well imagine there are very few minutes of the day that I am not thinking upon this great task of supplying the necessary munitions of war to Sir John French'.[34] When Lloyd George castigated the War Office for not realising the magnitude of the war, he was really blaming it for not sharing his concern for Russia. Kitchener was intuitively correct in deprecating the Chancellor's concern with supplies for Russia. Their reverses, like Sir John French's, were not due solely to a lack of munitions. Better tactics and generalship could have done much to improve their plight. The help Lloyd George offered the Russians merely further dissuaded them from organising their own industries for war.[35] It would have been better for the Entente if the British and Russians had put their own houses in order first. And that was just what Kitchener wanted Lloyd George to do in Britain. He wanted the Chancellor to confine himself to helping Askwith's committee to organise skilled labour for the existing armaments manu-facturers so that they could meet the needs of the British army.[36]

Ministers realised that the trade unions would not accept dilution unless the government prevented their employers from making very large profits from the national emergency.[37] Within the Cabinet there was little opposition to the principle of a government takeover of the arms firms. Churchill alone stood out against it, but only because he was intent on preserving the special relationship between his own department and the shipbuilders. At a time of clearly perceived national emergency *laissez-faire* scruples were thrown to the wind, even if departmental jealousies remained.[38]

Between 16 February and 25 March the Askwith Committee issued four reports. The first examined the problem of bad time-keeping, and the second and third recommended dilution of skilled labour and compulsory government arbitration in trade disputes. But, as Askwith told the Prime Minister on 10 March, that would not be possible unless the government took steps to 'assure the country that the needs of the nation in time of war must not be made the means of undue private gain'. Unless that were done, 'it is almost useless to struggle against the trouble there is going to be in the labour world, without whom we cannot wage war'.[39] To ensure that this assurance was given he had already recommended that the government should use the Defence of the Realm Act to take control of the munitions manufacturers. Following the model of the Railway Executive Committee the executive management of the firms should be left in the hands of the existing managers, and the shareholders should be compensated for any losses they sustained. At the same time the existing circle of suppliers had to be extended and to do this the government ought to set up an executive committee to organise new sources of supply. The government would then need to acquire powers to take possession of any factory or machinery it required to make munitions, to compel manufacturers to abandon private contracts in order to give priority to government work, and to compel them to release men to work on government contracts.[40] On 5 March the Askwith Committee told the government that if these steps were taken it would have 'the inestimable advantage of impressing on the nation a serious realisation of the fact that the country is at war, and must mobilise its industrial resources with definite and concentrated purpose for the successful prosecution of the war'.[41]

On the same day Lloyd George seized on Askwith's recommendations and, at a special meeting called by the Prime Minister to discuss munitions supplies, Kitchener reluctantly agreed that an executive committee for the engineering industry should be set up and that Home Office factory inspectors should survey all engineering factories in the country so that the government would know exactly what resources were available.[42] Lloyd George's next step was to persuade the Cabinet to accept his new Bill and then to present it to the House of Commons. In introducing the Defence of the Realm (Amendment No. 2) Bill to the Commons he made clear his final repudiation of 'business as usual'. He reminded MPs that Britain was at war, 'and we cannot conduct war and allow business to be conducted as usual. Instead of "business as usual", we want "victory as usual".'[43] The Act became law on 16 March.

Although the government now had the legal powers to carry out Lloyd George's policy, it was well aware that without the willing co-operation of both employers and employees the Act would be a dead letter. So Runciman then began negotiations with the two largest munitions firms, Vickers and Armstrongs, to secure their co-operation, and to do this he allowed them to propose their own terms of compensation. The companies knew they were in a strong position and drove a hard bargain, making the government pay dearly for their help.[44] However, no written agreement was actually signed. That had to wait until negotiations with the other manufacturers had been successful, and they dragged on until the fall of the Liberal government in May. But in the meantime the government felt that the talks had gone so well that it could open discussions with the trade unions. Lloyd George met representatives of twenty-three unions at the Treasury between 17 and 19 March, and the terms the government offered them were by no means as generous. The unions were not permitted to put forward their own terms and the Treasury agreement was drafted by Board of Trade officials. Vickers and Armstrongs were being asked to agree to limit their profits to a figure well above their pre-war dividends. The unions, in return for a mere promise to return to the status quo *ante bellum* at the end of the war, were asked to forgo the right to strike, to submit all disputes to arbitration, and to accept the dilution of skilled labour. In the face of a powerful appeal to their patriotism all but two unions agreed.[45]

The Treasury agreement marked the formal recognition of an important shift away from the government's prewar policy towards labour in wartime. Labour supply was not as plentiful as had been expected, but it was much more patriotic than had been feared. The government was now intent on playing on that patriotism to mobilise organised labour behind the war effort. The agreement also endorsed the establishment of an advisory committee of workers' representatives to help carry out its terms and thus marked the first, very hesitant, steps towards absorbing the labour leaders into the machinery of government.

Lloyd George next turned his attention to organising the remainder of the engineering industry to produce munitions. The Home Office survey showed that deliveries of all types of munitions were still seriously in arrears. Shell deliveries alone were 34 per cent behind contract times. The Chancellor was intent on wiping out these deficits and increasing production enormously, and to do this he was convinced that control of all munitions production had to be taken away from the War Office. On 23 March he persuaded Asquith to set up a committee, presided over by Lloyd George, to mobilise the engineering industry. The committee was to work in consultation with the War Office and Admiralty, but it had powers to take any necessary steps 'to ensure the promptest and most efficient application of all available productive resources of the country to the manufacture and supply of Munitions of War'.[46]

This marked the start of a bitter struggle between Lloyd George and Kitchener for the control of munitions supply. Kitchener objected to the Chancellor's interference on two grounds. He thought that the committee was part of a cabal to remove him from the War Office. This is unlikely, because although many Liberal ministers disliked him, they recognised that he still had the unbounded confidence of the nation.[47] Kitchener was also afraid that the Chancellor's proposals would delay the completion of current orders for the New Armies and the Expeditionary Force by drawing away already scarce supplies of labour and machinery from existing manufacturers. To prevent this he insisted that the

Chancellor's committee must not interfere with work on existing War Office contracts.[48] Kitchener was still wedded to transforming Britain into a 'nation in arms', and to do that he needed to equip the New Armies as quickly as possible. He was quite prepared to have Lloyd George as an assistant, but only on his terms. He wanted the Chancellor to confine himself to finding more labour for the machinery existing contractors already had but could not operate because they did not have enough men. The New Armies and Sir John French needed shells and guns immediately, so Kitchener had no pressing interest in developing new and problematic sources of supply which might be able to deliver orders in, as Lloyd George admitted, nine months' time. 'I feel sure', he wrote to Lloyd George, 'that the Committee will be the first to recognise that our main efforts should be directed towards getting all the machinery we already have into full working order'.[49]

Until the fall of the Liberal government the struggle between them revolved around whether to spread contracts to new manufacturers, as Lloyd George advocated, or whether to concentrate labour with existing contractors, as Kitchener wanted. Early in March the Board of Trade had held a series of exhibitions in engineering centres designed to show local firms the types of munitions the War Office wanted. The Board had hoped that manufacturers would attend the exhibitions and then tender for contracts, but the War Office wanted to use the exhibitions to find firms with suitable skilled men whom they could persuade to go to work in the factories of existing manufacturers. The exhibitions opened on 10 March and although a number of firms tendered for contracts the War Office refused to give them any. On 18 March the director of artillery explained that thanks to the decisions of the Cabinet Committee in October 1914,

> The armament firms had undertaken contracts very largely in excess of what they could fulfil. The Government had purchased for them large increases of plant, and it was not intended to place any further orders until their labour requirement had been met.[50]

To do this the War Office wished to use the powers of the Defence of the Realm (Amendment No. 2) Act to close firms working on private contracts and transfer their labour to their own contractors, and on 16 March Kitchener asked G. M. Booth, a Liverpool ship- and factory-owner, to head a committee to carry out this policy. Booth himself actually preferred Lloyd George's policy of spreading orders, but he did as Kitchener requested.[51] When Lloyd George discovered what the War Office intended he went to Asquith and explained the differences between them. After some hesitation Asquith imposed a typically Asquithian compromise on the two ministers, which meant that neither of them was really in charge of munitions supply. The Chancellor's Munitions of War Committee was given the authority to modify the War Office's policy as it saw fit, but the War Office retained the final right to veto its work because it could refuse to sign any contracts the Chancellor's Committee might negotiate.[52]

Such an agreement was unworkable, and the people involved could not make it work. Instead Lloyd George and Kitchener still tried to go their own ways. In April Booth, whose Armaments Output Committee was now openly acting as the executive arm of the Chancellor's Committee, tried to set up an 'A' and 'B' areas scheme. 'A' areas were within one hour's train journey of existing War Office contractors and here labour was to be transferred to the existing contractors. 'B' areas were other engineering centres where engineering firms were to be encouraged to pool their resources and tender for collective contracts.[53] Booth asked manufacturers in the 'B' areas to form committees to organise the pooling of their resources and suggested that as this might take up to two months they might release some of their men for that period to go to work for existing War Office contractors. This would benefit everyone. The existing contractors would have, at least temporarily, the men they needed, and in two months' time when the men returned to their old factories they would be trained in shell-making.[54] This compromise was obviously weighed against the War Office because after the trainees had returned to their former employers the War Offices' contractors would again be short of labour. Kitchener tried to protect his contractors by asking his former protégé Sir Percy Girouard, who was now a director of Armstrongs, to come to London. Girouard was prepared to accept the outline of Booth's scheme but he insisted that the existing manufacturers had to be given absolute priority in men, materials and machines. In his opinion, 'to attempt [the] organisation of small engineering factories in preference to main factories, is suicidal'.[55] He insisted that groups of manufacturers in 'B' areas should only be allowed to organise themselves under the supervision of managers of the existing War Office contractors, and thus the latter would be able to protect their own interests. The result of this was to pile confusion on confusion, and by 15 May Lloyd George was loud in his complaints: 'I am frankly disappointed at the slowness of our progress.'[56]

Against this background of bickering the 'shell scandal' came as a marvellous opportunity for both Lloyd George and Asquith.

Asquith seized upon it, and upon Admiral Lord Fisher's resignation, as a plausible justification for establishing a Coalition government. His purpose in doing so was to avoid the impending general election, which was certain to generate a great deal of harmful party warfare which might threaten national unity, and which he probably expected the Liberals to lose. On 17 May he called upon the entire Cabinet to resign, telling them:

> I have for some time past come, with increasing conviction, to the conclusion that the continued prosecution of the War requires what is called a 'broad-based' Government. Under existing conditions, criticism, inspired by party motives and interests, has full reign, and is an asset of much value to the enemy.
>
> The resignation of Lord Fisher, which I have done my best to avert, and the more than plausible Parliamentary case in regard to the alleged deficiency of high-explosive shells, would, if duly exploited (as they would have been) in the House of Commons at this moment, have had the most disastrous effect on the general political and strategic situation: in particular such a discussion might have had the result of determining adversely to the Allies the attitude of Italy.[57]

Lloyd George used the crisis to gain control of munitions supplies. He was given information about Sir John French's views by Repington and Brinsley Fitzgerald.[58] He believed everthing they told him as it appeared to confirm his own low opinion of Kitchener. On 19 May he wrote to Asquith and completely dissociated himself from any hint of having failed to produce all the munitions the army needed and claimed that for months the War Office had failed to tell him the true situation on the western front. He overlooked the fact that he had been present at the War Council meetings in January when Sir John had explained his case fully to the politicians. Although deliveries were considerably behind the inflated promises the Cabinet Committee had tried to extract from the manufacturers in the autumn of 1914, he also overlooked their still considerable achievements. Before the war the manufacturers were expected to deliver 162,000 18-pounder shells in six months.[59] They were now producing more than that in just four weeks. Nor did he recognise that his own proposals to spread contracts would, in the short term at least, have slowed down the rate at which supplies increased to meet the growing demands of the Expeditionary Force, and he was unaware that his concern for Russia was misplaced and only served to discourage it from developing its own industries.

Llewellyn Smith, who had been working in close collaboration with the Chancellor for several months, was the first to recognise that the 'shell scandal' had presented Lloyd George with the opportunity to oust Kitchener as a rival for the control of munitions supplies. He told him that 'the turn of events has made possible a really comprehensive reform which even a week ago seemed impossible'.[60] Consequently Lloyd George determined to resist pressure on him to become Secretary of State for War and instead he wanted to take over sole control of munitions production by establishing a new ministry. The real significance of the 'shell scandal' for Britain's future economic strategy was that it opened the way for Lloyd George to begin to implement his vision of a total war economy.

Notes: Chapter 10

1   PRO Cab. 41/35/40, Asquith to HM the King, 2 Sept. 1914; PRO Cab. 41/35/42, Asquith to HM the King, 8 Sept. 1914; PRO Cab. 41/35/47, Asquith to HM the King, 23 Sept. 1914; N. Stone, *The Eastern Front* (London, 1975), p. 154.

2   PRO Cab. 41/35/62, Asquith to HM the King, 4 Dec. 1914.

3   Lord Riddell, *Lord Riddell's War Diary, 1914–18* (London, 1933), p. 44; Emmott mss, diary entry, 1 Dec. 1914.

4   PRO Cab. 42/1/8, The War. Suggestions as to the military position, D. Lloyd George, 1 Jan. 1915.

5   A. J. P. Taylor (ed.), *Lloyd George. A Diary by Francis Stevenson* (London, 1971), pp. 22–3; Stone, *op. cit. Eastern Front*, p. 154.

6   PRO T 171/107, The United States of America, B. Blackett, 5 Jan. 1915.

7   PRO T 171/107, Russia, J. M. Keynes, 30 Jan. 1915.

8   Haldane mss 6108A (iv), Cabinet paper–decisions of the Paris conference, Feb. 1915; K. M. Burk, 'British war missions to the United States, 1914–18' (D. Phil. thesis, University of Oxford, 1976), p. 99; *History of the Ministry of Munitions*, Vol. 2, pt 8, p. 18.

9   69 HC Deb., 5s., col. 913, 15 Feb. 1915.

10 PRO WO 159/1, The War (August 1914 to 31 May 1915), Note by the Secretary of State. Lord Kitchener, 31 May 1915.

11 Asquith mss, Vol. 14, Lloyd George to Asquith, 19 May 1915; PRO T 181/65, Notes by Maj.-Gen. Sir S. von Donop, 6 July 1935. Major G. French, *The Life of Field Marshal Sir John French* (London, 1931), pp. 286, 290: Haldane mss 5911, Haig to Haldane, 24 Apr. 1915; Col. C. T. B. Mott (translator), *The Memoirs of Field Marshal Joffre* (London, 1932), Vol. 2, p. 596.

12 PRO T 181/68, Lord Aberconway (Thos. Firth & John Brown Ltd) to the Royal Commission ... ,2 Oct. 1935; PRO T 181/69, A. B. H. Clerke (Hadfields) to the Royal Commission ... , 16 Oct. 1935; letter to *The Times* of 10 June 1919 by Maj.-Gen. Mahon.

13 PRO Cab. 37/126/28, Output of munitions of war, R. McK[enna], 25 Mar. 1915; PRO T 181/50, Royal Commission on the private manufacture of, and trading in, arms, app. 5, Note on private arms manufacture in the Great War, Sir M. Hankey, May 1935; *History of the Ministry of Munitions*, Vol. 2, pt 2, p. 37.

14 PRO MUN 5/8/171/29, Board of Trade national clearing house, Demands for labour, 1 June 1915; PRO T 181/112, Q. 1329 (Sir S. von Donop).

15 Runciman mss box 112, Dawson to Runciman, 4 Jan. 1915.
16 D. Lloyd George, *War Memoirs* (London, 1934), Vol. 1, pp. 152–3; PRO MUN 9/1., J. S. S[imon] to Lloyd George, 18 Oct. 1914; Lloyd George mss C/5/7/23, Lloyd George to von Donop, 8 Apr. 1915; PRO Cab. 19/33, Dardanelles Commission, Minutes of evidence, Q. 4556 (Lord Haldane); C. Trebilcock, 'War and the failure of industrial mobilisation: 1899 and 1914', in J. M. Winter (ed.), *War and Economic Development* (London, 1975), pp. 157–8.
17 Trebilcock, 'War and the failure of industrial mobilisation', p. 156.
18 C. J. Wrigley, *David Lloyd George and the British Labour Movement in Peace and War* (New York, 1976), p. 92.
19 PRO Cab. 42/1/7 Limits of enlistment, A. J. Balfour, 5 Jan. 1915.
20 ibid.
21 PRO Cab. 42/1/14, Limits of enlistment. Note by Sir H. Llewellyn Smith, 11 Jan. 1915; *History of the Ministry of Munitions*, Vol. 1, pt 2, p.8.
22 PRO BT 13/603/E271908, Llewellyn Smith to R. H. Brade, 25 Jan. 1915.
23 PRO Cab. 42/1/21, Limits of enlistment. Statistical supplement to note by Sir H. Llewellyn Smith, 23 Jan. 1915.
24 PRO Cab. 42/1/24, Minutes of 131st meeting of the CID, 27 Jan. 1915.
25 ibid.
26 ibid.
27 PRO MUN 5/8/172/1, Munitions of War Committee, The effect of recruiting on the supply of armament labour, Sir H. Llewellyn Smith, 6 May 1915; David French, 'Some aspects of social and economic planning for war in Great Britain, *c.* 1905–15' (PhD thesis, University of London, 1978), pp. 252–3.
28 PRO Cab. 37/125/12, Third interim report of the Committee on Production in Engineering and Shipbuilding Establishments engaged on government work, 4 Mar. 1915; W. R. Scott and J. Cunnison, *The Industries of the Clyde Valley during the Great War* (London, 1924), pp. 139–41.
29 PRO MUN 5/8/171/29, Sir George Askwith to Runciman, 4 Feb. 1915; PRO MUN 5/8/180/3, Memorandum, shortage of labour, Sir G. Askwith, 28 Jan. 1915.
30 E. David (ed.), *Inside Asquith's Cabinet – from the Diaries of Charles Hobhouse* (London, 1977), p. 224.
31 PRO Cab. 37/124/40, Some further considerations on the conduct of the war, Lloyd George, 22 Feb. 1915.
32 PRO Cab. 37/124/47, Asquith to HM the King, 24 Feb. 1915.
33 Spears mss 2/3/83, copy of letter from Kitchener to Sir John French, 28 Dec. 1914.
34 Lloyd George mss C/5/7/16, von Donop to Lloyd George, 1 Mar. 1915.
35 Stone, *Eastern Front,* pp. 130–1; N. Stone, 'Organising an economy for war: the Russian shell shortage of 1914–17' in G. Best and A. Wheatcroft, (eds), *War, Economy and the Military Mind* (London, 1976), pp. 108–16.
36 PRO Cab. 1/11/33, Remarks on the Chancellor of the Exchequer's memorandum on the conduct of the war, Lord Kitchener, 25 Feb. 1915.
37 Gainford mss, diary entry, 2 Mar. 1915.
38 PRO Cab. 1/11/39, Armament firms, W. S. C[hurchill], 3 Mar. 1915.
39 Asquith mss, Vol. 14, Askwith to the Prime Minister, 10 Mar. 1915.
40 PRO WO 159/1, Sir G. Gibb to Kitchener, 1 Mar. 1915.
41 PRO Cab. 1/11/46, Fourth interim report of the committee on production in engineering and shipbuilding establishments engaged on government work, 5 Mar. 1915.
42 PRO Cab. 22/1/17, Minutes of the War Council, 3 Mar. 1915; Lord Hankey, *The Supreme Command* (London, 1961), Vol. 1, pp. 209–10; PRO MUN 5/6/170/22, Minutes of conference of ministers on the supply of munitions, held at 10 Downing St, 5 Mar. 1915; Hankey mss 1/1, diary entry, 5 Mar. 1915; Lloyd George mss C/3/3/2, Lloyd George to Balfour, 6 Mar. 1915.

43 70 HC Deb., 5s., col. 1460, 10 Mar. 1915.
44 PRO MUN 7/91, Project of taking over certain firms. Financial arrangements, 12 Mar. 1915.
45 PRO MUN 5/10/180/17, Mobilisation of war industries. Conference between the government and the representatives of the trade unions and federations held at the Treasury on 17, 18 and 19 Mar. 1915; PRO Cab. 37/126/16, Memorandum of proposals which the workmen's representatives agreed to recommend to their members at a conference with the Chancellor of the Exchequer and the President of the Board of Trade, held at the Treasury on 17–19 Mar. 1915; PRO MUN 5/10/180/18, Treasury conference with the ASE. Minutes of proceedings, 25 Mar. 1915; Wrigley, op. cit., pp. 102 *ff.*
46 PRO MUN 5/8/172/3, Munitions of War Committee, 8 Apr. 1915; PRO 30/57/82, Asquith to Kitchener (and enc.), 23 Mar. 1915; Earl of Oxford and Asquith, *Memories and Reflections* (London, 1928), Vol. 2, p. 67.
47 Oxford and Asquith, op. cit., Vol. 2, p. 68; David (ed.), op. cit., p. 231.
48 PRO 30/57/82, Kitchener to Asquith, 25 Mar. 1915.
49 PRO 30/57/82, Kitchener to Lloyd George, 26 Mar. 1915.
50 PRO MUN 5/8/171/29, Runciman to Llewellyn Smith (and enc.), 19 Mar. 1915.
51 D. Crow. *A Man of Push and Go. The Life of George Macaulay Booth* (London, 1965), pp. 91–2.
52 PRO MUN 5/8/172/3, op. cit.; Lloyd George mss C/3/3/4, Lloyd George to Balfour, 8 April 1915.
53 David French 'Some aspects of social and economic planning', p. 267.
54 PRO MUN 5/7/171/1, Minutes of meetings of the Armament Output Committee – 1st meeting, 20 Apr. 1915.
55 PRO MUN 5/8/171/21, Sir Percy Girouard's first scheme for central organisation for labour supply, 25 Mar. 1915.
56 Lloyd George mss C/1/2/16, Lloyd George to U. Wolff, 15 May 1915.
57 PRO Cab. 37/128/19, Asquith to the Cabinet, 17 May 1915; M. D. Pugh, 'Asquith, Bonar Law and the first Coalition', *Historical Journal,* vol. 17 (1974), pp. 815–17.
58 Lloyd George, op. cit., p. 199.
59 HMSO, *Statistics of the Military Effort of the British Empire* (London, 1922), p. 471.
60 Lloyd George mss C/7/5/21, Llewellyn Smith to Lloyd George, 21 May 1915; C/7/5/22, Llewellyn Smith to Lloyd George, 22 May 1915.

11

Conclusion: The Unresolved Dilemmas of Economic Strategy

By May 1915 it was obvious that Kitchener was correct in expecting a long war. On 8 August Churchill had told the Admiralty to plan for a war lasting nine months. Nine months later, with victory no nearer, he increased his estimate by another nineteen months.[1] The myth of the short war was dead. But even after nine months of war the Cabinet was still undecided on how best to organise the economy to support the war effort. It was pursuing three incompatible policies, and the time was rapidly approaching when it would have to choose between them. Runciman was still intent on supporting 'business as usual'. Addressing a meeting of the Association of Trade Protection Societies of the United Kingdom on 12 May, he told his audience that 'business as usual' still had a vital role to play in the Entente's war effort. He remained convinced that

> In so far as we had been able to conduct our great business concerns as though no war were interfering with them, we had added to our national strength and had been able to give material assistance to our Allies, who were less fortunately placed than we were.[2]

Defeating Germany by proxy was anathema to Kitchener. He was still intent on placing the New Armies in the field as soon as possible and maintaining them there until Germany was beaten and Britain could impose its own peace terms on an exhausted Europe. On 18 May he defended his handling of shell supplies in the House of Lords, and ended his speech with a call for another 300,000 men.[3] He was not blind to the need for munitions, and he specifically told his listeners that he did not want men engaged in munitions production to enlist. But unlike Lloyd George, he was not concerned with the need to supply Russia. The Chancellor's vision of the British economy organised for total war contained elements of both of these strategies. He agreed with Runciman and McKenna that it was vital for the navy to retain command of the sea, because without it Britain would starve. He recognised that it had to maintain its financial power if it was to continue to subsidise its allies. He was also in accord, at least to a certain extent, with Kitchener's desire for a larger army, although on this point he was just beginning to waver. In his Cabinet paper of 22 February he had agreed that perhaps another $1\frac{1}{2}$ million men could be raised. But in his budget speech of 4 May he indicated that he was aware that there were limits to the size of the army Britain could put into the field. If too many men enlisted, trade and industry might collapse and Britain would be bankrupted. He told MPs:

> We have raised enormous numbers of men in this country, but I say now speaking purely from the point of view of finance, that the time has come when there should be discrimination, so that recruiting should not interfere with the output of munitions of war, and that it should interfere as little as possible with the output of those commodities which we export abroad, and which enable us to purchase munitions for ourselves and our Allies.[4]

The key word in this passage was 'discrimination'. It was a euphemism not just for conscription but for a much tighter control of all economic resources. The New Armies were rapidly depriving the economy of the human and material resources necessary to pursue 'business as usual'. Lloyd George realised that if Kitchener's creation were allowed to continue to expand haphazardly it might do more harm than good to the Entente's war effort. By May 1915 Britain was faced by a problem which had not been dreamed of before 1914. It was becoming increasingly difficult to pay for the war. Churchill's estimate of 1 August that 'the naval war will be cheap – not more than 25 millions a year' was wildly wrong.[5] Even Sir George Clarke's belief that a great war would cost £200–300 million was already an underestimate by March 1915. Up to 31 March 1915 the government had spent £359,786,000 on the war. Of this sum £280,545,000 had been spent on the army and navy, and the remainder had gone on loans to the allies and dominions, on buying food and on various miscellaneous items. Britain was facing a growing deficit on its balance of payments because of the war.[6] In the first nine months of the conflict the deficit on visible trade had increased by £160–170 million. Most of this increase was due to a fall in the value of manufactured exports, which fell by £117 million compared with the 1913 figure. According to the Chancellor this was due to the fact that about 4 million men had been withdrawn from their normal occupations. They had either enlisted or gone to make munitions.[7] This had happened at the very moment when imports were increasing because, as Runciman explained, 'we have to purchase enormous quantities of supplies for the army and navy as well as for the civilian population from America', and without these Britain and its allies could not sustain their war effort.[8] Before the war the gap on visible trade had been made good by interest payments on overseas investments and by payments for British shipping and financial services abroad. But the war had adversely affected these and they were no longer enough to compensate for the shortfall in Britain's visible exports. In December the rate of exchange in New York had begun to go against sterling. By February 1915 E. C. Grenfell, of the merchant bankers Morgan, Grenfell & Co., who were the government's purchasing agents in America, was pressing the Treasury to do something to support the exchange rate. But Lloyd George was preoccupied with other matters, and the situation was allowed to deteriorate.[9]

Britain's resources were too limited to permit it to pursue all three strategies at once. By the spring of 1915 it was coming to be felt that unless the government applied some single-minded direction to the economy, victory might be jeopardised. For some months Unionists like Walter Long had been urging that conscription for both the army and industry was the answer.[10] By May several prominent Liberals, including C. P. Scott and Sir Edward Grey, were beginning to believe that he was right. Grey recognised that voluntary methods had provided the army with plenty of recruits, but they could not control all the other resources needed to prosecute the war. If victory was to be secured, the government would have to ape the Germans and control all the nation's human and material resources. At the start of the war it had been assumed that if the Germans did not overrun France quickly, the Russians would eventually crush them. This no longer seemed likely. There appeared to be little prospect of a swift German collapse, and consequently, he concluded, 'staying power and the development of the supply of munitions of war are, in the long run, going to decide the issue'.[11] It was thus vital for Britain to husband and organise all its resources.

It has long been argued that the greatest failure of the Asquith Cabinet in the early months of the war was its inability to recognise the need to assume the kinds of controls over the economy Grey had spoken of. This has normally been explained by its supposed addiction to the principles of *laissez-faire*. Arthur Marwick, in his otherwise illuminating study of the impact of the war on British society, *The Deluge,* argues that the government was faced by a simple choice between *laissez-faire* and assuming a greater degree of state control.[12] But in fact this was not the real choice facing them. Debates about strategy, not about economics, dominated their discussions. The government had begun the war believing that the word strategy meant little more than the conduct of naval and military operations and that wars were fought by professional soldiers and sailors. The proper role of the civilian was to suffer the hardships of war in silence. But by May 1915 it was becoming obvious that modern wars between industrial societies must necessarily involve whole societies unless one side or the other was prepared to make a compromise peace. In May 1915 neither the British nor the Germans were ready to begin negotiations for peace, and so willy-nilly both sides were beginning to realise that they would have to throw all their resources into the fight before a decision was reached. Hitherto Britain's strategy had been chaotic because it believed it could fight the war successfully by waging less than total war. The collapse of 'business as usual', and the dawning realisation that Kitchener's 'nation in arms' was creating as many problems as it was solving, made it slowly apparent to Lloyd George that the only road to victory lay through total war.

There were two reasons why this took so long to become apparent to the government and why it acted so slowly. The structure of Cabinet government was ill-adapted to the conduct of war and the political situation within which it operated seriously restricted the courses of action open to it in 1914. The dilemmas facing the government might have been made more apparent sooner if the machinery of Cabinet government had been better suited to the problems posed by modern war. Its shortcomings in the conduct of military operations are already well known. The absence of a properly constituted General Staff to which the government could turn for military advice was sorely felt.[13] The Cabinet was similarly handicapped in conducting the war at home because of the absence of an economic general staff. If such a body had existed it might have been able at least to warn the Cabinet that its economic and strategic policies were incompatible. In August the most obvious body which might have undertaken this duty was the secretariat of the Committee of Imperial Defence. But hardly had the measures detailed in the War Book been put into operation when the Committee's staff began to disperse as the assistant secretaries took up active service appointments. Even Hankey tried to rejoin the Royal Marines. He was not allowed to do so, but within a few weeks he was left with only one assistant.[14] It is easy to see why no one before 1914 recognised the need for an economic general staff. Once the pre-arranged plans had been put into operation to safeguard trade and employment, the government's direct intervention in the economy was expected to be minimal. 'Business as usual' would function automatically.

But 'business as usual' did not function automatically. As the war progressed the state came to interfere increasingly in areas of economic life it had left untouched before 1914. This piecemeal extension of the government's powers was not matched by any corresponding and systematic extension in the machinery of government to use these powers. The government tried to exercise its growing control through a steadily increasing number of *ad hoc* committees. Between August 1914 and 1 March 1915 no less than thirty-eight of them were formed. They were of two kinds. There was a handful of Cabinet committees, which consisted of a group of Cabinet ministers advised by some senior civil servants and possibly outside business experts. This arrangement had some undoubted merits. It enabled the Cabinet to draw on the advice of a wide number of experts. For example, the Cabinet committee which dealt with the financial crisis on the outbreak of war drew on the advice of, among others, a former Chancellor of the Exchequer, Austen Chamberlain, the Governor of the Bank of England and the permanent secretary to the Treasury. Cabinet committees could formulate policies, but any major decisions they wanted to make had to be ratified by the full Cabinet. The second type of committee performed a more purely executive function. It harnessed the knowledge of outside experts to carry out policies that the Cabinet had already ratified. For example, the Admiralty's Advisory Committee on the Diversion of Shipping was the body through which the Admiralty controlled the movements of merchant ships around the coast. Its chairman, a vice-admiral, was advised by representatives of all of the war risk insurance associations and Lloyd's.[15]

Some of these committees, like the Railway Executive Committee, came into being automatically on the outbreak of war because they had been written into the War Book. Others, like the Cabinet Committee on Food Supplies, were established by the Cabinet as part of the government's emergency measures in August 1914. The great lacuna in this procedure was that there was no established machinery to co-ordinate the policies of the new committees. The only person with the time or inclination to do so was Hankey. In August 1914 he told a former colleague: 'Now I spend all my time trying to co-ordinate everyone's efforts.'[16] Even Asquith was unaware of what the new committees were supposed to do, so on 20 August he told Hankey to prepare a directory of all of them. Hankey tried to persuade the secretaries of the committees to send him copies of their minutes so that he could follow the

Prime Minister's instructions to keep abreast of their activities and so co-ordinate their efforts. This, however, proved to be impossible. Like the Cabinet itself, the Cabinet committees did not keep minutes, and the secretaries of the other committees were too overworked to help Hankey. The next expedient that was tried was for Hankey to become a member of some of the committees so that he would have personal knowledge of what they were doing. By October he was sitting on nine of them.[17] But there were limits to what even he could do, especially as he was excluded from the Cabinet committees which actually formulated policy.

Asquith was determined to retain the power to make policy in the hands of Cabinet ministers and, if possible, in the hands of the whole Cabinet. He still remembered the jealousy the Committee of Imperial Defence had provoked. As he admitted in his memoirs, the greatest problem facing the government as it tried to conduct the war was how to combine rapid decision-making with the maintenance of Cabinet responsibility and control.[18] This was a problem which he never solved, and it probably could never be solved. The peacetime organisation of the Cabinet was not compatible with rapid and effective action in wartime. It was not designed to maintain a close and continuous watch on the progress of the war or to reach rapid decisions. The Cabinet remained a collection of departmental ministers who were increasingly submerged by a growing volume of work. Herbert Samuel, for example, who was busy organising relief measures, could not even leave his desk for lunch on 20 August. He began work at 9.30 a.m. and worked continuously until 8.30 p.m. Grey, who was in relatively poor health even before August, nearly broke down completely under the strain of the war.[19] In January 1915 Runciman confessed to his wife: 'I have found myself breathless and only half way up my hill of papers, exhausted with interviews, and never a word written to you.'[20] Under this pressure of departmental work it was difficult for many ministers to find time to survey the broader strategic issues of the war.

Between 2 August and 30 October 1914 the Cabinet met on an average once every three days.[21] Ministers soon found these frequent meetings very tiring and time-consuming. Cabinet business was not well organised. The Cabinet was too large to conduct business quickly. It had twenty-one members, some of whose departments were only remotely connected with the war. It kept no minutes, nor even a formal record of its decisions beyond the Prime Minister's letter to the King. As the Cabinet's desultory discussions on the raising of the New Armies indicated, this lack of system could breed confusion. It was difficult to summon such a large number of ministers quickly to discuss a sudden emergency.[22] Lord

Emmott, a newcomer to the Cabinet in August 1914, described some of its shortcomings thus in January 1915:

> My chief disappointment in Cabinet work is the difficulty of obtaining a hearing and the insufficient time given to consideration of questions brought before us. The Prime Minister writes letters and weighs in at the end with very sound and weighty opinions; but the rest seem to worry things out as best they can among themselves. Were it not for Winston and L. G. [Lloyd George] asking Kitchener questions we shd. have precious little enlightenment on military questions.[23]

In an attempt to rectify some of these shortcomings Asquith set up the War Council on 25 November. It was much smaller that the Cabinet; its original members were the Prime Minister himself, Lloyd George, Crewe, Churchill, Kitchener and Grey. They were advised by the First Sea Lord, Lord Fisher and the Chief of the Imperial General Staff, Sir James Wolfe Murray. However, the last was so much in awe of Kitchener that he never spoke. Hankey was the Council's secretary and he kept the minutes of its discussions. But the new system still had many drawbacks, and it may even have slowed down the process of reaching decisions on questions of policy. Its powers were ill-defined. Hankey considered that it was neither a Cabinet committee nor a subcommittee of the Committee of Imperial Defence.[24] It had no executive powers as a committee, but individual members could give orders to their own departments after taking part in its discussions. Its decisions were reported to the full Cabinet, and although the latter often agreed with them, it did so only after having discussed them again. This produced the worst of both worlds. The Council breached the doctrine of the Cabinet's collective responsibility for all decisions taken in its name. Junior Cabinet ministers who did not sit on the Council were placed in an invidious position. As Emmott explained, they 'are compelled either to accept responsibility for decisions without full information of the grounds on which the decisions are based or to make themselves an intolerable nuisance to harried and overworked colleagues in asking for explanations'.[25] And secondly, because the Cabinet often trod the same ground as the Council did it merely ensured that matters were discussed twice before a decision was reached. As Montagu pointed out in March 1915, often the only difference between the deliberations of the two bodies was 'a different set of spectators'.[26] The Council also developed other faults. Its meetings were irregular and they were too widely spaced to permit it to exercise any kind of close control over the war. Between November 1914 and May 1915 it met only nineteen times, or an average of once every nine days. Between 6 April and 14 May it did not meet at all. Its membership also grew, thus often needlessly prolonging its deliberations.

Discussions of purely economic issues were confined to the Cabinet or to a handful of *ad hoc* committees. For example, the committee which discussed manpower in January 1915 was an *ad hoc* subcommittee of the Committee of Imperial Defence. All the discussions of Lloyd George's Defence of the Realm (Amendment No. 2) Bill took place in the full Cabinet. The point which must be emphasised is that these discussions did not take place as part of a continuous and wide-ranging review of national policy. Naval and military strategy was decided apart from economic policy. The War Council's business was dominated by the concerns of the Admiralty and War Office. Problems of economic policy did not come within its purview. It did not, for example, ever consider the likely economic repercussions of launching the Dardanelles operation on the merchant shipping situation.[27]

Much of the responsibility for failing to recognise that economic policy ought to be considered side by side with naval and military strategy must rest with Asquith. He believed that war was too serious a business not to be left to the generals (and admirals). He was content to leave the direction of the war very much in the hands of the two service ministers and their professional advisers.[28] He relied heavily on the advice of just three ministers, Kitchener, Churchill and, later in the spring of 1915, Lloyd George. It was difficult for other ministers to put forward policies if one of these three objected to them.[29] The composition of Asquith's inner Cabinet goes some way towards explaining why, by May 1915, Kitchener's 'nation in arms' was overtaking 'business as usual', and was in turn being challenged by Lloyd George's strategy of total war. Runciman and McKenna did not have Asquith's ear on major strategic questions as Kitchener, Churchill and Lloyd George did.

These adminstrative shortcomings contributed significantly to the Cabinet's failure to pursue a single coherent strategy. But that does not imply that this problem could have been rectified in the political circumstances of 1914–15. The decision to raise the New Armies was crucial because it made 'business as usual' increasingly impossible and it prefixed Lloyd George's drive to increase munitions supplies. The Cabinet was correct to raise a continental-scale army because, as it transpired in 1917, the French and Russian armies were not strong enough to defeat Germany alone. Nor did the Royal Navy prove to be the decisive offensive weapon the navalists had hoped it would be. But the New Armies posed fundamental economic problems. The great advantage of 'business as usual' was that it minimised both the demands the state had to make on the economy and the degree of control the government had to exercise over it. The New Armies created a situation in which men and materials became scarce, and in 1914–15 a more rational use of scarce resources, particularly manpower, could only have been achieved through conscription. Conscription would have made it possible for the government to have regulated the flow of men joining the army, and to have balanced the country's military and economic needs. The economic disruption caused by recruiting would have been minimised, and Kitchener would not have been placed in the embarrassing position of having large numbers of unarmed recruits. But conscription was not politically practical in the circumstances of 1914, and the Cabinet, with the exception of Churchill, recognised that fact. If it had tried to introduce it it would have divided the nation at a time of the gravest national peril. Nor was there an alternative government in 1914 waiting to enter office and united behind such a policy.

The history of the Liberal Cabinet in the early months of the war was one of administrative muddle but, above all, of confusion of purpose. The Cabinet was not divided between supporters of *laissez-faire* on the one hand and more state intervention on the other. The major lines of division were between proponents of different strategies. Divisions over abstract political principles were very much a secondary issue. By May 1915 it was becoming apparent that 'business as usual' would not defeat the Germans and that Kitchener's 'nation in arms' might do so, but only at the cost of bankrupting the nation. Lloyd George held out the promise of victory by blending the best elements of the two together, but no one knew what would be the cost of his policy of total war. But the ultimate choice of which strategy to pursue now no longer lay solely with the Liberals. It was one of the problems which was to vex and torment the new Coalition government.

Notes: Chapter 11

1 PRO Adm. 1/8388/235, Churchill to the Secretary of the Admiralty, 11 May 1915.
2 *The Times*, 13 May 1915.
3 18 HL Deb., 5s., cols 1017–22, 18 May 1915.
4 71 HC Deb., 5s., col. 1014, 4 May 1915.
5 R. S. Churchill (ed.) *Winston S. Churchill*, Vol. 2: *Companion, Part III* (London, 1969), p. 1,997.
6 PRO T 171/109, First Budget, 1915. Treasury I (n.d., but *c*. April 1915).
7 Sir G. Mallett and C. O. George, *British Budgets. Second Series, 1913/14 to 1920/21* (London, 1920), p. 57

8 Runciman mss box 89, Effects of diminished exports on foreign exchange, W. R. Runciman, 2 June 1915.
9 K. M. Burk, 'British war missions to the United States, 1914–18' (D.Phil. thesis, University of Oxford, 1976), pp. 12–16; J. M. Cooper Jr, 'The command of gold reversed: American loans to Britain, 1915–17', *Pacific Historical Review,* vol. 45 (1976), pp. 209–27; Roberta A. Dayer, 'Strange bedfellows: J. P. Morgan & Co., Whitehall and the Wilson administration during World War One', *Business History,* vol. 18 (1976), pp. 127–34.
10 Bonar Law mss, 36/2/46, Long to Bonar Law, 27 Jan. 1915.
11 PRO FO 800/95, Memorandum for the Cabinet, 13 May 1915 [E. Grey].
12 A. Marwick, *The Deluge. British Society and the First World War* (London, 1967), ch. 5, *passim.*
13 J. Gooch, *The Plans of War* (London, 1974), pp. 299–333; R. R. James, *Gallipoli,* (London, 1974), *passim.*
14 Lord Hankey, *The Supreme Command* (London, 1961), vol. 1, p. 232.
15 PRO Cab. 42/2/2, CID paper 214B, List of committees appointed to consider questions arising during the present war [M. P. A. Hankey], 1 Mar. 1915.
16 Grant Duff mss 1/2, Hankey to Grant Duff, 14 Aug. 1914.
17 Hankey, op. cit., Vol. 1, p. 226–7.
18 Earl of Oxford and Asquith, *Memories and Reflections* (London, 1928), Vol. 2, p. 23.
19 Samuel mss A/157/723, Samuel to his wife, 20 Aug. 1914; K. Robbins, *Sir Edward Grey* (London, 1971), p. 298.
20 Runciman mss box 303, Runciman to his wife, 6 Jan. 1915.
21 PRO Cab. 19/33, Dardanelles Commission, Minutes of evidence, Q. 1160 (W. S. Churchill).
22 Hankey, op. cit., Vol. 1, pp. 177, 209–10.
23 Emmott mss, diary entry, 4 Jan. 1915.
24 PRO Cab. 19/33, op. cit., Q. 184 (Hankey).
25 Emmott mss box 5, Emmott to Asquith, 31 May 1915.
26 Hankey mss 4/7, Montagu to Hankey, 22 Mar. 1915.
27 PRO Cab. 19/33, op. cit., QQ. 740 (Grey); 976 (Hankey).
28 R. Jenkins. *Asquith* (London, 1964), p. 350.
29 PRO Cab. 19/33, op. cit., QQ. 1110 (W. S. Churchill); 5929 (Asquith).

Select Bibliography

Only works cited in the footnotes or which were found to be especially important are cited here.

1 *Departmental Records in the Public Records Office, London.*
  Admiralty
  Board of Trade
  Cabinet
  Home Office
  Ministry of Transport
  Ministry of Munitions
  Treasury
  War Office

2 *Private Papers*
H. H. Asquith mss (Bodleian Library, Oxford).
A. Bonar Law mss (House of Lords Record Office, London).
H. Creedy (Kitchener) mss (Public Record Office, London).
Cromer mss (Public Record Office).
J. E. Edmonds mss (Liddell Hart Centre for Military Archives, King's College, London).
A. Emmott mss (Nuffield College, Oxford).
Esher mss (Churchill College, Cambridge).
B. Fitzgerald mss (microfilm, Imperial War Museum, London).
Viscount French mss (Imperial War Museum, London).
Lord Gainford mss (J. A. Pease) (Nuffield College, Oxford).
A. Grant-Duff mss (Churchill College, Cambridge).
Grey of Fallodon mss (Public Record Office, London).
H. A. Gwynne mss (Bodleian Library, Oxford).
R. B. Haldane mss (National Library of Scotland, Edinburgh).
E. W. Hamilton mss (Public Record Office, London).
M. P. A. Hankey mss (Churchill College, Cambridge).
Harcourt mss (Bodleian Library, Oxford).
Kitchener mss (Public Record Office, London).
Llewellyn Smith mss (in private hands).
Lloyd George mss (House of Lords Record Office, London).
MacDonald mss (Public Record Office, London).
McKenna mss (Churchill College, Cambridge).
Mance mss (Public Record Office, London).
Montagu mss (Trinity College, Cambridge).
Mottistone mss (Nuffield College, Oxford).
Murray mss (Public Record Office, London).
Rawlinson mss (Churchill College, Cambridge).

Runciman mss (University of Newcastle upon Tyne Library).
St Loe Strachey mss (House of Lords Record Office, London).
Samuel mss (House of Lords Record Office, London).
Slade mss (microfilm, National Maritime Museum, London).
Spears mss (Liddell Hart Archives, King's College, London).
Trevelyan mss (University of Newcastle upon Tyne Library).
Von Donop mss (Imperial War Museum, London).
Wilson mss (microfilm, Imperial War Museum, London).

3 *Official Publications*
General Staff, War Office, *Combined Training, 1905* (London, 1905).
General Staff, War Office, *Field Artillery Training, 1906* (London, 1906).
General Staff, War Office, *Field Service Regulations, Part I, Operations (1909)* (London, 1909).
General Staff, War Office, *Field Artillery Training, 1912 Provisional* (London, 1912).
General Staff, War Office, *Field Artillery Training, 1914* (London, 1914).
General Staff, War Office, *Field Service Pocket Book, 1914*, (London, 1914, repr. Newton Abbott, 1971).
HMSO, *Hansard Parliamentary Debates*, 4th and 5th Series.
HMSO, *History of the Ministry of Munitions*, 8 Vols (London, 1918–22).
HMSO, *Parliamentary Papers*.
HMSO, *Statistics of the Military Effort of the British Empire* (London, 1922).
Hozier, H. M., 'Commerce in maritime war', Admiralty Library, p. 642 (1904).

4 *Memoirs, collections of documents, etc.*
Addison, C., *Four and a Half Years. A Personal Diary from June 1914 to January 1919* (London, 1934), Vol. 1.
Amery, L., *My Political Life: War and Peace* (London, 1953).
Asquith, H. H., *The Genesis of the War* (London, 1923).
Asquith, Earl of Oxford and, *Memories and Reflections* (London, 1928).
Bahlman, D. W. R. (ed.), *The Diary of Sir Edward Hamilton* (London, 1972).
Beveridge, W., *Power and Influence* (London, 1953).
Blake, R. (ed.), *The Private Papers of Douglas Haig* (London, 1952).
Brett, M. V. (ed.), *Journals and Letters of Reginald, Viscount Esher* (London, 1934–8).
Callwell, Maj.-Gen. Sir C. E., *Experiences of a Dug-out* (London, 1920).
Chamberlain, Sir A., *Politics from Inside: An Epistolary Chronicle, 1906–1914* (London, 1936).
Churchill, W. S., *The World Crisis, 1915* (London, 1923).
French, Viscount, *1914* (London, 1919).
Gooch, G. P. and Temperley, H. (eds), *British Documents on the Origins of the War, 1898–1914* (London, 1926–38).
Grey, Sir E., *Twenty-Five Years, 1893–1916* (London, 1925).
Hankey, Lord, *The Supreme Command* (London, 1961).
Johnson, Elizabeth (ed.), *The Collected Writings of J. M. Keynes* (London, 1971), Vol. 16.
Kemp, Lieutenant Commander P. (ed.), *The Papers of Admiral Sir John Fisher* (London, 1964).

Lloyd George, D., *War Memoirs* (London, 1934).
Marder, A. J. (ed.), *Fear God and Dread Nought. The Correspondence of Admiral of the Fleet Lord Fisher of Kilverstone* (London, 1956).
Midleton, Earl of, *Records and Reactions, 1859–1939* (London, 1939).
Mill, J. S., *Principles of Political Economy, with Some of their Applications to Social Philosophy* (London, 1848).
Morgan, K. O., (ed.), *Lloyd George. Family Letters, 1885–1936* (London, 1973).
Morley, J. *Memorandum on Resignation* (London, 1928).
Mott, Col. C. T. B. (translator), *The Memoirs of Field Marshal Joffre* (London, 1932).
Oppenheimer, Sir F., *Stranger Within* (London, 1960).
Parnell, Sir H., *On Financial Reform* (London, 1831).
Repington, Lt Col., *The First World War, 1914–18* (London, 1920).
Riddell, Lord, *Lord Riddell's War Diary, 1914–18* (London, 1933).
Seely, J. E. B., *Adventure* (London, 1930).
Seymour, C. (ed.), *The Intimate Papers of Colonel House* (London, 1926).
Smith, A., *An Inquiry into the Nature and Causes of the Wealth of Nations* ed. R. H. Campbell, A. S. Skinner and W. B. Todd, (Oxford, 1976; first published 1776).
Sydenham, Lord, *My Working Life* (London, 1927).
Taylor, A. J. P. (ed.), *Lloyd George. A Diary by Francis Stevenson* (London, 1971).
United States Government, *Papers relating to the Foreign Relations of the United States, Supplement, 1914* (Washington, DC, 1915).
Winch, D. (ed.), *James Mill. Selected Economic Writings* (Edinburgh, 1966).

5   *Published secondary sources*

Angell, N., *The Great Illusion. A Study of the Relation of Military Power to National Advantage* (London, 1909).
Arthur, Sir G., *Life of Lord Kitchener* (London, 1920).
Ashworth, W., *An Economic History of England, 1870–1939* (London, 1972).
Barnett, C., 'Strategy and society', *Royal United Services Institute Journal*, vol. 121 (1976), pp. 11*ff.*
Bartlett, C. J., *Great Britain and Sea Power, 1815–53* (Oxford, 1963).
Becke, Maj. A. F., 'British heavy and siege batteries in France, August to November 1914', *Journal of the Royal Artillery*, vol. 50 (1923–4), pp. 168*ff.*
Bell, A. C., *A History of the Blockade of Germany, Austria-Hungary, Bulgaria, and Turkey, 1914–18* (London, 1937).
Beveridge, W. H., *British Food Control* (Oxford, 1928).
Bidwell, S., *Gunners at War* (London, 1970).
Blake, R., *The Unknown Prime Minister. The Life and Times of Andrew Bonar Law, 1858–1923* (London, 1955).
Bourne, K., *The Foreign Policy of Victorian England* (London, 1970).
Brand, R. H., *War and National Finance* (London, 1921).
Broad, Lt. Col. C. N. F., 'The development of artillery tactics, 1914–18', *Journal of the Royal Artillery*, vol. 49 (1922), pp. 62–72.
Brooke, Lt. Col. A. F., 'The evolution of artillery in the Great War', *Journal of the Royal Artillery*, vol. 51 (1924–5), pp. 250–66.

Bullock, A., and Shock, M. (eds), *The Liberal Tradition* (Oxford, 1967).

Callwell, Maj.-Gen. Sir C. E., *Field Marshal Sir Henry Wilson, his Life and Diaries* (London, 1927).

Cassar, G. H., *Kitchener: Architect of Victory* (London, 1977).

Cecco, M. de, *Money and Empire. The International Gold Standard, 1890–1914* (Oxford, 1974).

Challener, R. D., *The French Theory of the Nation in Arms, 1866–1939* (New York, 1955).

Checkland, S. G., 'The mind of the City, 1870–1914', *Oxford Economic Papers*, vol. 9 (1957), pp. 261–74.

Churchill, R. S. (ed.), *Winston Churchill*, Vol. 2: *Young Statesman, 1901–14* (London, 1967), and *Companion* volumes.

Clapham, J. H., *The Bank of England, a History, 1797–1944* (London, 1944).

Clinton, A., 'Trades councils during the First World War', *International Review of Social History*, vol. 15 (1970)), pp. 202–34.

Cooper Jr, J. M., 'The command of gold reversed: American loans to Britain, 1915–17', *Pacific Historical Review*, vol. 45 (1976).

Corbett, Sir J., *History of the Great War. Naval Operations* (London, 1920).

Crammond, E., 'International finance in time of war', *Quarterly Review* (October, 1910).

Crow, D., *A Man of Push and Go. The Life of George Macaulay Booth* (London, 1965).

Cunningham, H., *The Volunteer Force* (London, 1975).

Dangerfield, G., *The Strange Death of Liberal England* (London, 1935).

David, E., 'The Liberal party divided, 1916–18', *Historical Journal*, vol. 13 (1970,) pp. 509–32.

David, E. (ed.), *Inside Asquith's Cabinet – from the Diaries of Charles Hobhouse* (London, 1977).

Dayer, Roberta A., 'Strange bedfellows: J. P. Morgan & Co., Whitehall and the Wilson administration during World War One', *Business History*, vol. 18 (1976), pp. 209–27.

Dunlop, Brig.-Gen., Sir John, 'The Territorial Army – the early years', *Army Quarterly and Defence Journal*, vol. 84 (1967), pp. 53–9.

Emy, H. V., 'The impact of financial policy on English politics before 1914', *Historical Journal*, Vol. 15 (1972), pp.103–31.

Emy, H. V., *Liberals, Radicals and Social Politics, 1892–1914* (Cambridge, 1973).

Esher, Lord, *The Tragedy of Lord Kitchener* (London, 1921).

Fayle, C. E., *A History of the Great War. Seaborne Trade* (London, 1920).

Faylr, C. E., *The War and the Shipping Industry* (London, 1927).

Feldman, G., *Army, Industry and Labour in Germany* (Princeton, NJ, 1966).

Fischer, F., *War of Illusions: German Policies from 1911 to 1914* (London, 1975).

French, D., 'Spy-fever in Britain, 1900–15', *Historical Journal*, vol. 21 (1978), pp. 355–70.

French, Maj. G., *The Life of Field Marshal Sir John French* (London, 1931).

Gash, N., 'After Waterloo. British society and the legacy of the Napoleonic Wars', *Transactions of the Royal Historical Society*, 5th ser., vol.28 (1978), pp. 145–59.

Gibb, D. E. W., *Lloyd's of London. A Study in Individualism* (London, 1957).

Giffen, Sir R., 'The necessity of a war chest in this country, or a greatly increased gold reseve', *Royal United Services Institute Journal*, vol. 52 (1908), pp. 1,329–40.

Gooch, J., *The Plans of War. The General Staff and British Military Strategy, c. 1900–16.* (London, 1974).

Gooch, J., 'Sir George Clarke's career at the Committee of Imperial Defence', *Historical Journal*, vol. 18 (1975), pp. 555–69.

Gooch, J., 'Soldiers, strategy and war aims in Britain, 1914–18', in B. Hunt and A. Preston (eds), *War Aims and Strategic Policy in the Great War, 1914–18* (London, 1977), pp. 21–40.

Gordon, M. R., 'Domestic conflict and the origins of the First World War: the British and German cases', *Journal of Modern History*, vol. 46 (1974), pp. 191–226.

Grant, Sokolov, 'The origins of the War Book', *Journal of the Royal United Services Institute*, vol. 117 (1972), pp. 65–70.

Haggie, P., 'The Royal Navy and war planning in the Fisher era', *Journal of Contemporary History*, vol. 8 (1973), pp. 113–33.

Hammond, M. B., *British Labour Conditions and Legislation during the War* (New York, 1919).

Hancock, W. K. and Gowing, M. M., *British War Economy* (London, 1949).

Hardach, G., *The First World War, 1914–18* (London, 1977).

Harrison, R., 'The war emergency workers national committee' in A. Briggs and J. Saville (eds), *Essays in Labour History, 1886–1923* (London, 1971) pp. 185–232.

Harrod, R. F., *The Life of John Maynard Keynes* (London, 1951).

Hazlehurst, C., 'Asquith as Prime Minister, 1908–16', *English Historical Review*, vol. 85 (1970), pp. 502–31.

Hazlehurst, C., *Politicians at War, July 1914 to May 1915. A Prologue to the Triumph of Lloyd George* (London, 1971).

Headlam, Gen. Sir J., *The History of the Royal Artillery, (1899–1914)* (London, 1937).

Hendrick, B. J., *The Life and Times of Walter Hines Page* (London, 1930).

Hill, Sir N., *War and Insurance* (London, 1927).

Hilton, B., *Corn Cash, Commerce* (London, 1977).

Hinsley, F. H., (ed.), *British Foreign Policy under Sir Edward Grey* (London, 1977).

Hirst, F. W., *The Political Economy of War* (London, 1915).

Hobson, J. A., *Richard Cobden. The International Man* (London, 1919, repr. 1968).

Hogg, O. F., *The Royal Arsenal* (London, 1963).

Howard, M., *The Continental Commitment* (London, 1974).

Hurwitz, S. J., *State Intervention in Great Britain. A Study of Economic Control and Social Response, 1914–19* (New York, 1949).

Imlah, A. H., *Economic Elements in the Pax Britannica* (New York, 1958, repr. 1969).

Irving, R. J., 'New industries for old? Some investment decisions of Sir W. G. Armstrong, Whitworth & Co. Ltd., 1900–14', *Business History*, vol. 17 (1975), pp. 150–75.

James, R. R., *Gallipoli* (London, 1974).

Jenkins, R., *Asquith* (London, 1964).

Kennedy, P. M., 'The development of German naval operation plans against England, 1896–1914', *English Historical Review*, vol. 89 (1974), pp. 48–76.

Kennedy, P. M., *The Rise and Fall of British Naval Mastery* (London, 1976).

Kirkaldy, A. W., *British Shipping* (London, 1914, repr. 1974).

Lammers, D., 'Arno Mayer and the British decision for war in 1914', *Journal of British Studies*, vol. 11 (1973), pp. 137–64.

Lloyd, E. M., *Experiments in State Control at the War Office and the Ministry of Food* (London, 1924).

Lowe, C. J. and Dockrill, M. L., *The Mirage of Power* (London, 1972).

Mackintosh, J. P., 'The role of the Committee of Imperial Defence before 1914', *English Historical Review*, vol. 77, (1962), pp. 490–503.

Mallett, Sir G., and George, C. O., *British Budgets. Second Series, 1913/14 to 1920/21* (London, 1920).

Marder, A. J., *From the Dreadnought to Scapa Flow*, Vol. 1: *The Road to War, 1904–14* (London, 1961).

Marder, A. J., *The Anatomy of British Sea Power* (London, 1964).

Marwick, A., *The Deluge. British Society and the First World War* (London, 1967).

Marwick, A., *Britain in the Century of Total War* (London, 1970).

Mayer, A. J., 'The domestic causes of the First World War', in L. Krieger and F. Stern (eds), *The Responsibility of Power* (London, 1968).

McCord, N., *The Anti-Corn Law League* (London, 1958, repr. 1975).

McCord, N., 'Cobden and Bright in politics, 1846–57', in R. Robson (ed.), *Ideas and Institutions of Victorian Britain* (London, 1969), pp. 87–114.

McCord, N., *Free Trade. Theory and Practice from Adam Smith to Keynes* (Newton Abbot, 1970).

McGill, B., 'Asquith's predicament, 1914–18', *Journal of Modern History*, vol. 39 (1967), pp. 283–304.

Money, L. G. Chiozza, 'British trade and the war', *Contemporary Review*, vol. 106 (October 1914), p. 475.

Monger, G. W., *The End of Isolation. British Foreign Policy, 1900–7* (London, 1963).

Morgan, E. V., *Studies in British Financial Policy, 1914–25* (London, 1952).

Morgan, K. O., *Keir Hardie, Radical and Socialist* (London, 1975).

Morley, J., *The Life of William Ewart Gladstone* (London, 1908).

Morris, A. J. A., *Radicalism against War, 1906–14* (London, 1972).

Morris, A. J. A., (ed.), *Edwardian Radicalism, 1900–14* (London, 1974).

Ombrain, N. d', *War Machinery and High Policy* (London, 1973).

Peacock, A. T., and Wiseman, J., *The Growth of Public Expenditure in the United Kingdom* (London, 1967).

Pollard, S., *The Development of the British Economy, 1914–67* (London, 1969).

Pratt, E. A., *The Rise of Rail Power in War and Conquest* (London, 1915).

Pratt, E. A., *British Railways and the Great War* (London, 1921).

Pugh, M. D., 'Asquith, Bonar Law and the first Coalition', *Historical Journal*, Vol. 17 (1974), pp. 813–36.

Robbins, K., *Sir Edward Grey* (London, 1971).

Robbins, Lord, *Political Economy, Past and Present* (London, 1976).

Roseveare, H., *The Treasury. The Evolution of a British Institution* (London, 1969).

Roskill, S., *Hankey. Man of Secrets* (London, 1970).

Rowan-Robinson, Maj. H., 'More accurate methods with field artillery', *Royal United Services Institute Journal*, vol. 58 (1914), pp. 111*ff.*

Sayers, R. S., 'The development of central banking after Bagehot', *Economic History Review*, 2nd ser., vol. 4 (1951), pp. 109–16.

Sayers, R. S., *The Bank of England* (London, 1976).

Scheiber, H. N., 'World War One as entrepreneurial opportunity: Willard Straight and the American international corporation', *Political Science Quarterly*, vol. 84 (1969), pp. 486–511.

Scott, J. D., *Vickers, a History* (London, 1962).

Scott, W. R., and Cunnison, J., *The Industries of the Clyde Valley during the Great War* (London, 1924).

Searle, G. R., *The Quest for National Efficiency* (Oxford, 1971).

Sherwig, J. M., *Guineas and Gunpowder. British Foreign Aid in the Wars with France, 1793–1815* (Cambridge, Mass. 1969).

Siney, Marion C., *The Allied Blockade of Germany, 1914–16* (Ann Arbor, Mich., 1957).

Spender, J. A. and Asquith, C., *Life of Henry Herbert Asquith. Lord Oxford and Asquith* (London, 1932).

Steiner, Zara, *Britain and the Origins of the First World War* (London, 1977).

Stone, Col. F. G., 'The heavy artillery of a field army: a comparison', *Royal United Services Institute Journal*, vol. 52 (1908), pp. 925–31.

Stone, N., *The Eastern Front* (London, 1975).

Stone, N., 'Organising an economy for war: the Russian shell shortage of 1914–17,' in G. Best and A. Wheatcroft (eds), *War, Economy and the Military Mind* (London, 1976), pp. 108–20.

Taylor, A. J. P., 'Politics in the First World War', in A. J. P. Taylor (ed.), *Essays in English History* (London, 1976), pp. 218–53.

Terraine, J., *Douglas Haig, the Educated Soldier* (London, 1963).

Towle, P., 'The debate on wartime censorship in Britain, 1902–14', in B. Bond and I. Roy (eds), *War and Society. A Yearbook of Military History* (London, 1975), pp. 103–13.

Travers, T. H. E., 'The offensive and the problem of innovation in British military thought, 1870–1915', *Journal of Contemporary History*, vol. 13 (1978), pp. 531–55.

Trebilcock, C., 'A special relationship: government, rearmament and the Cordite firms', *Economic History Review*, 2nd ser., vol. 19 (1966), pp. 254–72.

Trebilcock, C., 'Spin-off in British economic history. Armaments and industry, 1760–1914', *Economic History Review*, 2nd ser., vol. 22 (1969), pp. 474–90.

Trebilcock, C., 'Legends of the British armaments industry, 1890–1914: a revision', *Journal of Contemporary History*, vol. 5 (1970), pp. 1–19.

Trebilcock, C., 'British armaments and European industrialisation, 1890–1914', *Economic History Review*, 2nd ser., vol. 26 (1973), pp. 364–79.

Trebilcock, C., 'War and the failure of industrial mobilisation: 1899 and 1914', in J. M. Winter (ed.), *War and Economic Development. Essays in Memory of David Joslin* (London, 1975), pp. 139–64.

Trebilcock, C., *The Vickers Brothers* (London, 1977).

Trevelyan, G. M., *Grey of Fallodon* (London, 1937).
Tryon, Admiral Sir G., 'National Insurance: a practical proposal', *United Services Magazine* (May 1890), pp. 184–92.
Tryon, Admiral Sir G., 'National Insurance – III', *United Services Magazine* (July 1890), pp. 289–98.
Weinroth, H. S., 'The British radicals and the balance of power, 1902–14', *Historical Journal*, vol. 13 (1970), pp. 653–82.
Weinroth, H. S., 'Norman Angell and the "Great Illusion"; an episode in pre-1914 pacificism', *Historical Journal*, vol. 17 (1974), pp. 551–74.
Whittam, J., *The Politics of the Italian Army* (London, 1976).
Williams, D., 'The evolution of the sterling system', in C. R. Whittlesey and J. S. G. Wilson (eds), *Essays in Money and Banking in Honour of R. S. Sayers* (Oxford, 1968), pp. 266–97.
Williamson, S. R., *The Politics of Grand Strategy* (Cambridge, Mass., 1969).
Wilson, T., *The Downfall of the Liberal Party* (London, 1968).
Wilson, T., 'Britain's "moral commitment" to France in August 1914', *History*, vol. 64 (1979), pp. 380–91.
Winch, D., *Adam Smith's Politics* (Cambridge, 1978).
Wright, C., and Fayle, C. E., *A History of Lloyd's* (London, 1928).
Wrigley, C. J., *David Lloyd George and the British Labour Movement in Peace and War* (New York, 1976).
Wynne, G. C., *If Germany Attacks* (London, 1940).

6 *Unpublished theses*
Burk, K. M., 'British war missions to the United States, 1914–18' (D. Phil. thesis, University of Oxford, 1976).
French, David, 'Some aspects of social and economic planning for war in Great Britain, c. 1905–15' (PhD thesis, University of London, 1978).
Ranft, B. McL., 'The naval defence of British seaborne trade, 1860–1905' (D. Phil. thesis, University of Oxford, 1967).
Summerton, N. W., 'The development of British military planning for a war against Germany, 1904–14' (PhD thesis, University of London, 1970).

7 *Works of reference and newspapers*
Contemporary Review.
Dictionary of National Biography.
The Economist.
Mitchell, B. R. and Deane, Phyllis, *An Abstract of British Historical Statistics* (Cambridge, 1962, repr. 1976).
Quarterly Review.
The Spectator.
The Times.
Who Was Who.

Index